93

917
.304
Blo

Blockson, Charles L.
   Hippocrene guide to the underground railroad /
Charles L. Blockson. -- New York : Hippocrene Books,
c1994.
   380 p. : ill., maps.

   Includes bibliographical references (p. 367-370) and
index.
   07424752 LC:94011174 ISBN:0781802539

   1. Underground railroad - Guidebooks. 2. Historic sites
- United States - Guidebooks. 3. Historic sites -
(SEE NEXT CARD)

1298   94AUG22   26/   1-00634263

THE UNDERGROUND RAILROAD

Native Americans and a group of escaping slaves.
(Artist Jerry Pinkney, private collection, Charles
L. Blockson)

HIPPOCRENE GUIDE TO

THE UNDERGROUND RAILROAD

Charles L. Blockson

HIPPOCRENE BOOKS
New York

For information, address:
HIPPOCRENE BOOKS, INC.
171 Madison Avenue
New York, NY 10016

Library of Congress Cataloging in Publication Data
Blockson, Charles L.
    Hippocrene guide to the underground railroad /
Charles L. Blockson.
        p.   cm.
    Includes bibliographical references and index.
    ISBN 0-7818-0253-9 : $22.95
    1. Underground railroad—Guidebooks. 2. Historic
sites—United States—Guidebooks. 3. Historic sites—
Canada—Guidebooks. 4. United States—Guidebooks.
5. Fugitive slaves—United States—History.   I. Title.
    E450.B65   1994
917.304'929—dc20   94-11174

Printed in the United States of America.

Dedication

This book is respectfully dedicated to the memory of those brave souls who represented the morality of antebellum America. They served an admirable purpose of organizing the Underground Railroad—that mysterious, formidable enemy of slavocracy—with an uncompromising commitment to freedom.

Contents

Branding a slave on the West Coast of Africa.

Introduction

The Underground Railroad seems to excite people of all ages, everybody is talking about the subject. This guidebook provides students, historians, vacationers, travel agents, and government agencies, such as the National Park Service, with information concerning the location of historic sites connected to the Underground Railroad. My fascination with the Underground Railroad began when I was a boy of ten; my grandfather told me that his father escaped from Seaford, Delaware to Canada in 1856. Throughout my life in numerous towns, cities and villages along the Atlantic Coast and extending as far west as Kansas, people have mentioned the homes, churches, caves and tunnels alleged to have been station stops on the Freedom Train. From the outset, I was faced with the heart-breaking task of exclusion when writing this book.

Some of the most exciting homes connected with the Underground Railroad are restricted because of private ownership. Through urban renewal and other capital improvement projects, important landmarks, especially private homes, connected with the Underground Railroad have been demolished. Other buildings are falling into decay through neglect.

Today, slaves are too often portrayed as passive victims waiting to be led out of slavery. But long before the invisible Underground Railroad was organized, slaves in Colonial America had frequently escaped alone or with others from their owners to seek freedom.

Their routes were many and varied, they often traveled in disguise, through woods and farms, by wagon, boat and train, hiding in stables and attics and store-rooms, and fleeing through secret passages; but the destination they sought was always freedom. In areas where escaped slaves often traveled, stories or legends of the Underground Railroad's routes and stations still persist. No one knows how many fled from bondage along its invisible tracks: as many as 100,000 before 1830 and 1860? As few as 30,000? No one may ever know, because secrecy was crucial; few records of the railroad's activities survive.

Some Underground Railroad stations existed in the South. Many southerners risked their lives and property by giving aid and comfort to escaped slaves. Native Americans were among the earliest friends of escaped slaves. The Seminoles permitted runaway slaves from Georgia and South Carolina as well as Alabama and Florida to live with them in swamps and the wilderness. Legend says that most slaves simply walked to freedom, "Guided by the north star alone, towards Canada the 'Promised Land'"—it had no fugitive slave law. Others dared to remain—for them the danger of discovery and recapture was real. Overemphasis on the Quakers' role as aides in the Underground Railroad has led to ignorance about the participation of other religious groups who equally participated in the operation. Some of the individuals who helped escaped slaves were important figures in American history.

In 1990 Congress passed Public Law 101-628, which recognized the significance of the Underground Railroad to American history. The legislation, directed by the Secretary of Interior, led the National Park Service to conduct a study of the historic Underground Railroad. Largely because of my twenty-five years of research on the subject and the publication of my article "Escape from Slavery: The Underground Railroad" in *National Geographic* Magazine (July 1984), I was selected as the Chairperson of the Advisory Committee to examine the historical significance of various sites covering twenty states and territories including link-age to Canada, Mexico, and the Caribbean.

Until now, no single guide has been devoted solely to explore the Underground Railroad. The sites in this guide are arranged by geographic regions. Each entry contains a description of the site with information about its history. As much as possible, included in the sites at the end of each entry is important visitor information, directions, contact addresses, and telephone numbers. If you plan to visit any of the sites listed in this guide, call at least two weeks in advance to make the necessary arrangements. Many of the sites are subject to uncertain fundings. Visitor's hours may vary from season to season.

With these words I hope that this guide will encourage you, the reader, to follow the trail of the Underground Railroad.

It is a story that thrills the heart and soul as it does the mind.

Abduction from the coast of Africa.

Chronology: A Historical Review of the Underground Railroad

1526   The first group of Africans to set foot on what is now the United States are brought by a Spanish explorer to South Carolina, to erect a settlement. However, they soon escape to the interior and settle with native Americans.

1619   The origin of slavery in English colonies began, with the arrival of twenty Africans in Jamestown, Virginia, on Dutch vessels as indentured servants, later condemned to slavery.

1640-   Punitive fugitive laws applying to both indentured servants
1699   and slaves are erected in the English colonies. The Virginia Law, passed in 1642, penalizes people sheltering escaped slaves 20 pounds worth of tobacco for each night of refuge granted. Slaves are branded after a second escape attempt.

1672   Virginia—A law is enacted providing for a bounty on the heads of "Maroons," escaped Africans who form communities in the mountains swamps and forests surrounding the Great Dismal Swamp boarding Virginia and North Carolina.

1688   Germantown (now Philadelphia), Pennsylvania, Mennonite Quakers sign an anti-slavery resolution, the first formal protest against slavery in the Western Hemisphere.

1740   North Carolina enacts law to prosecute any person caught assisting escaped slaves.

1766   George Washington orders that one of his "Negroes, 'Negro Tom,'" who had run away, be sold in the West Indies for molasses, rum, limes, tarmarinds, sweet meats, and good old spirits.

1733   Two African-American ministers, George Lile and Andres Bryan organize the first African-American Baptist Church at Savannah, Georgia. In later years this church became an important station on the Underground Railroad.

1775   In Philadelphia a society was founded by Quakers and others in April. Its proper title was lengthy: The Pennsylvania Society for Promoting the Abolition of Slavery, the Relief of Negroes Unlawfully Held in Bondage, and for improving the condition of the African Race.

1786   George Washington writes to a friend about fugitive slaves in Philadelphia "which a Society of Quakers in the city (formed for such purposes) have attempted to liberate."

1787   Congress outlaws slavery in the Northwest Territory. The Free African Society is organized in Philadelphia by Richard Allen and Absolom Jones. Members of this society assisted escaped slaves.

1793   The Fugitive Slave Act becomes a federal law. It allows slave-owners, their agents or attorneys to seize fugitive slaves in free states and territories.

1793   The Emanicpation Act of Upper Canada became the law of all of Canada on July 9, 1793, by Lieutenant Governor John Graves Simcoe. "An Act to prevent the future introduction of slaves, and to limit the terms of contracts within this province." ·

1794   Mother Bethel African Methodist Episcopal Church is established in Philadelphia. Shortly thereafter, the church will become an important station on the Underground Railroad.

1800   Nat Turner and John Brown are born. Betrayal of Gabriel Prosser's plans to lead thousands of free blacks and slaves in an attack on Richmond, Virginia. Prosser and 15 of his followers are later hanged.

1804   The Underground Railroad is "incorporated" after slave owner General Thomas Boudes of Columbia, Pennsylvania refuses to surrender a young slave to authorities.

1816   The Seminole War begins in Florida, as a result many escaped slaves from Georgia, South Carolina and Alabama are given refuge by the Seminole Indians.

1817   Frederick Douglas is born in Tuckahoe, Maryland.

1817   As a response to the Fugitive Slave Act (1793), Anti-Slavery advocates use the Underground Railroad to assist slaves to escape into Ohio and Canada.

1820   The Missouri Compromise provides for Missouri's entry into the Union as a slave state. There are now 12 slave states and 12 free states in the United States. All territory north of 36-30 is declared free: all territory south of that line is open to slavery.

1821   William Still, the great African-American Underground Railroad agent and author is born in Burlington County, New Jersey.

1822   The Denmark Vesey slave conspiracy in Charleston, South Carolina is exposed, thirty six collaborators are hanged.

1823   Mary Ann Shadd Cary is born in Wilmington, Delaware. As an Underground Railroad agent, teacher and editor, she assisted John Brown and preached permanent emigration from the United States.

1829   David Walker, a free African-American from North Carolina published his famous militant anti-slavery pamphlet, *An Appeal to the Colored People of the World* in Boston.

1831   Nat Turner stages the greatest slave revolt in the history of the United States in Southampton County, Virginia.

         In Boston, Abolitionist William Lloyd Garrison publishes his famous anti-slavery newspaper, *The Liberator*. African-American entrepreneur James Forten of Philadelphia becomes the chief financial contributor to the publication.

1831   The World Anti-Slavery Convention opens in London, England. Among the many topics discussed is the protection of escaped slaves.

1832   The New England Anti-Slavery Society is established by 12 whites at the African Baptist Church in Boston.

1833   Founding of Ohio's Oberlin College, intergrated from the outset and a leader in the abolitionist cause and the Underground Railroad movement.

By Imperial Order, all slavery was abolished in the British Empire, including Canada.

1837   Reverend Elijah P. Lovejoy is murdered by a mob in Alton, Illinois after refusing to stop publishing anti-slavery materials and for his connections with the Underground Railroad.

1838   At the age of twenty-one Frederick Douglass escapes from Maryland through Underground Railroad connections. Robert Purvis becomes chairman of the General Vigilance Committee and "president" of the Underground Railroad in Philadelphia.

1842   The capture of George Latimer, an escaped slave, precipitates the first of several famous fugitive slave cases in Boston.

An early challenge to the Fugitive Slave Act (of 1793) occurs when the Supreme Court rules in *Prigg vs. Pennsylvania* that state officials are not required to return fugitive slaves.

1845   Frederick Douglass' narrative of his life is published. A song entitled "The Fugitive Song," dedicated to Douglass is published the same year.

1847   Frederick Douglass and Martin R. Delaney publish *The North Star*, an anti-slavey newspaper.

1848   Henry Box Brown makes his famous escape nailed in a box.

1849   Harriet Tubman, soon to be called "Moses," escapes from Maryland.

1850   The infamous Fugitive Slave Law is enacted strengthening the 1793 Fugitive Slave Act. Federal officers are now offered a fee for the slaves they apprehend.

1851   Sojourner Truth addresses the National Women's Suffrage

Convention in Akron, Ohio and delivers her famous lines in her "Ain't I a Woman" speech.

1851 The Fugitive Slave Rebellion in Christiana, Pennsylvania occurs. Along with John Brown's raid, it was a major episode in Underground Railroad history.

1852 Harriet Beecher Stowe publishes her famous book *Uncle Tom's Cabin*.

1854 The Kansas-Nebraska Act of 1854 modified the Missouri Compromise leaving the question of slavery open to territorial legislatures.

1856 Pro-slavery forces sack the town of Lawrence, Kansas; John Brown arrives to defend anti-slavery members.

1856 Margaret Garner, an escaped slave from Kentucky, kills her child rather than allowing her daughter to be taken back in to slavery.

1857 The United States Supreme Court declares in the Dred Scott decision that slaves do not become free when taken into free territory.

1859 John Brown and his men attack Harpers Ferry, Virginia; a number of his men are killed; Brown is later hanged for attempting to liberate slaves in the South.

1863 President Abraham Lincoln issues the Emancipation Proclamation, declaring all slaves in rebellious areas to be free.

1865 The Civil War ends, the Underground Railroad ends, and the Thirteenth Amendment is added to the United States Consitution abolishing slavery permanently.

MID-ATLANTIC

Delaware

Wilmington, Delaware
Mother African Union Protestant Church

Most historians and other writers in the past failed to record the important contributions of the African-American churches and their connection with the Underground Railroad. Their ministers were noteworthy leaders and their church buildings were used as stations. Their contributions were all the more significant because active abolitionists were few among white congregations in Delaware. Mother African Union Protestant Church was organized in 1813; the Reverend Peter Spencer, through his impressive personality and moral conviction, established it as a major stop on the road to freedom. His congregation provided food, clothing and shelter to scores of escaping slaves. The church still stands today, and there is a plaza whose name honors the popular minister. Peter is buried at the site of the marker that honors him.

Location: Peter Spencer Plaza is located on French Street
              between Eight and Ninth Streets.

For further information contact:

Mother African Union Protestant Church
(302) 994-3410
Historical Society of Delaware
Wilmington
(302) 655-7161

Wilmington, Delaware
The site of Thomas Garrett's Plaque

A Quaker, Thomas Garrett wore no pistol and carried no knife. He was born in Upper Darby, Pennsylvania, on August 21, 1789. The fearless Garrett was known from end to end of the Atlantic Coast states for his quiet but firm defiance of law officers, slave hunters and overseers. He is credited with aiding more than 2,700 fugitive slaves with the assistance of Wilmington's free African-American community, particularly the Abraham Shadd family. He worked openly for 40 years, sheltering slaves and pleading their cause. In 1848, after he helped a freedman carry his enslaved family from Delaware to Philadelphia, a court assessed damages at $5,400. Garrett was not deterred by physical threats or financial penalties. He told the court defiantly, "I have assisted over 1,400 in 25 years on their way to North, and I now consider the penalty imposed might be as a license for the remainder of my life. If any of you know any slave who needs assistance, send him to me."

His friend, William Lloyd Garrison, said that Garrett was "among the manliest of men, and the gentlest of spirits." Harriet Tubman stopped at Garrett's home on numerous occasions seeking food, shelter and money as she passed through Delaware. Underground Railroad historian William Still devoted an entire chapter on Garrett in his book *The Underground Railroad*. Although his former home has been demolished, a historical plaque is dedicated to Thomas Garrett. Also located in the Peter Spencer Plaza, French Street between Eight and Ninth Streets, is a monument to the Underground Railroad that honors Thomas Garrett and Harriet Tubman.

Location: Garrett's plaque is located on the corner of 4th
              and Shipley Streets.

The headstone of Garrett's grave can be viewed at the Friends Meetinghouse in Wilmington.

Smyra, Delaware
The Clearfield Farm

Located in Blackbird Hundred, a sparsely populated section of the state during the antebellum period, was Daniel Corbet's Clearfield Farm. Built circa 1755, the house was added to in 1840. When fugitive slaves needed help in escaping on the Underground Railroad, the Corbet family aided them. The house, which stands a short distance from Duck Creek Meetinghouse, had several places of concealment for slaves. Above the bedroom on the second floor of the original section of the home is a crawl space in the attic. A large fireplace, also in the original part of the house, is connected to a ten-by eight-foot cellar where slaves were hidden. There are also places of concealment in the 1840 addition of this large house; in one room a sliding panel matches a paneled wall. Daniel Corbet is listed with Thomas Garrett and John Hunn as an important stationkeeper on the Underground Railroad in Delaware.

Location: At the Clearfield Farm in Smyrna
For further information contact:

>Historical Society of Delaware
>505 Market Street
>Wilmington, DE 19801
>(302) 655-7161
>Delaware Tourism Office, 1-800-441-8846

Dover, Delaware
John Dickinson Plantation

This imposing Georgian mansion was built in 1740 for Samuel Dickinson, a judge for the Court of Common Pleas in Kent County. His son John inherited the mansion and large plantation lands located along the St. Jones River after his father's death. Dickinson is known in American history books as the "Penman of the Revolution" for his provacative essays on Colonial rights and liberty. Dickinson signed the

United States Constitution in 1787 as a delegate from Delaware.

His slaves were responsible for overseeing the production of grains and managing the orchards and the meadowlands. In 1777, largely influenced by Quakers, Dickinson executed a manumission that freed his slaves. In contrast to the large manor house, the site also includes a log dwelling that enhances the interpretation of plantation slave life 200 years ago. Listed as a National Historic Landmark, the Dickinson Plantation staff offers a special focus tour on African-American culture and history.

Location: Six miles south of Dover, Delaware on Kitts
              Hummock Road, just off Route 113 and
              southeast of Dover Air Force Base.

For further information contact:

The Afro-American Historical Society
512 E. 4th Street
Wilmington, DE 19801
(302) 652-1313
John Dickinson House
RD 3, Box 257
Dover, Delaware 19901
(302) 739-3277

Camden, Delaware
Wild Cat Manor and Great Geneva

Many Quakers in Delaware caught the Abolition fever from the Pennsylvania Quakers. The Hunn family has owned Wild Cat Manor and Great Geneva for over two hundred years. Wild Cat manor and Great Geneva, by all documented accounts were important stations on the Underground Railroad. Jonathan Hunn who worked with Thomas Garrett lost all of his property except Wild Cat Manor and Great Geneva for assisting escaped slaves. These properties are located within walking distance of each other. Many local residents have seen the cellar room behind a revolving shelf of canned goods, however the ceiling of the room collapsed a few years ago.

Harriet Tubman was well acquainted with this family, for their homes were the first known Underground Railroad stops in her route to freedom. William Still also knew their family. In his book *The Underground Railroad*, Still describes Jonathan Hunn:

> He was well known to the colored people far and near, and was especially sought with regards to business pertaining to the Underground Railroad, as a friend who would never fail to assist, as far as possible in every time of need. Through his agency many found their way to freedom, both by land and water.
>
> He was not without friends, however for even near by, dwelt a few well-tried Abolitionists, Ezekiel Jenkins, Mifflin Warner and others.

Although Wildcat Manor and Great Geneva are privately owned today, the houses are opened to the public on "Dover Day" when tours are given. Occasionally the properties are open to visitors if the prearrangements are scheduled.
For further information contact:

Delaware State Museums
102 South State Street
P.O. Box 1401
Dover, Delaware   19903
(302) 739-5316 or
Delaware Tourism Office
99 King's Highway
P.O. Box 1401
Dover, Delaware   19903
1-800-441-8846

Star Hill, Delaware
Star Hill African Methodist Episcopal Church

Located in a sparsely populated section of the state, Star

Hill African Methodist Episcopal Church was a station on the Underground Railroad. Although it was not unusual that this small rural free African-American church should open its doors to escaping slaves, because Delaware's free African-American population outnumbered slaves twenty to one. Still, it was an act of tremendous bravery in a slave state. The present members of Star Hill African Methodist Episcopal Church have confirmed that their church formally sheltered escaped slaves.

Location: Route 13, east of Country Road and Route 330
For further information contact:
        Delaware Tourism Office
        99 Kings Highway
        P.O. Box 1401
        Dover, Delaware 19903
        (800) 441-8846
        or call:
        Star Hill African Methodist Episcopal Church
        (302) 697-9903

Dover, Delaware
Woodburn, The Governor's House

Woodburn, as the mansion is now called, was built around 1790 for Charles Hillyard. During the mid-nineteenth century, the home was owned by Henry Cowgill, a Quaker. His family was active in helping fugitive slaves to escape, and used its large home as a station on the Underground Railroad. On other occasions, family members would take food and clothing to fugitive slaves who were harbored in their barn. A marker at the mansion tells of Woodburn's connection with the Underground Railroad. *The Entailed Hat*, written by George Alfred Townsend, also gives details pertaining to Woodburn's connection to the Underground. The notorious Patty Cannon's gang of slave kidnappers once entered the house and attempted to make off with several African-Americans who had been given permission to dance in the house by the Cowgill family. However, the gang members were driven off. Today Woodburn serves as the Governor's Mansion.

Location: At King's Highway and Pennsylvania Avenue
For further information pertaining to tours contact:
Woodburn
151 Kings Highway
Dover, Delaware 19901
(302) 739-5656
(302) 739-3260

Odessa, Delaware
Appoquinimink Friends Meetinghouse

This little, red-brick structure, about 20 feet square, with a pitched roof and pent eaves across the gable ends, was built in 1793. Braving the rage of the slaveholding countryside, the Friends hid fugitive slaves at this station from Delaware, Maryland and Virginia in the loft of their little building until it was safe to send them on their way to other stations. Harriet Tubman often stayed at this meetinghouse. Her route through the state included Camden, Dover, Blackbird, Laurel, Concord, Seaford, Millsborough, Smyrna, Delaware City, Middletown, Georgetown, Lewes, Milford, Frederica and New Castle on her way to Wilmington and Philadelphia.

Location: South side of Main Street, west of U.S. Route 13
For further information contact:
Historic Houses of Odessa
Main Street
P.O. Box 507
Odessa, Delaware 19730
(302) 378-4069

Reliance, Delaware
Patty Cannon, the Woman Who Ran the Underground Railroad in Reverse

Lucretia (Patty) Cannon was a tall, robust and attractive woman, with auburn hair and burning eyes. Tough Patty had the beauty of a lady; she also had the strength of a man and could wrestle most men to the ground. Charming, smooth-talking Patty Cannon was also a manipulative woman. Regardless, there were those who said she had the heart of seven devils. Coarse and salty language was her trademark.

Few persons, in the North or South, spoke kindly of her, yet no accurate account of the Underground Railroad can be written without telling her story. Patty Cannon's name is still used to strike terror into the hearts of children along the Delmarva Peninsula, that part of the Eastern Shore that connects the states of Delaware and Maryland.

Patty and her gang of kidnappers operated their Underground Railroad station in reverse at a place known as Johnson's Crossroads, where Dorchester and Carolina Counties, Maryland join Sussex County, Delaware, in what might be called "No Man's Land."

There were many similarities between Patty Cannon's Underground Railroad running south into slavery and the one running north into freedom. Both employed black and white conductors and agents, both had a system of station houses and both relied upon secrecy and passengers. It was at that time the clever and wicked woman saw the necessity of bringing all of her artfulness of deception into action.

One year it was estimated that as many as 20 African-American children were kidnapped from Philadelphia and surrounding suburbs. At the piers in Philadelphia and Camden, New Jersey, Patty Cannon's spies watched ships arriving from the South, always ready to kidnap their victims. In her former home and tavern at Johnson's Crossroads was a bloodstained oak door and wrought-iron rings on the walls where shackled African-Americans awaited purchase and shipment to the Deep South. All of Patty Cannon's former property has disappeared. Only a state historical marker records her foul deeds and her gang of kidnappers. In the end, she cheated death by hanging by taking poison with her own hands the night before she was to be hanged.

Location: A few yards west of the boundary where Reliance, Delaware, joins Dorchester County and Caroline County, Maryland.

For further information on Patty Cannon contact:
Historical Society of Delaware
505 Market St.
Wilmington, DE 19801
(302) 655-7161
Delaware Tourism Office
1-800-441-8846

District Of Columbia

Washington, D.C.
Emancipation Statue

The idea of the Emancipation Proclamation and its implementation occupied President Abraham Lincoln's mind for months. He had hoped to achieve the monumental task by a Congressional act; however, the plan caused controversy and confusion within Congress. Lincoln had waited for a victory to move against slavery. Antietam was the answer, and a preliminary proclamation in September, 1862 gave warning that he would free the slaves in the South.

It expressely permitted those slave states or parts of them fighting on the Union side to keep their slaves. The real purpose of the Emancipation Proclamation is found near the end of the document: "Negroes of suitable condition will be received into the armed services of the United States to garrison forts, positions, stations and to man vessels of all sorts in said service." Lincoln favored colonization for African-Americans, and several hundred former slaves were shipped to Haiti, where their plight soon became desperate. A warship was sent for them, and they were settled in Arlington. The Emancipation Statue was unveiled in 1876, with Frederick Douglass reading the Proclamation aloud at the dedication ceremonies.

Location: Lincoln Park, East Capital Street between
Eleventh and Thirteenth Streets, NE

Washington, D.C.
Mt. Zion United African Methodist Episcopal Church

African-Americans of Washington, D.C., free and slave, sometimes took matters into their own hands, and the Underground Railroad had several important stopping places in the city. Leonard A. Grimes, for instance, operated as a hackman, accumulating enough money to purchase a number of horses and carriages, which he used for Underground purposes. Grimes later moved to Boston and became pastor of the Twelfth Street Baptist Church, where he established a major station of the Underground Railroad. According to oral tradition, Mt. Zion United A.M.E. Church was likewise an important stopping point on the Road to Freedom, and fugitive slaves were hidden in a burial vault in Mt. Zion's cemetery. The church is reported to have the oldest African-American congregation in the city. Francis Henderson, a former fugitive slave, told Underground Railroad chronicler Benjamin Drew in 1856 that he was a member of this church before escaping to Canada. It is probable that Harriet Tubman also knew this church, since she operated around Washington as well as on the Eastern Shore.
Tours by appointment only.
Location: 1334 29th Street, S.W.
             (Georgetown) Washington, D.C. 20007

Washington, D.C.
District of Columbia Wharf

At the time of President James Polk's administration, Washington had become an important station on the Underground Railroad, by means of which Southern slaves were smuggled northward to freedom. A spectacular Underground Railroad rescue was attempted in April, 1848 when

76 house slaves belonging to prominent local families were carried off at night on a small vessel that reached the Potomac River's mouth. There it was captured. In the resulting public outcry, a mob stormed the office of Dr. Gamaliel Bailey's abolitionist weekly, *The National Era*, demanding that the editor remove his printing press. Although no violence ensued, the Capital was the most thoroughly alarmed it had been since the British invasion of 1814.

Throughout its operation the Underground Railroad included sea captains who were loyal to the cause. The District of Columbia Wharf served as an important station on the fugitive network. Anthony Bowen, who later founded the first YMCA in Washington, D.C., often met incoming vessels at this wharf and led fugitives to his home, formerly located at 85 East E. Street, now the present site of L'Enfante Plaza.

Location: Sixth Street SE

For further information contact:

> The Association for the Study of
> AFRO-American History
> 1407 14th Street
> N.W. Washington, D.C. 20005
> (202) 667-2822
>
> Washington Visitor Information Center
> 1455 Pennsylvania Avenue, N.W.
> Washington, D.C. 20004
> (202) 357-2700

Washington, D.C.
Capitol Hill

Our impressive capitol dominating all of Washington stands in spacious grounds on the crest of a hill where the north-south and east-west axes of the Federal metropolis intersect. At the top of the dome is Thomas Crawford's 19-foot bronze statue of Freedom. Jefferson Davis, who was Secretary of War at the time of the statues unveiling and in

NEGROES
FOR SALE.

I will sell by Public Auction, on Tuesday of next Court, being the 29th of November, *Eight Valuable Family Servants*, consisting of one Negro Man, a first-rate field hand, one No. 1 Boy, 17 years o' age, a trusty house servant, one excellent Cook, one House-Maid, and one Seamstress. The balance are under 12 years of age. They are sold for no fault, but in consequence of my going to reside North. Also a quantity of Household and Kitchen Furniture, Stable Lot, &c. Terms accommodating, and made known on day of sale.

Jacob August.
P. J. TURNBULL, *Auctioneer.*
Warrenton, October **28,** **1859.**

Printed at the *News* office, Warrenton, North Carolina.

charge of the construction of the capitol, compelled Crawford to alter the headgear on the statue because the liberty cap, as it is called, represented slave liberation. Ironically, the statue of Freedom was erected and put in place by an African-American slave, Phillip Reed.

Thomas Smallwood, an important African-American Underground Railroad conductor in Washington, D.C. explained in his book *The Narrative of Thomas Smallwood* that not much could be done in the way of Underground Railroad activities in Washington until the Reverend Charles T. Torrey made his appearance there. Torrey was arrested in Annapolis, Maryland, for anti-slavery activities, but upon returning to Washington continued his Underground Railroad work.

For further information about Capitol Hill and The White House contact:

> Smithsonian Information Center
> Smithsonian Institution
> Washington, D.C. 20560
> (202) 357-2700

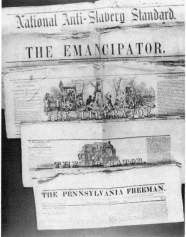

Anti slavery newspapers, these journals were a power. One of the most important papers was Garrison's Liberator.

$100 REWARD.

Ran away from the subscriber, living eight miles from Baltimore, on Falls turnpike road, on Tuesday 22d July, 1814,

Negro Job.

He is a stout black man, about 35 years of age, 5 feet 10 or eleven inches high, stoops when walking fast, flat footed and turns his toes out when in the act of walking, stutters a little in common conversation, but when alarmed increases it—a lump or mark on his shin occasioned by a kick from a horse, has no whiskers and but a small beard—he is fond of dress and occasionally wears a watch, he also is fond of company, and if he drinks any spirits is very apt to use words which he doth not understand the signification of—and amongst his companions he is very noisy, calls himself Joseph Chew—he was seen in the neighborhood of York Haven, about the 1st of January 1817, has been employed by John Gross near York Haven and by John Shelly, on Shelly's island, but he may have left that.

I will give the above reward if he is secured in any jail so that I get him again, and all reasonable charges if brought home or lodged in Baltimore jail.

THOMAS JOHNSON.

Rockland, July 20, 1819.

Washington, D.C.
The White House

The White House, executive mansion of the United States, stands proudly among the world's great residences of state in charm and dignity. Yet manacled slaves had marched under its windows to the auction block at Decatur House on Lafayette Square, just across Pennsylvania Avenue. Solomon Northrup, a free citizen of New York State, who had been kidnapped and was on his way to slavery in New Orleans, recalled that the voices of patriotic representives boasting of freedom and equality and the rattling of the slaves' chains commingled.

Northrup also remembered that in Williams' slave pen, in one of the cellars of which he found himself unaccountably confined, were slaves who had attempted to escape by themselves or with the assistance of others. His celebrated narrative, *Twelve Years a Slave*, was so successful that the book was reprinted several times.

Location: 1600 Pennsylvania Avenue
             Washington, D.C.

Washington, D.C.
Metropolitan A.M.E. Church

Established in 1822, the Metropolitan African Methodist Episcopal Church was built by former slaves when a group of dissatisfied African-Americans broke away from a predominantly white church. The present massive red brick edifice, in the Victorian Gothic style, was dedicated in 1886, and has been called an architectural landmark. According to oral tradition, the original church's congregation shielded and fed fugitive slaves within the church's walls. In 1895, the funeral of Frederick Douglass was held in the Metropolitan A.M.E. Church, and was attended by 2,500 mourners. The Union Wesley Church, another African-American church, also served as an important station on the

Underground while it was under the leadership of Pastor
J.W. Anderson.
Location: 1518 M Street NW
              Washington, D.C. 20002
              (202) 331-1426

Washington, D.C.
Cedar Hill, Former Home of Frederick Douglass

Frederick Douglass lived in this imposing house on Cedar
Hill during the last years of his life. Located in Old Ana-
costia on a nine-acre hillside, it is now maintained by the
National Park Service. The house was never connected with
the Underground Railroad. Douglass purchased this home,
which he called Cedar Hill, in 1877 for $6,700. His second
wife, a white woman named Helen Pitts, arranged for the
home to be preserved as a memorial to the great leader after
his death. Douglass, who was himself of mixed parentage,
caused quite a stir when he took Helen Pitts as his second
wife. He later stated, "I took as my first wife the race of my
mother and as my second wife the race of my father."
Location: 1411 W Street, SE.
              It can be reached from central Washington by
              taking I-395 to the Eleventh Street Bridge, then
              proceeding straight ahead on Martin Luther
              King, Jr. Avenue.
              (202) 426-5961

Maryland

Baltimore, Maryland
President Street Station

Not all fugitive slaves escaped on the "Trackless Train:" some of them used real locomotives to deliver them to freedom. Most of the terminology connected with the Underground Railroad, such as agents, conductors, passengers, stockholders, stationmasters, baggage, brakemen and switching stations were terms associated with regular railroading. In fact, to avoid possible lawsuits, the Pennsylvania, Wilmington and Baltimore, like many other rail lines, posted a notice in 1858 saying,

All Colored People (Bond or Free) wishing to travel on the P.W. & B. Railroad, will be required to bring with them to the ticket office, President Street Depot, some responsible White Person, a citizen of Baltimore known to the undersigned, William Crawford, Agent.

In 1848, prior to the building of the President Street Station, two of the boldest and most ingenious escapes in Underground Railroad history passed through Baltimore, and later became topics of conversation throughout the nation. Henry "Box" Brown, who had himself shipped in a box from Richmond, Virginia, stopped in Baltimore on his way to freedom in Philadelphia. William and Ellen Craft, husband and wife, escaping from Macon, Georgia, were delayed at the old Pratt and Charles Street depot, but eventually were permitted to travel on to Philadelphia.

Other fugitive slaves passed through the President Street Station. In 1857 an unnamed young woman arrived in Philadelphia in a box after traveling through President Street; she was a seamstress and had punched airholes in her container with her scissors. Her bold and dangerous escape to freedom is documented in William Still's book, *The Underground Railroad*.

President Street Station's name derived from an attempt on President-elect Abraham Lincoln's life, prevented by the famous detective and secret-serviceman Allan Pinkerton when he had Lincoln's train re-routed to avoid the Baltimore site of the planned assasination.

Location: President and Fleet Streets
For further information contact:
           Maryland Historical Society
           201 West Monument Street
           Baltimore, MD 21201
           (410) 685-3750

Baltimore, Maryland
The Orchard Street Church and the Watkins Family

Baltimore was a pivotal point on the Underground Railroad, a city divided, with both an anti-slavery society and a slave auction block. The Orchard Street African Methodist Episcopal Church began more than 150 years ago, with prayer meetings held in the home of a Caribbean-born former slave named Truema Le Pratt. Free African-Americans and slaves labored by torchlight to build the first church. Nearly century and a half later, in 1882, the present church was built on the original site, replacing a second structure. According to oral tradition, the first and second church buildings served as stops on Baltimore's Underground Railroad. During the early 1970s, a tunnel was uncovered beneath the church by construction workers.

Connected with Baltimore's fugitive slave network was William Watkins, a noted African-American teacher and abolitionist. His home was a major station, and several members of his family were connected with the Orchard Street A.M.E. Church. Watkin's famous niece, Frances Ellen Watkins Harper, was born in Baltimore. When she settled in Philadelphia, Harper worked with William Still and offered her home as a safe house to escaped slaves. By the 1850s she had won considerable fame as an anti-slavery poet, novelist and speaker. She became associated with Frederick Douglass and assisted him with his newspaper, the *North Star*.

Despite the buffetings and erosion of time, Orchard Street A.M.E. Church still stands proudly today, serving as the headquarters of Baltimore's Urban League and as an African-American cultural museum.

Location: 512 Orchard Street (and David Hill)
             Baltimore, MD 21201
             (410) 523-8150

Baltimore, Maryland
The Great Blacks in Wax Museum
Frederick Douglass' Life-Size Wax Figure

Located in Baltimore is the "Great Blacks in Wax" Museum. It features over 150 lifelike figures of prominent African-Americans, including Harriet Tubman and Frederick Douglass.

Douglass was an exasperating slave, and often suffered because of his indomitable spirit; he bore the marks of many beatings and whippings on his body. Born in February of 1817 in Tuckahoe, Talbot County, he was the son of the slave Harriet Bailey and an unidentified white man. Once, when Douglass was asked exactly when and where he was born, he declared, "I cannot answer, don't know my age, slaves have no family records." In Baltimore he labored as a slave at Fells Point, as a ship caulker. In 1838, when he was 21, he

Reverend Henry Highland Gar-
net, an escaped Maryland slave.
Garnet later became an impor-
tant agent on the Underground
Railroad, an editor and orator.

Frederick Douglass

escaped to New Bedford, Massachusetts, on the Underground Railroad. Still a fugitive slave, he continued his
dangerous travels as an orator, speaking publicly and de-
nouncing slavery. The publication in 1845 of his narrative
made it obvious who his owner was. Later in his life,
Douglass wrote a powerful autobiography revealing the
names of the friends who had assisted him on the road to
freedom.

Recently the museum has re-created a portion of a slave
ship and its hold, that will become a permanent part of the
museum.

Scenes that have been re-created also include the branding of a woman, and a mutiny of a man trying to starve
himself to death to avoid slavery.

Location: Baltimore's Great Blacks in Wax Museum

1601 East North Avenue
Baltimore, MD 21213
(410) 563-3404

The Eastern Shore, Maryland
Birthplace of Prominent Underground Railroad Conductor
It is evident from the works of William Still and other Underground Railroad historians that more slaves escaped into the North from this region than from any other area of Maryland. It produced many of the leading African-American revolutionaries, including Harriet Tubman, the Reverend Samuel R. Ward, James W.C. Pennington, Hezekiah Grice and the Reverend Henry Highland Garnet. Other fugitive slaves told William Still that they had escaped from the following towns and counties; Hagerstown, Frederick, Westminster, Laurel, Bel Air, Towson, Havre de Grace, Elkton, Easton, Cambridge and Hereford. Many slaves found refuge in vessels sailing from the ports of Annapolis and Baltimore, while others were transported in small boats on the Chesapeake Bay into the Susquehanna River and delivered to waiting conductors in Pennsylvania.

Bucktown, Maryland
Harriet Tubman's Birthplace Marker

I have seen hundreds of escaped slaves, but I never saw one who was willing to go back and be a slave. I think slavery is the next thing to hell.
Harriet Tubman

Dark of skin and medium in height, with a full, broad face often topped by a colored kerchief, Harriet Tubman possessed extraordinary physical endurance and muscular strength as well as mental fortitude. As a young woman in her 20s, Harriet set off one dark summer night in 1849 from her master Edward Brodas' plantation in Bucktown to follow the North Star. After great lengths she crossed the

45

Harriet Tubman, one of the most popular conductors on the Underground Railroad.

Mason-Dixon Line into Pennsylvania, and, penniless and "a stranger in a strange land" as she later remembered, she joined and inspired the Underground Railroad.

At least 19 times Tubman returned to the South, rescuing perhaps 300 slaves, including her own family, from "the jaws of hell." She signalled her people with a song, and, although she could not read, she knew her Bible and felt no fear. "My train never ran off the track and I never lost a passenger," said "the Woman called Moses."

Location: Harriet Tubman's birthplace marker is located eight miles south of U.S. 50 on Maryland Route 397. A short distance away from the historical marker is Bazzel Methodist Episcopal Church, built on the site where Harriet Tubman worshipped in open-air services during her early youth.

For further information contact:
Dorchester County Tourism Office
410-228-1000

Sharpsburg, Maryland
The Kennedy Farm: John Brown's Headquarters

Today the Kennedy Farm is a historical site located in a pleasant mountain setting. In 1859, it was an old farm house across the Potmac River from Harpers Ferry that John Brown had rented under the alias of Isaac Smith. Visitors were unwelcome; Brown's 16-year-old daughter Annie and 17-year-old Martha, wife of his son Olive, kept lookout and cooked for the men. Brown had gathered a number of supporters and a collection of arms. On one occasion, "Old Brown" traveled to Chambersburg, Pennsylvania, to keep a rendezvous with his friend, Frederick Douglass, in a stone quarry. Douglass failed to discourage him in making his raid on Harpers Ferry, and refused to join him. However, Shields Green, a fugitive slave from Charleston, whom Douglass had harbored, came with Brown and was later killed in the attack on Harpers Ferry on Sunday, October 16, 1859, when Brown revealed his true identity. It had been such a well-kept secret that when the raid first occurred, early newspaper reports indicated that it was not known who was in charge.

On exhibit at the Kennedy Farm are a lifelike mannequin of John Brown and other memorabilia related to his famous raid on Harpers Ferry.

Location: United States Route 340, near Maryland entrance
              to the old Harpers Ferry Bridge
For further information contact:
The Kennedy Farm
2604 Chestnut Grove Road
Sharpsburg, MD 21782
301-432-2666

New Jersey

Timbuktu, New Jersey

Named for the fabled desert city in West Africa, Timbuktu, New Jersey, has been an African-American community from its inception in the early 1820s. While the ancient city in the desert was known as a trading post and a center of learning, her New Jersey namesake was during the antebellum period a noted haven for freed and escaped slaves surrounded by concealing woods. Although fugitive slaves normally could feel reasonably safe from their masters in Timbuktu, in 1860 the town was involved in the "Battle of Pine Swamp," when a posse of slave hunters attempted to recapture several runaways. The slave hunters were beaten back, and shortly thereafter Timbuktu became known on the Underground Railroad grapevine as a place where members of the community would protect their fugitives. The three focal points of Underground activity were the African Methodist Episcopal Church, the schoolhouse and the camp meeting ground. Many escaped slaves came across the Delaware River from the state of Delaware; some settled in Timbuktu, while others continued on to New York State and Canada. Contemporary maps have shortened the name to Bukto.

Location: About two miles south of Mount Holly on the
             road from Rancocas to Mount Holly, in
             Westampton Township.

Mannington, New Jersey
The Tide Mill Farm

The Tide Mill home of Quaker George Abbotts, built in 1845, was often reached by escaping slaves who propelled logs across the flooded Mannington Meadows to get there. Once safe on dry land, slaves were taken to the Abbott Farmhouse, fed and given shelter before they were moved on to the next station. In 1985 a secret room was discovered under the floor of one of the rooms in the old home. An air vent was found to lead several feet underground from the room to the middle of the yard.

The house has since been turned into a bed and breakfast inn.

Location: 100 Tide Mill Road
             Mannington, NJ 08079
             (609) 935-2798

Mt. Holly, New Jersey
The Ashurst Mansion

While fugitive slaves were resting and sleeping in this spacious house, the Ashurst family provided suitable wagons and drivers to take passengers to distant stations. The home was well adapted to harbor escaping slaves. The mansion is now used as a law office.

Location: Ashurst Lane and Garden Street
             Mt. Holly, NJ 08060

Princeton, New Jersey
The Witherspoon Presbyterian Church

Built in 1840, Witherspoon Presbyterian Church is located in a section of Princeton that was called "African Lane" during the 19th century. Oral tradition states that this church and members of its congregation were connected with the Underground Railroad; Princeton was certainly situated on a main route that led into New York State.

At the turn of the 20th century, the church was pastored by William Drew Robeson, a former slave who was born on a plantation in Martin County, North Carolina, and escaped in 1860 at the age of 15, making his way north on the Underground. He married Maria Louisa Bustill, a school teacher whose father and mother, Charles and Emily Bustill, were connected with the Underground Railroad in Philadelphia. William and Maria Robeson were the parents of one of the world's charismatic personalities, Paul Leroy Robeson, reowned athlete, scholar, singer, actor and humanitarian.

Location: 124 Witherspoon Street
              Princeton, NJ 08542
              (609) 924-1666

Haddonfield, New Jersey
Edgewater: Station on the Underground

Built in 1748, this imposing, three-and-a-half story masonry and sandstone structure was a station stop on the Underground Railroad operated by Thomas and Josiah Evans. The brothers concealed fugitive slaves in the haymow or attic, and, after feeding them, drove them in the middle of the night to Mt. Holly, where they were sheltered during the day. On one occasion when Thomas Evans was apprehended for assisting an escaped slave named Joshua Sadler, he was forced to purchase the man to ensure his freedom. Sadler settled near Westmont later in life and started a school for African-American children known as Sadlertown.

Location: Mill Road, along the Haddonfield/Cherry Hill
              border.
              Haddonfield, NJ 08033
For further information contact:
              Cherry Hill Township Recreation Dept.
              820 Mercer Street
              Cherry Hill, NJ 08002
              (609) 488-7868

Lumberton, New Jersey
The D.B. Cole House

The D. B. Cole house, once a station on New Jersey's Underground Railroad, is now a tenant house on the farm of Lester C. Jones, Sr. No one knows how many fugitive slaves sneaked through the carriage house to hide in a false well that was reached by sliding down a chute. Under the well is a room, 20 feet at the highest point of its arched ceiling, that was large enough for the Underground Railroad, but is now a reminder of the passage of time. This venerable Burlington County hiding place can still be seen today. The farm is located on a former Indian trail.

Location: Creek Road
             Lumberton, NJ 08048
Tours by appointment:
             (609) 261-7176

Lawnside, New Jersey
The Peter Mott House

According to oral tradition handed down from one generation to another within the African-American community, the Peter Mott house was a key stop on the Underground Railroad. Mott, who came to Lawnside from the state of Delaware, was a farmer and a preacher. He was one of the few African-American property owners in Camden County. According to descendents of the famous Still family, Mott worked with noted agents William Still and his brother James, hiding fugitive slaves behind a double door above his cellar, feeding them and passing them on to Mt. Laurel and Mt. Holly. The Mott house is one of the few remaining structures of its kind in Camden County. In 1990, the former station was saved from demolition (it occupies two prime building lots) when local residents petitioned for it to be placed on the National Register of Historical Places. The small white wood frame house that was built in 1845 still stands today.

"On to Liberty," in Theodor Kauman's sympathetic portrayal of the route to freedom.

THE UNDERGROUND RAILROAD

Location: Gloucester Road and White Horse Pike
For further information contact:
Clarence Still
137 E. Oak Avenue
Lawnside, NJ 08045
(609) 546-8172

Lawnside, New Jersey
Mount Pisgah A.M.E. Church

The town that is now known as Lawnside was once a station on the Underground Railroad, aptly named Free Haven. Originally located in a densely wooded area, the whole community consisted of African-Americans, both slaves and free, and became a natural safe haven. The homes were deliberately located in the woods to conceal fugitive slaves from slave hunters. A number of the early residents were themselves escaped slaves from Snow Hill, Maryland.

Lawnside is connected with one of the most famous names in Underground Railroad history, that of William Still. The Stills have lived in this community, even now predominatly African-American, for generations. Their ancestors, Levin and Charity Still, were both born in slavery, but they were able to buy Levin's freedom, while Charity succeeded in escaping and joining him with two of her daughters. The Stills eventually raised a family of 18, and most of their children were conductors on the Underground Railroad. William Still documented his family history in his famous book, *The Underground Railroad*. The Still's family church, Mount Pisagh A.M.E. Church, dates its foundings from the year 1792, and is the oldest Methodist church in Camden County. It also was a station on the Underground Railroad.

Members of the Still family, and Civil War veterans, as well as a naval veteran of the War of 1812 are buried in the church's intriguing cemetery.

Location: The intersection of Warrick and Moudly Roads

54

For further information contact:
Clarence Still
137 East Oak Avenue
Lawnside, NJ 08045
(609) 546-8172

Salem, New Jersey
Abigail Goodwin House

Salem County's proximity to the South, as well as the anti-slavery sentiments of a number of its Quaker families, gave it a prominent role in the Underground Railroad. As early as 1795, Salem County Justice of the Peace Thomas Sinnickson was quoted as dictating to the local jailor, "You have herewith committed to your custody a negro man who calls himself Jack Wilson taken up as a runaway." Harriet Tubman directed her passengers through this community on several occasions. Among those who took a most active part in hiding escaped slaves was a courageous Quaker woman named Abigail Goodwin, who was aided by her sister Elizabeth. Goodwin was active in the anti-slavery cause as early as 1836. Although her own clothes were often more ragged than those of the runaways who knocked at her door, she organized sewing societies, saved her own and borrowed others' money to support the Underground Railroad. Abigail Goodwin helped fugitive slaves for nearly 36 years until her death in 1867. William Still devoted a chapter in *The Underground Railroad* to Goodwin and her sister. The two "friends of the fugitive" occasionally sent their passengers on to Edward Turner, the well-known station keeper in Cape May.

Location: The Goodwin House is located at 47 West Market Street downtown Salem and is privately owned.
Salem, NJ 08079

Harriet Beecher Stowe

Reverend Henry Ward Beecher

New York

Brooklyn, New York
The Bridge Street African Methodist Episcopal
Wesleyan Church

The Bridge Street African Methodist Episcopal Wesleyan
Church is the oldest African-American Church in Brooklyn.
The earliest records of the church show that in 1766,
Wesleyan British Army Captain Thomas Webb conducted
outdoor services in Brooklyn. Later in 1794, a small inte-
grated congregation built Sands Street on the same location
where the outdoor services were held regularly. Sometime
later, friction developed among white and African-American members and separation was imminent. As a result, the
African Wesleyan Methodist Episcopal Church was formed
in 1818. This church later became a major station on the
Underground Railroad in Brooklyn, and provided refuge
for hundreds of escaped slaves. The church also provided
shelter, food and clothing as well. In addition, the church
also provided funds to establish Wiberforce University located in Ohio. The present church is in the Bedford-Stuyve-
sant Community.

Location: 273 Stuyvesant Avenue
             Bedford-Stuyvesant
             Brooklyn, NY 11216
             (718) 452-3936

Brooklyn, New York
Plymouth of the Pilgrims

Henry Ward Beecher, the brother of Harriet Beecher Stowe, was a popular preacher, editor and abolitionist. He was also an ardent supporter of women's rights and was the only man ever to serve as president of the American Suffrage Society. A popular expression during the years when he served as pastor of the Plymouth Church of the Pilgrims was, "If you want to hear Henry Ward Beecher preach, take the ferry to Brooklyn and then follow the crowd." His church seated over 2,500 visitors. People stood in lines two deep for a couple of blocks waiting to get into his church to hear him preach. From his pulpit Beecher hurled invective at all slaveowners, shouting that a gun was a greater moral agency than the Bible. He once held a mock slave auction, auctioning off a slave girl for her freedom.

Standing in the Hills Arcade, a statue of Beecher as a liberator graces the Orange Street garden. Like his father, the Reverend Lyman Beecher, he supported the Underground Railroad. There is a legend that cannot be documented that slaves were hidden in the tunnel-like spaces beneath the church, which has been called the Grand Central Terminal of the Underground Railroad. In 1875 Beecher welcomed the nationally-known Fisk Jubilee Singers to his church. Their spirituals drew tears and the waving of handerchiefs from the crowd for their soul-stirring singing. Several of their songs were connected with the Underground Railroad.

Among those who have spoken in the church are Horace Greeley, Ralph Waldo Emerson, Wendell Phillips, Charles Sumner, Clara Barton, Booker T. Washington and Martin Luther King, Jr. This historic church still stands today.

Location: 75 Hicks Street
             Brooklyn, NY 11201
             (718) 624-4743

Brooklyn New York
Siloam Presbyterian Church

Prior to the Civil War, Siloam Presbyterian Church was a center of anti-slavery activities and used its quarters to shelter escaped slaves. They were sometimes concealed by members of this church until the word was given to travel to the next Underground Railroad station. Members of the congregation provided funds when it was necessary. This African-American church still stands today.

Location: 260 Jefferson Avenue
              Bedford-Suyvesant
              Brooklyn, NY 11216
              (718) 789-7050

New York City, New York
Mother Zion African Methodist Episcopal Church

Apart from being the oldest African-American church in New York state, Mother Zion African Methodist Episcopal Church also enjoys the distinction of having assisted hundreds of fugitive slaves during its early years. The first church was located on Leonard Street; its cornerstone was laid on July 30, 1800. The Reverend James Varick spoke forcefully from its pulpit against slavery and offered the church as a station on the Underground Railroad. Mother Zion A.M.E. Church, affectionately called "Mother Zion," was also known as the "Freedom Church" because of its abolitionist ties. It was the founding church of the A.M.E. Conference of Churches; many conference churches likewise served as stations on the Underground Railroad. Mother Zion A.M.E. later moved to its present location in Harlem, where the Reverend Benjamin Robeson, brother of Paul Robeson, served as pastor for nearly 25 years. He led civil rights crusades that attracted such notables as Langston Hughes, James Baldwin and Dr. W.E.B. Dubois, and his pulpit was often the platform for social and political activism.

Location: 140 137th Street
            Harlem, NY 10030
            (212) 234-1545

Barker, New York
David Barker Home

David Barker and his wife Vania, a Quaker couple with no children of their own but eight foster children in their home, built this large red brick house with bricks from Barker's brickyard. David Barker made frequent trips to Niagara Falls, explaining that he had grain to be ground into flour. As often as not, he was transporting fugitive slaves. The Barkers' passengers usually came to them by following what would later become the route of the Rome, Watertown and Ogendenburg Railroad. Passengers received food and shelter at the Barker home as well as transportation when it was time for them to make the last leg of their journey. The house is identified by historic marker stating that Barker was the founder of this Quaker community and a conductor on the Underground Railroad.
Location: 1707 Quaker Road
For further information contact:
            Castellani Art Museum
            Niagara University
            Niagara Falls, NY 14109
            (716) 286-8581 (phone and fax)

Lewiston, New York
Tyron's Folly

The Reverend Amos Tyron was an agent for the Underground Railroad who assisted escaped slaves in crossing the Niagara River to freedom in Queenston, Onatario, Canada. His home was referred to as a "folly" because of its extravagant antiquarian design typical of the romanticism of the late 18th and early 19th centuries. It made an excellent sanc-

tuary and getaway point due to its terraced layout of two
main living areas above four underground cellars leading
to the river bank. Although the spacious home has been
remodeled many times since it was built in the 1820s, it
retains its place in local history as a important station on the
Underground Railroad. Set back on a bluff, with a commanding view of the Niagara River, Tyron's Folly is today
a private riverside residence.

Location: 4772 Lower River Road (Route 18F)
For further information contact:
          Castellani Art Museum
          Niagara University
          Niagara Falls, NY 14109
          (716) 286-8581

Pekin, New York
The Thomas Root House

Abolitionist Thomas Root built this house in the 1850s and
used it as the last stop on the Underground Railroad in the
U.S. Fugitive slaves were hidden in the cellar and barn of
the house and transported to the Canadian border in farm
wagons containing produce. The Root home is one of the
few documented stations in this area.

One house lying east of Lockport in the section that is
today known as Chestnut Ridge was, according to local
legend, a station on the Underground. Isaac Terry, the former owner of the house was known for his anti-slavery
views. He was acquainted with Frederick Douglass, who, it
was said, visited Terry's home.

Location: Thomas Roots's house is at 3106 Upper Mountain
          Road.
For further information contact:
          Castellani Art Museum
          Niagara University
          Niagara Falls, NY 14109
          (716) 286-8581

Lockport, New York
Lockport Y.M.C.A.

Known as the Moss house during the era of the Underground Railroad, this building was once a private home where runaway slaves were hidden. Now housing the Y.M.C.A., it is a historic landmark that bears a plaque on the facade noting its service in the name of freedom.

Location: 32 Cottage Street
Lockport, NY 14094
(716) 434-8887

Niagara Falls, New York
St. John's African Methodist Episcopal Church

Located in the heart of Niagara Falls' African-American community, St. John's African Methodist Episcopal Church was the first church founded in Niagara County by people of African descent and was a station on the Underground Railroad. The county is dotted with Underground stations where fugitive slaves gathered before slipping into Canada, where the Emancipation Act of 1793 had prohibited the importation of slaves.

Location: 917 Garden Avenue
Niagara Falls, NY 14305
(716) 285-6432

New York, New York
Isaac T. Hopper Home

Quaker Issac T. Hopper had become the friend of men and women of African descent when he was nine, as a young boy in Philadelphia. By the time Hopper was 17, he was giving what support he could to runaways, and by 1787 was actively assisting escaped slaves. Before long he joined the Philadelphia Manumission Society, and his home became a station stop on the "Lightning Train."

One of the African Americans that he aided was the

Isaac Hopper of Philadelphia and New York who was active as early as 1787, assisting escaped slaves.

Reverend Richard Allen, founder of the African Methodist Episcopal Church. Although Allen was a highly respected member of the Philadelphia community, he was nevertheless arrested by a slave hunter as a fugitive. After a short trial, in which Hopper paid the cost of the defense, Allen was declared free.

When Hopper moved to New York City in 1829, his home once again became a noted station on the Underground. In 1835, he attracted notoriety when he was falsely accused of harboring a fugitive slave in his store on Pearl Street.

Today the Isaac T. Hopper Home is known as an organization that helps families in need.

Location: 110 Second Avenue
             New York, NY 10003
             (212) 674-1163

Ithaca, New York
Cemetery Inscription of a Former Fugitive Slave

Located in the city cemetery of Ithaca, New York, is a tombstone with in inscription that has withstood time and the elements. It bears the following message:

> 1814-1889; Faithful Daniel Jackson; Born a slave, he followed the North Star to Freedom; He returned to bring his aged mother and tenderly care for her a long as he lived. They were not long parted, for she survived him but five days. Daniel Jackson was 75 and his mother 103 years of age. This tribute belongs of right to faithfulness and filial affection.

Location: University and Court Streets
Ithaca, NY 14850

Niagara Falls, New York
The Whirlpool Rapids Bridge

The old wooden suspension bridge that was located near the swirling pools of Niagara Falls was used by Harriet Tubman and hundreds of other liberty-seeking slaves, for it spanned the cut-off point between slavery and freedom, which was the United States border to Canada. The original structure known by Tubman has since been demolished and replaced by the Robling Bridge, named for its builder, now called the Whirlpool Rapids Bridge.

Although the old span located in Lewiston was also a suspension bridge, it did not have railroad tracks on which fugitives could ride what Harriet Tubman called the "iron horse" to freedom. This bridge is listed on page 76, the Lewiston, NY "Suspension Bridge."
Location: Whirlpool Street

Buffalo, New York
The Michigan Avenue Baptist Church

The Michigan Avenue Baptist Church was an important

William Wells Brown, an escaped slave, anti-slavery lecturer and the first African-American to write a play or novel.

way station on the Underground Railroad, a haven for slaves traveling through the area. Shortly after his escape from slavery, William Wells Brown hired himself out at the age of 21 to a lake captain, and later worked at various jobs in Cleveland, then Buffalo. Here he became associated with the members of this church. In 1847 he was called by William Lloyd Garrison to serve as a lecturer and Underground Railroad agent. Although Brown could not rival Frederick Douglass as an orator, he lectured almost without interruption. On one occasion in Buffalo he assisted a fugitive slave when the owner attempted to return the man to bondage in the South. A prolific author, Brown became America's first African-American man of letters. To him belong the multiple distinctions of being the first African-American novelist, dramatist, historian and travel writer. Brown was also s self-taught doctor and practiced medicine after the Civil War.

Location: 511 Michigan Avenue
              Buffalo, NY 14203
              (716) 854-7976

Troy, New York
The National City Bank Building

Fugitive slave hunting became a profitable business when the Fugitive Slave Law of 1850 offered a fee for the capture of runaway slaves and delivery to federal officers in the North. Members of the Underground Railroad network had the double duty of rescuing escaped slaves first from Southern slave hunters, then from Northern captors.

For example, Charles Nalle, an escaped slave from Culpepper County, Virginia, was discovered in Troy, New York, in Harriet Tubman's home territory, and was taken against his will to the United States Commissioner's office. As news of Nalle's arrest spread, an angry crowd gathered, Harriet Tubman among them. Exposing herself to the full fury of the pro-slavery forces in Troy, she entered the office of the commissioner and forcefully rescued Nalle. Although another African-American was killed and Tubman herself injured, Nalle was able to make his escape into freedom. In 1908, a half century later, the citizens of Troy erected a memorial at the National City Bank Building that is inscribed as follows:

> *Here was begun*
> *April 27, 1860*
> *The Rescue of*
> *Charles Nalle*
> *An Escaped Slave who had been Arrested*
> *Under the Fugitive Slave Law.*

It is there to this day.

Location: Northeast corner of First and State Streets
            Troy, NY 12180

Rochester, New York
Susan B. Anthony House

Rochester was the home of Susan B. Anthony. Raised to be self-supporting by a Quaker father, Anthony spoke out

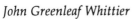

John Greenleaf Whittier

Thomas Garrett

Lucretia Coffin Mott

Levi Coffin

for temperence, women's rights and abolition, despite vehement prejudice against women in public affairs. When Harriet Tubman was not staying with the Frederick Douglass family or at the African Methodist Episcopal Church at Spring and Favor Streets, she stayed with the Anthonys and in other local abolitionist homes.

Susan B. Anthony's brother Merritt had fought with John Brown in a bloody skirmish in Kansas against pro-slavery forces. The Susan B. Anthony House is a National Historic Landmark and is open for tours. Large groups should shedule a tour.

Location: 17 Madison Street
Rochester, NY 14608
(716) 235-6124

Rochester, New York
Frederick Douglass Moument

Frederick Douglass published his newspaper, the *North Star*, in Rochester and his print shop and home were stations on the Underground Railroad. Although his first house burned to the ground, hundreds of fugitive slaves passed through his station in Rochester during these years. On one occasion, Harriet Tubman brought thirteen slaves to his home at once. Douglass, a former fugitive slave himself, recognized the superior contributions made by Tubman. He once wrote:

> Most of that I have done has been in public, and I have received much encouragement ... applause of the crowd ... While the most that you have done has been witnessed by a few trembling, scared and footsore bondsmen ... The midnight sky and the silent stars have been the witnesses of your devotion to freedom and your heroism.

The Douglass monument was dedicated by Governor Theodore Roosevelt in 1899.

Location: Central Avenue and St. Paul Street in
Highland Park

Reverend Jermain Loguen

William Whipper

For further information contact:
      The Hamm House
      301 Adams Street
      Rochester, NY 14608
      (716) 464-8828

Syracuse, New York
The Reverend Jermain Loguen Gravesite

Syracuse was an active center for abolitionists, and the Reverend Jermain Loguen was the superintendent of the fugitive slave network in this city. Son of a Tennessee master and a slave woman, Loguen spoke from experience when he said, "No day dawns for the slave, nor is it looked for. It is all night—night forever." After his escape to Canada, he returned to New York and lived for short periods in Rochester, Utica, Ithaca and Bath before settling in Syracuse, where he and his wife Caroline established two major Underground Railroad terminals, their home and his church. Loguen helped 1,500 escaped slaves to freedom, and started schools for African-Americans in New York State. He was

69

an intimate friend of Harriet Tubman and Frederick Douglass; Douglass' son married his daughter. When the Lougen home was filled to capacity with fugitives, he sent the overflow to the home of the Reverend Samuel J. May.

Location: Oakwood Cemetery, Section 6
            Syracuse, NY 13210

Syracuse, New York
Monument Honoring a Fugitive Slave

Escaped slave Jerry McHenry had been living as a free man for several years in Syracuse when a detective employed by his former master discovered his whereabouts in 1851. He was seized by slave hunters to be returned South, but was rescued from the Journal Building, where he was being held, by a group of abolitionists led by millionaire philanthropist Gerrit Smith, and William Seward who was later to become United States Secretary of State. The rescue was in such open defiance of the law that prosecution was deemed futile. This inimical act inflicted such fatal wounds to the Fugitive Slave Law of 1850 that the law could hardly be enforced.

The public was outraged to hear that McHenry had been found lying on the floor, bloody, almost naked and bound in chains. After his ordeal, he was sent on to Canada, where he worked as a barrel maker. In the late 1980s, a monument honoring his celebrated rescue was erected.

Location: Clinton Square and West Water Street, near the
            Canal

Rochester, New York
Austin Steward Memorial

Austin Steward, a fugitive slave turned grocer and conductor on the Underground Railroad was, along with Frederick Douglass, an important station keeper in Rochester. His home, which no longer stands, was known as a haven to escaping slaves who traveled through the city.

Frederick Douglass as a young man.

Henry Bibbs

Sojourner Truth

Reverend Samuel Ringgold Ward

Steward was at one time the president of Wilberforce Colony in Canada, and in 1857 published his autobiography entitled *Twenty-Two Years a Slave, and Forty Years a Freeman.*
Location: 120 East Main Street, Genesee Plaza Holiday Inn
            Rochester, NY 14604
            The memorial is on the second level connecting the bridge to the convention center
For further information and a self-directed tour which can
            be obtained from:
            Greater Rochester Visitors Assoc.
            126 Andrews Street
            Rochester, NY 14604
            (716) 546-3070
Or contact: Historical Society of Rochester
            485 East Avenue
            Rochester, NY 14607
            (716) 271-2705

Auburn, New York
William H. Seward House

The home of William H. Seward was an important station on Auburn's Underground Railroad as a well as a publishing center for anti-slavery literature. It was here that Frederick Douglass's celebrated autobiography was printed. Seward had an unassailable reputation as a friend of the fugitive slave. He opened his home to runaways and, as Governor of New York State, he purchased a small property for his friend Harriet Tubman, payable on easy terms. He also participated in the famous rescue of fugitive slave Jerry McHenry. During President Abraham Lincoln's administration he was appointed Secretary of State. Seward's Cayuga County home has been declared a National Historic Landmark.
Location: 33 South Street
            Auburn, NY 13021
For touring and information:
            (315) 252-1283

Ithaca, New York
St. James African Methodist Episcopal Zion Church

St. James African Methodist Episcopal Zion Church is one of the rare surviving pre-Civil War African-American houses of worship. The Reverend Samuel Perry, pastor of the church during the era of the Underground Railroad, used it as a way station, hiding escaped slaves in the basement or in the homes of his congregation. Assisting the Reverend Perry in his clandestine operations was one of Ithaca's most prominent citizens, Edward Esty, owner of a tannery reputed to be among the largest in New York State. Harriet Tubman worshipped in this church when on her way to Auburn and Canada.

Location: 116-118 Cleveland Avenue
Ithaca, NY 14850
(607) 272-4053

Fort Edward (Washington County), New York
Early Residence of Solomon Northup

Solomon Northup, the freed African-American who lived 12 years in slavery after having been kidnapped and put on the auction block, spent his early years at Old Fort House. In his celebrated narrative written in 1853, *Twelve Years a Slave*, Northup noted:

> The only respite from constant labor the slave has through the whole year is during the Christmas holidays ... It is the only time to which they look forward with any interest or pleasure. It is a time of feasting and frolicking and fiddling—the carnival season with the children of bondage. They are the only days when they are allowed a little restricted liberty, and heartily indeed do they enjoy it.

Location: 29 Lower Broadway
Fort Edward, NY 12828
(518) 747-7600
For further information contact:

Eighteen-year-old Lear Green escaping in a chest from Baltimore, Maryland. After her successful escape, she lived in Elmira, New York.

A bold stroke for freedom—escaped slaves defending themselves against armed slavehunters.

Washington County Historical Society
167 Broadway
Fort Edward, NY, 12828
(518) 747- 9108
(The Washington County Historical Society
operates Fridays from 12-4p.m.)

Jamestown, New York
Catherine Harris House

Among the most brave and adventuresome African-American women in New York was safe house keeper Catherine Harris. She was a devout member of Blackwell Chapel and the African Methodist Episcopal Zion Church in Jamestown. Her home is today marked by New York State as a memorial of Underground Railroad history, as her cellar was a congenial hiding place for fugitive slaves.
Location: 1610 Spring Street
             Jamestown, NY 14701
For further information contact:
             Fenton Historical Society
             67 Washington St.
             Jamestown, NY 14701
             (716) 664-6256

Peterboro, NewYork
Gerrit Smith Land Office

The Peterboro mansion and land office of Gerrit Smith was a place of refuge for Harriet Tubman and hundreds of other conductors and passengers on the Freedom Train. Born in Utica in 1797, Smith was the son of Peter Smith, John Jacob Astor's partner in the fur trade and other enterprises. Gerrit Smith took over his father's real estate interests and extended them throughout New York State, becoming a millionaire in the process. He did not betray his humanitarian values, and was known for never turning a good person or a good cause from his door. His famous cousin, Elizabeth Cady Stanton, shared his devotion to conviction. Smith used his barn and a room under the kitchen floor to harbor escaped slaves. He made a large contribution to John Brown for the attack on Harpers Ferry, and, when Brown was captured and presently hung, Smith had himself committed to an insane asylum until the threat of his own hanging had passed, and it was safe to return to normal life.

His home burned in 1936, just before it was to become a state historical site. There is a small museum, open by appointment only, that includes information on Gerrit and other African-Americans who settled in the area.

Location: Peterboro Area Museum
c/o John Andrezejek
R.R. 1, Oxbow Road
Cazenovia, NY 13035
(315) 684-7003

Lewiston, New York
The Suspension Bridge

Located about four miles from Niagara Falls, Lewiston served as the final stop on the Underground Railroad route to Canada. A monument to freedom-seeking fugitive slaves is located at the First Presbyterian Church on Cayuga Street.

Located also in Lewiston are the remains of two large granite columns that once supported the famous Suspension Bridge. Built in 1850, this bridge was once a welcome sight for hundreds of fugitive slaves, including Harriet Tubman, for just across the Niagara River was Canada, the Promised Land. Midway across the Suspension Bridge the United States ends and Canada begins. Harriet Tubman, who had traversed this bridge on numerous trips and who, like most fugitive slaves, crossed it on foot, knew from a slight descent on the Canadian side that her passengers had "crossed the line." For a similar bridge see the Niagara Falls, NY bridge entry on page 64.

Location: The two large granite columns that supported the
             Suspension Bridge are located in Art Park on
             River Road

Lewiston, New York
Riverside Inn

To stroll through historic Lewiston is to relive history.
During the War of 1812, the village was burned to the ground
during a British assault on Fort Niagara. Determined settlers rebuilt the village in a matter of two years.

As related through oral tradition, during the era of the
Underground Railroad, the Riverside Inn, located at the
base of Niagara Falls, served as a hiding place for fugitive
slaves before they made their final crossing to freedom in
Canada.

Location: River Road, a short distance from Art Park
             115 S. Water St.
             Lewiston, NY 14092
             (716) 754-8206

Lewiston, New York
The Niagara Frontier Bible Church

This large church/residence was once a monastery. During the era of the Underground Railroad, fugitive slaves
were provided with shelter here until they were transported
across the Niagara River to Canada. In the summer and fall,
some slaves swam across the river to freedom when the
water was calm; others were rowed across in small boats. In
the winter, when the river was frozen, many slaves walked
across the ice to the Promised Land.

Location: Mohawk and River Roads
             Lewiston, NY 14092
             (716) 745-2210

Harriet Tubman's home in Auburn, New York, was never a station on the Underground Railroad. A few years before she died in 1913, Tubman turned it into a home for the aged.

Auburn, New York
Harriet Tubman Home

This house was never a station on the Underground Railroad. Harriet Tubman purchased it (see Wm. Seward p. 72) for herself and her parents after serving as a spy, nurse and scout during the Civil War, despite that she was denied a pension for her services. She lived here until the last years of her life. The home has been restored to its late 19th century appearance, and contains some of her possessions.

When she was active on the Underground Railroad, Tubman was accustomed to saying, "Keep going; if you are tired, keep going; if you are scared, keep going; if you are hungry, keep going; if you want to taste freedom, keep going." She numbered among her friends Frederick Douglass, Senator Charles Sumner, John Brown, William

John Brown

Lloyd Garrison, Thomas Garrett, Sarah Bradford and Secretary of State William H. Seward. A group of her relatives and friends gathered to sing "Swing Low, Sweet Chariot" on the evening of March 10, 1913, upon her death. She was buried with military honors in Fort Hill Cemetery in Auburn. One year after her death, Auburn's citizens unveiled the Harriet Tubman Plaque, which may still be seen at the entrance to the Cayuga County Courthouse.

Location: 180-182 South Street
Auburn, NY 13021
(315) 252-2081

North Elba, New York
John Brown's Home and Grave

In 1848, John Brown took time out from his wool business of Perkins and Brown to help build a colony for African-American farmers in New York State called Timbucktoo.

The settlement was located in North Elba in Essex County, and was part of l00,000 acres set aside for freed and fugitive slaves by wealthy abolitionist and philanthropist Gerrit Smith. In 1849, Brown purhased 244 acres of land at a dollar an acre high in this Adirondack wilderness.

After he was hanged for his ill-fated attack on Harpers Ferry, Brown's widow and a group of abolitionist friends buried him on this farm at North Elba, so his grave would not be molested. The farm had never been used as an Underground Railroad station. Mrs. Brown sent an empty hearse by another route to delude would-be violators. Other Browns are also buried near his gravesite, including sons Watson and Oliver, who were killed at Harpers Ferry. In the small house are memorabilia of the Brown family, and overlooking the scenic view of the Adirondack Mountains is a large statue of Brown himself. No more need be said of Osawatomie Brown, whose "...soul goes marching on."

Location: Six miles south of Lake Placid on State Route 73
For further information and tours contact:
The John Brown Farms Historic Site
Edward Cotter, Jr.
2 John Brown Road
Lake Placid, NY 12946
(518) 523-3900
This site is closed from Oct. 24 - May.
Slide shows and other presentations are highlights.

Pennsylvania

Downingtown, Pennsylvania
Zebulon Thomas Home

Zebulon Thomas' home, now the Downingtown Public Library, was a station on the Liberty Line. It was constructed of fieldstone from local quarries in 1800. Thomas also owned a house across the road on Old Lancaster Pike, and built a connecting tunnel so he could transport escapees between the houses. As a girl's boarding school in the 1840s, his home was the site of an attempted kidnapping of a black slave woman by slave hunters and the successful kidnapping of a young black girl.
Location: 330 East Lancaster Avenue
             Downingtown, PA 19335
             (610) 269-2741

Lionville, Pennsylvania
Vickers Tavern

Runaway slaves were once harbored in the Vickers Tavern, the former home of John Vickers, a well-known conductor on Chester County's Underground Railroad. He was given the sobriquet "Quaker Abolitionist." Slaves in flight were hidden in a crawl space until it was safe to move them on, or the Vickers family sometimes hid them in the kiln, in their piles of cordwood, or under the straw covering pottery as they took them to the next station. Vickers made it a

Robert Purvis, president of the Philadelphia Underground Railroad and in the city's African-American community.

practice of sending a letter of introduction along with the slaves signed "Friend Potts," alerting his fellow Underground Railroad workers. The door to a crawl space where he hid passengers may still be seen in the tavern, which is now a restaurant serving French and Continental cuisine.

Location: Gordon Drive off Route 100 in Lionville, near Exton.

(610) 363-7998

Philadelphia, Pennsylvania
Former Home of Robert Purvis

Born free in Charleston, South Carolina, of wealthy parents, Purvis was sent at an early age to Philadelphia. While attending Amherst College in Massachusetts, he met William Lloyd Garrison, whose speeches and writing influenced Purvis to devote his life to the liberation of African-Americans. Although he was fair enough to pass for white, Purvis lived as an African-American. When the Pennsylvania legislature enacted a law in 1838 to deprive African-Americans the right to vote, he published " The Appeal for Forty Thousand Citizens Threatened with Disenfranchisement, to the People of Pennsylvania." He was a charter member of the Pennsylvania Anti-Slavery Society, president of the Philadelphia Underground Railroad and served on the Philadelphia Vigilance Committee. While living in his mother's home at Ninth and Lombard Streets, he used the house as a major station on the Underground. This house contained a secret room in the basement reached by a trapdoor for emergency concealment. Purvis kept a record of the fugitives he aided. However, later he was forced to destroy the records for the safety of his family. Upon moving to Byberry in Bucks County, he again used his home and farm as a station. When the Fugitive Slave Law of 1850 was enacted, the mild-mannered Purvis declared at the annual meeting of the Pennsylvania Anti-Slavery Society held at West Chester on October 17, 1850, "Should any wretch enter my dwelling, any pale-faced spectre among ye to execute this law on me or mine, I'll seek his life, I'll shed his blood." At this site, his last home, a Pennsylvania Historical and Museum Commission marker is dedicated to Robert Purvis, although this house was not connected with the Underground Railroad.

Location: 1601 Mt. Vernon Street
              Philadelphia, PA 19130

Philadelphia, Pennsylvania
William Still

William Still was the most energetic and perhaps the most famous Underground Railroad agent and conductor in the nation. Still had been born free in New Jersey, but his parents had undergone the hardships of escape, his father was forced to work for many years to purchase his freedom from the master who had recaptured them. William Still devoted a major part of his life assisting other escapees, with

*William Still, indefatigable
agent in the Pennsylvania
Underground Railroad. Still
kept records of escaped slaves
which were published in 1872.*

such effect that, it is recorded, 19 out of every 20 fugitive slaves passing through Philadelphia stopped at his house. In 1847, he served as a clerk in the Pennsylvania Anti-Slavery Society and later served as secretary of the Philadelphia Vigilance Committee. Among the famous Underground Railroad escapees whom he assisted were William and Ellen Craft, Harriet Tubman, Henry "Box" Brown and William Parker. Still also worked closely with Frederick Douglass, John Brown, William Lloyd Garrison, Lucretia Mott and J. Miller McKim. After seven years of owning a coal stove business in 1860, he found himself prosperous with both coal and lumber yards.

In addition to founding the first African-American YMCA, he wrote his classic book, *The Underground Railroad*, in 1872. Although the last house that William Still lived in was demolished in 1992, a Pennsylvania Historical and Mu-

The Johnson House (Germantown) Philadelphia, Pennsylvania.

seum Commission marker indicates its former location today.

Location: 224 South 12th Street
              Philadelphia PA 19107

Philadelphia, Pennsylvania
The Johnson House

Located in historic Germantown, this two-story stone
house has an interesting history. It was built in 1765 by
Quaker Derick Jansen for his son John Johnson, who had
Anglicized his name. The house figured prominently in the
Battle of Germantown of October 4, 1777, and bullets and
cannonballs left their mark on it, noted on three doors and
the northwest wall. John Johnson, Sr., married Rachel Live-
sey, also a Quaker, and their children and grandchildren
operated the home as a station on the Underground Railroad, adding third-floor dormer windows to provide better
light and ventilation for the slaves who were staying there.

Runaway slaves came up the Schuylkill River and were reported to have hidden by day in the industrial mills that lined Wissahickon Creek. By night they continued up the creek, then followed a small stream up to the Johnsons' home in Germantown. From there they were sent on to Norristown or to Plymouth Meeting, a predominantly Quaker Village where the Liveseys, relatives of Johnsons by marriage, operated a fugitive slave station along with the Corsons to whom they were also connected by marriage. The Johnsons and their network were allied with the larger anti-slavery community: according to a written account by family member Jennett Johnson, William Still and Harriet Tubman met in her grandparents' house to discuss important matters. Bronson Alcott, Louisa May Alcott's father, may also have been involved with the Johnsons and their Underground activities in Germantown when Alcott served as principal of the Germantown Academy, where he was known for his anti-slavery sentiments. He was fired from the Academy in 1834 after having admitted an African female student.

Location: 6300 Germantown Avenue near
              Washington Lane
              Philadelphia, PA 19144
              (215) 843-0943

Philadelphia, Pennsylvania
William Whipper

William Whipper was born in Little Britain, Lancaster County, in 1804. As a child, Whipper was raised in the home of a white Columbia, Lancaster County, lumber dealer where his mother served as a maid. Later, as an adult, Whipper and his cousin Stephen Smith became partners in a properous lumber business. His home and lumber yard was a major station on the Underground Railroad. Whipper told his friend William Still: "I know that it has been asserted, far down in the slave region that Smith and Whipper, the Negro lumber merchants, were engaged in secreting fugitive slaves." On two occasions attempts had been made to set fire to their yard for the purpose of punishing them for such illegal acts. Fugitive slaves first came to York and crossed the Susquehanna River at Wrightsville. The long bridge from Wrightsville to Columbia was the only outlet after 1847. Whipper and cousin Smith sent fugitives to Pittsburgh by boat and railroad lumber cars to Philadelphia. By 1834, Whipper had moved to Philadelphia, founded a Reading Room Society, edited a magazine and served as treasurer of the Philadelphia Building and Loan Association. Although his former home and lumber yard in Lancaster County no longer exist, his home in Philadelphia still stands today, but is a private residence.

Location: 919 Lombard Street
             Philadelphia, PA 19147

Philadelphia, Pennsylvania
Frances Ellen Watkins Harper

Although she may not rank with African-American poets Langston Hughes, Gwendolyn Brooks and Maya Angelou, Frances Harper is part of the tradition that goes back to Phillis Wheatley. During her day, she was one of the nation's leading anti-slavery poets. Her friend, William Still, called Frances Harper the "leading colored poet" of his day, and stated that her home was station on the Underground Railroad "where she frequently hid passengers and heard their tales of suffering and wrong." Harper was born free in Baltimore, Maryland. She was forced into exile in 1853 and pledged herself to the anti-slavery movement. As a lecturer, Harper was so effective that the Pennsylvania Anti-Slavery Society hired her. Her contributions as a lecturer, writer and poet were numerous and include her famous poems "The Slave Mother" and "Bury Me In a Free Land." This house is a private residence.

Location: 1006 Bainbridge Street
             Philadelphia, PA 19147

Frances Ellen Watkins Harper, anti-slavery lecturer, writer, poet, temperance reformer and Underground Railroad station-keeper.

Philadelphia, Pennsylvania
Campbell African Methodist Episcopal Church

Originally called the "Second Bethel" Church, the Campbell African Methodist Episcopal Church was founded by Frankford blacks in 1817 at the home of Sarah Congo, a charter member of the church, on Bowser Lane. It was rebuilt on Oxford Street in 1848. It was the first formal institution created by Frankford blacks and the only all-black church in that section of Philadelphia until 1869. The African Colored School held its first classes in this church between 1838 and 1840. During the antebellum period, members of this church were valiant workers on the Underground Railroad. Many fugitive slaves seeking freedom passed through its doors.

Location: 167 Kinsey Street
             Philadelphia, PA 19124

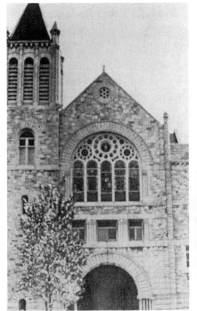

Reverend Richard Allen, a former slave and founder of Mother Bethel. He assisted escaped slaves and became a promoter of the self-help philosophy.

Mother Bethel African Methodist Episcopal Church, Philadelphia, Pennsylvania. During its early years the church was a major station on the Underground Railroad.

Philadelphia, Pennsylvania
Mother Bethel African Methodist Episcopal Church

Affectionately known as Mother Bethel, this church was founded by Bishop Richard Allen in 1794. The first church was oganized in a blacksmith's shop. In 1830, Allen led the first African-American convention in Philadelphia, the first large formal organizaiton dedicated to anti-slavery agitation. Altogether there have been four churches built on the same plot of ground that is oldest piece of real estate in America owned continuously by African-Americans. However, it was the second church, which was built in 1805, that served as a major station on the Underground Railroad. The most vigorous organizers of networks "to freedom" were African-American ministers. For example, Morris Brown, Edward Waters, William P. Quinn, Willis Nazrey and Daniel A. Payne, who served as bishops of Mother Bethel from 1828 to 1852, were all active stationmasters on the Underground. Large sums of money were collected to aid and comfort fugitives who were sheltered within the church. Known abolitionists such as Frederick Douglass, Harriet Tubman and Lucretia Mott visited and spoke at Mother Bethel.

Location: 419 South Sixth Street, about five blocks South of
              Independence Square
              Philadelphia, PA 19147
              (215) 925-0616

Philadelphia, Pennsylvania
Washington Square

As one of William Penn's five squares, Washington Square was originally called Congo Square. During America's colonial period, slaves were brought to this square once a month before they were sold and transported to other counties in Pennsylvania and elsewhere. At Congo Square, some of the slaves prayed, danced, cooked traditional African food and conversed in various languages. Some slaves took this opportunity to escape, with the assistance of the Free African-American community. The name "Congo" referred to that part of Africa now called Zaire. The square started as a pasture. Later Congo Square served as a burial ground (Potter's Field). Many American and British Revolutionary War soldiers lie here, along with white and black victims of the yellow fever epidemic of 1793.

Location: Sixth to Seventh Streets and Walnut to Locust
              Streets.
For further information contact:
              Independence National Historical Park

313 Walnut Street
Philadelphia, PA 19106
(215) 597-8974

Philadelphia, Philadelphia
The Liberty Bell

Near Independence Hall, where American liberty was claimed and proclaimed, there is housed the historic symbol that we reverently preserve as the voice of human rights and human freedom. The Liberty Bell was, in fact, commissioned by a slaveholder, Isaac Norris. In 1751, Norris was speaker of the Pennsylvania Assembly and proposed the installation of a bell in the newly-erected steeple of Philadelphia's State House (now Independence Hall) in commemoration of the fiftieth anniversary of William Penn's Charter of Privileges. First hung in 1753, the bell bore the inscription, "Proclaim Liberty throughout the Land unto all the Inhabitants thereof." Exactly how the bell got its familiar name is unknown. However, the earliest reference to it as the "Liberty Bell" is connected with a radical anti-slavery group known as the Friends of Freedom. This group of abolitionists and Underground Railroad figures called for immediate liberation of the slaves and continued promotion of the security, protection and improvement of free African-Americans.

Founded in Boston in 1839, this group issued a famous series of publications entitled "The Liberty Bell by the Friends of Freedom." Included in the 1839 issue of the annual publication was a sonnet whose description read, "suggested by inscription on the Philadelphia Liberty Bell."

Location: Market between Fifth and Sixth Streets on
Independence National Historical Park.
313 Walnut Street
Philadelphia, PA 19106
(215) 597-8974

Upper Darby, Pennsylvania
Abraham L. Pennock
Abolitionist and Underground Railroad Stationmaster and Sellers Hall

The Pennsylvania Historical and Museum Commission marker now standing on this site is dedicated to Abraham L. Pennock and his home, Hoodland. Pennock once met President John Quincy Adams and discussed the elimination of slavery in the nation's capital. Pennock's quiet manners gave no hint of his bravery. Delaware County fugitive slaves were duly cared for by the Pennock family after they were sent to them by Edward Garrett of Upper Darby, the brother of Wilmington, Delaware's, famous conductor, Thomas Garrett. Pennock often sent fugitive slaves to his father-in-law, John Sellers, II, whose large home, Sellers Hall, was a station stop. Sellers Hall still stands today, and also has a Pennsylvania Historical and Museum Commission marker to identify it. Pennock also founded *The Non-Slaveholder*, an anti-slavery newspaper, and he provided an illustration of Paul Cuffe's vessel, the *Traveller*. Notable visitors to Hoodland included John Greenleaf Whittier and James Russell Lowell. The Pennock, Sellers and Garrett families were instrumental in building Pennsylvania Hall in 1838. This majestic structure was located in Philadelphia and was burned to the ground three days after its opening by an anti-abolitionist mob. Ironically, Alvan Stewart, an abolitionist from Utica, New York, had hope that the hall would be a "moral furnace in which the fire of free discussion would burn day and night."

Location: Hoodland was formely located at 76 State Road, Upper Darby. Sellers Hall is now the Old Rectory of St. Alice's Church, 150 Hampton Road, in Upper Darby, PA 19082.

Lima, Pennsylvania
The Honeycomb A.M.E. Church

African-Americans had arrived in Delaware County as early as 1639 with the Swedes. (Contrary to popular belief, it was the Swedes, not William Penn, who were the first Europeans to set foot here.) By the 1840s, a small community of African-Americans had settled in the county. The Honeycomb African Methodist Episcopal Church was founded by members of a nearby Springfield church in 1852, and served as a station on the Underground Railroad. Led by the Reverend Hildenbrand, members of this church harbored fugitive slaves, who were usually traveling along a route that led from the state of Delaware into Philadelphia. William Spradley, John Peters and George Smith came to Lima during the Civil War as slaves who served as scouts for the Confederate Army. While reconnoitering Delaware County, these men escaped and joined the Honeycomb A.M.E. Church, which still stands today.

Location: 166 Barren Road and Van Leer Avenue
             Lima, PA 19063

Norristown, Pennsylvania
Church Opened Its Door to Anti-Slavery Speakers

A decision to form a Baptist congregation in December 1832 initiated the First Baptist Church of Norristown. Once located on the corner of Airy and Swede Streets, it was the only church in the county (aside from some Quaker and Unitarian institutions) open to anti-slavery lectures.

The Reverend Samuel Aaron, the pastor between 1841 and 1844, represented the more radical wing of the anti-slavery movement, which called for immediate emancipation of the slaves. An eloquent orator himself, the pastor invited celebrated abolitionists such as William Lloyd Garrison, Frederick Douglass, Lucretia Mott, Mary Grew and others to speak. Henry "Box" Brown spoke at this church after he made his famous escape; his visit is recorded in the church's history. These fiery abolitionists strengthened the anti-slavery sentiment in the community. At the same time, they incited violent opposition from the pro-slavery segment of the community, which threatened to burn the church to the ground.

One night a mob threatened Lucretia Mott and Frederick Douglass when they left the church arm-in-arm. That a woman was permitted to deliver an address was insult enough, but that she walked arm-in-arm with a black man was an assault on white motherhood. Mrs. Mott and Douglass were saved by the anti-slavery group also leaving the church.

In 1971, the First Baptist Church left its historic location near the Montgomery County Courthouse and moved to Burnside Avenue in West Norriton Township.

Location: Burnside Avenue, West Norriton Township
             Norristown, PA 19403

Plymouth Meeting, Pennsylvania
Linden Grove

Built in 1785, the original dwelling included 128 acres. Around 1810 Peter Dager, the owner of a marble quarry, built the newer part of the house entirely of unpolished marble. Dager was a member of the Plymouth Meeting and the Whitemarsh Township Underground Railroad, working as a conductor with the Corson family. One day in 1829, John Lewis' owner found him in Dager's stable. Shortly thereafter Lewis' brother, Westley, was captured while in the same place. Both slaves were tied up and taken by wagon to a magistrate four miles away in Norristown, where they were awarded to their Southern master. Dager, however, had summoned a friend, Ezra Comfort, and the two hurried to the magistrate to buy the men from their owners. Dager bought John Lewis and his freedom for $600, and Comfort bought Westley for $300.

The two abolitionists asked slave owner Christian Miller

J. Miller McKim, agent on Pennsylvania's Underground Railroad.

how he knew the whereabouts of his slaves. Miller said he heard of their whereabouts from a free black man from Lauden County, Maryland.

It was reported that Dager had tunnels dug on the property that have long since been closed off; however, they were opened accidently when modern sidewalks were installed.

Location: Linden Grove is located on the Corner of Spring
                   Mill Road and Ridge Pike.

For further information contact:

> Montgomery County Historical Society
> 1654 Dekalb Street
> Norristown, PA 19401
> (610) 272-0297

La Mott, Pennsylvania
Mott's "Roadside" Home Historical Marker

Only a gatehouse remains to mark the existence of "Roadside," the home of Lucretia and James Mott dating from 1857 and a notable stop along the Underground Railroad. A Quaker who was the village's spiritual leader and a diminutive woman who never weighed more than one hundred

pounds, Lucretia Mott was nonetheless doughty enough to draw many of her neighbors into social and political movements against slavery. The Mott's Roadside home saw persons, famous and obscure, American and foreign, men and women, dedicated to the abolitionist movement as constant guests. Among them were William Lloyd Garrison, Frederick Douglass, John Greenleaf Whittier, British actress Frances Kemble and the widow of the famous John Brown who was hanged at Harpers Ferry. A Pennsylvania State Historical Marker provides information on the former site.
Location: Old York Road, near Beech Avenue

Plymouth Meeting, Pennsylvania
Abolition Hall

Abolition Hall was built in 1858 as a meeting place for those advocating the abolition of slavery. It was also a refuge for fugitive slaves making their way north to freedom via the Underground Railroad. It was built by George Corson, of the noted Quaker and abolitionist Corson family of Plymouth Meeting, and comfortably accommodated one hundred and fifty persons. There, members could carry on their work without disturbance. People dedicated to abolition were guests at the hall, among them the famous and the obscure, Americans and foreigners. It was a focal point for abolitionist feeling: so strong was the faith in this Quaker community that many fugitive slaves were sent there by families that were sheltering them. Dr. Hiram Corson was well aware of Dan Ross, a black conductor who lived in a spacious two-and-a half story frame house on Green Street near Jacoby in Norristown. For twenty years Ross and his wife worked as conductors on the Underground Railroad.

The Hall later served as a studio for the noted American artist Thomas Hovenden, who married into the Corson family. Here he painted his well-known painting "John Brown's Last Moment."

Location: Behind the intersection of Germantown Pike and
             Butler Pike.
For further information contact:
             Plymouth Meeting Historical Society
             Box 156
             Plymouth Meeting, PA 19426
             (610) 828-3635

Plymouth Meeting, Pennsylvania
The Maulsby House

A quiet country town where four square homes and
stately trees continue to resist the change of centuries, Plymouth Meeting once played an important role in a turblent
period of American history. While abolitionists thundered
protest and wily slave hunters scanned Philadelphia newspapers for descriptions of fugitives from the South, Plymouth Meeting calmly functioned as the nearest point of the
Underground Railroad to the great city. Samuel Maulsby's
home was a major station.

As early as 1820 Maulsby had spoken openly against
slavery along with Allen Corson and his brother Joseph, and
his large stone house was a haven for such anti-slavery
orators and writers as Lucretia Mott, Abbey Kelly, William
Wells Brown, Benjamin Lundy and William Lloyd Garrison.
So well known was it that slave hunters and anti-abolition-
ists threatened to burn it down, yet today the 270+-year-old
structure still stands, virtually unchanged, among the hum
of the Quaker community.

Irish-born artist Thomas Hovenden, who married Corson's daughter, Helen, used simple people, neighbors and
local folk that he knew, as his models. He lived in this house
for a number of years. Dedicated to the anti-slavery cause,
Hovenden executed several works related to the anti-slavery movement. The Maulsby house is owned by one of his
descendants.

Location: On the corner where Butler Pike doglegs into

THE UNDERGROUND RAILROAD

The last moments of John Brown. The bravery of the martyr is conveyed; from the original painting.

Below: The Fugitive Slave Law of 1850 gave slaveholders, or those hunting slaves, the power to organize a posse at any point in the United States to aid them in running down their slaves.

Germantown Pike. This is now a private home; anyone seeking to tour the property must ask for permission.
For further information contact:
Nancy Corson
Plymouth Meeting Historical Society
P.O. Box 156
Plymouth Meeting, PA 19462

West Grove, Pennsylvania
Anna Preston Home

Anna Preston was one of the members of the first graduating class (1851) of the Woman's Medical College in Philadelphia. Her home was an important station on the Underground Railroad network. Anna Preston once dressed a runaway in Quaker clothes and drove her in a horse-drawn buggy towards Oxford, PA. Here they happened upon a group of slave hunters who did not stop them, assuming they were Quakers.

Location: State and Rose Hill Roads (A private residence)
             West Grove, PA 19390

Kennett Square, Pennsylvania
John and Hannah Cox

There were no greater staunch abolitionists than John and Hannah Cox. The husband and wife knew intimately most of the leading anti-slavery champions of their day. Poet John Greenleaf Whittier commemorated the Coxes' fiftieth anniversary of marriage with his poem "Golden Wedding at Longwood:"

Blessing upon you, what you did for each sad, suffering one.
Some homeless, faint and naked, unto our Lord was done.

Their former tract of five hundred acres and home, Edgewood Farm, is now called Du Point Pierce Park Estate. As recorded in *Recollection and Experiences of an Abolitionist* by Dr. Alexander Ross,

> The house of this noble woman [Hannah Cox] had for many years been one of the principal stations on the Underground Railroad for fugitive slaves escaping from Maryland and Delaware, where many poor fugitives have come with bleeding and tattered garments, relying upon the humanity of this noble woman who shielded the outcasts from their pursuers. Hannah Cox was a member of Society of Friends.

Location: One half mile west of the Anvil on Nottingham Road—now Route l. Private estate—must ask for permission to tour the property.

For further information:
> Brandywine Valley Tourist Information Center
> (entrance on Longwood Gardens)
> Route 1
> Kennett Square, PA 19348
> (610) 388-2900

Oxford, Pennsylvania
Hosanna A.U.M.P. Church

Founded by the African-Americans who settled in Upper and Lower Oxford Township in 1829, this small church served as an anti-slavery meetinghouse and station stop on the Underground Railroad. Many distinguished lecturers such as Frederick Douglass, Harriet Tubman and other anti-slavery leaders spoke here. In 1843, the building was formally organized as the African Union Methodist Protestant Church, but was often referred to as the "African Meetinghouse." In its cemetery are tomstones bearing the original African names of the church's members. Also buried in the small churchyard are the remains of 17 veterans of the famous 54th Massachussets Infantry Regiment who fought in the Civil War.

The church is located on the wooded campus of historic Lincoln University, founded in 1854.

Hosanna A.U.M.P. Church still stands as a former station on the Underground Railroad. Courtesy, Lincoln University, Public Information Office.

Location: Route 1 two miles northeast of Oxford.
For further information contact:
>Chester Historical Society
>225 North High Street
>West Chester, PA 19380
>(610) 692-4800
>or:
>Public Relations Office
>Lincoln University
>Lincoln University, PA 19352
>(610) 932-8300

Kimberton, Pennsylvania
Sunnyside: The Home of the Lewis Sisters

Many years ago Wayne Homan, a local journalist wrote: "Looking at Graceanna Lewis, no casual observer would have suspected her as the operator of a 'station' of the

Underground Railroad. Neither she nor her sisters, Mariann and Elizabeth, looked the part." The sisters were members of the Society of Friends. William Still, the great African-American agent of the Underground Railroad, said that the sisters were among "the most faithful, devoted and quietly efficient workers in the anit-slavery cause" in his book *The Underground Railroad*.

The large Lewis farm and house was the setting for several marriages between slaves. In 1851, while law officers throughout the nation were looking for William Parker, who was involved in the Christiana Resistance (see p. 111) Parker was hiding at Sunnyside. Many of the fugitive slaves who were harbored by the Lewis sisters were forwarded to Elijah Pennpacker at Phoenixville, one of the greatest conductors of Pennsylvania's Underground.

Frequently, though, professional slave-hunters suspected the sisters, and Graceanna permitted them to search the farm and the imposing house. She issued one restriction: "No gentleman would peer into a lady's bedroom," she told the slave-hunters. "Surely you gentlemen agree." Invariably the slave-hunters agreed. As one would guess, slaves were hiding in her bedroom until the searchers left the premises. After the Civil War, Graceanna turned to a less adventuresome pursuit, and wrote a definitive work, the *Chart of the Animal Kingdom*, which won acclaim.

Although Sunnyside still stands today, the house and property are private, and not open to the public.

Location: Old Kimberton Road, two miles south of
             Kimberton Lake

For further information contact:

Chester County Historical Society.
225 N. High St.
West Chester, PA 19380
(610) 692-4800

Longwood Quaker Meetinghouse, at Kennett Square, Pennsylvania was known as an Abolitionist Center. William Lloyd Garrison and Sojourner Truth lectured in this meetinghouse.

Kennett Square, Pennsylvania
Longwood Progressive Friends Meetinghouse and Cemetery

Not all the Quakers in Chester County took an active part in Underground Railroad activities. However, those who did not take an active part did not talk about the activities of those who did. In the graveyard of Longwood Meetinghouse sleep great conductors of the Underground Railroad. Cox, Darlington, Medenhall, Taylor; all were members of this progressive meeting house. They concealed fugitive slaves and spirited them away from the meetinghouse under the noses of pro-slavery spies and informers who knew of their activity but could neither prove nor prevent it. Because not all Quakers were anti-slavery, the Longwood Meetinghouse was formed in 1854 by "Friends" who had been cast out by their co-religionists due to their anti-slavery sentiments. Many prominent leaders in the anti-slavery movement spoke here. Among them were Thomas Garrett, John Greenleaf Whittier, Sojourner Truth, Susan B. Anthony, Lucretia Mott and William Lloyd Garrison. Today the meetinghouse, newly restored, is the site of the Brandywine Tourist Information Center. A permanent exhibit tells the story of the Underground Railroad. This building is open to visitors daily.

Location: At the entrance to Longwood Gardens
              Route 1
              Kennett Square
For further information contact:
              Brandywine Valley Tourist Information Center
              Kennett Square, PA 19348
              (610) 388-2900

Phoenixville, Pennsylvania
The Schuylkill Friends Meetinghouse

This small meetinghouse was used both as a station on the Underground Railroad and as a gathering place where anti-slavery speakers such as poet John Greenleaf Whittier could air their views. Henry "Box" Brown also visited this meetinghouse. Brown made his ingenious escape by freighting himself to freedom. A "model slave" from Richmond, Virginia, he had himself nailed in a box with a bladder of water and a few biscuits and shipped himself to the Philadelphia Vigilance Committee. Though he traveled upside down part of the way, he arrived safely. But the white Virginian who helped him, Samuel A. Smith, was sentenced to prison for a subsequent attempt to freight slaves to freedom. Henry "Box" Brown demonstrated his escape to freedom at this meetinghouse.

Location: Route 23 and White Horse Road
For further information contact:
              Chester County Historical Society

225 N. High St.
West Chester, PA 19380
(610) 692-4800

Williamsport, Lycoming County, Pennsylvania
Ebenezer Baptist Church

Ebenezer Baptist Church was organized in April, 1890.
During its first decade, there existed an organization among
the congregation made up of individuals who escaped from
slavery. They called themselves the Underground Railroad
Club. During the construction of the sanctuary, which was
completed in 1899, this group donated a stained glass window with its insignia on it "The Underground Railroad
Club." As a part of Ebenezer Baptist Church's annual activities, an Underground Railroad Club Service has been established.
Location: 527 Park Avenue
For further information contact:
               Rev. Clifton R. White
               (717) 322-7415 or
               (717) 322-2060

Willow Grove, Pennsylvania
The Charles Kirk Homestead

In 1841 Charles Kirk, for whom a road is named, bought
this property, with a history that dates back to 1682 when
John Hart first came to Pennsylvania after purchasing it
from William Penn. Hart, a Quaker who was in 1688 a clerk
of the Byberry Meeting, commended the German Quakers
of Germantown for adopting the first declaration against
slavery made in the New World.

In 1846 Charles Kirk visited the Quaker meetings. He
recorded his thoughts on the issue of slavery: "It was during
one of these that the conviction came to me of the wrong I
was doing partaking of slave labor." Hart thereafter refused

to partake of any slave-prepared food and purchased products made only by free labor. It was also during this period that Hart used his large home as a station on the road to freedom for escaping slaves. Slaves were hidden in the second cellar. This cave section of the basement extends under the front porch and yard and nearly to the well. The large stone house still exists today, and it is designated Quarters A by the Willow Grove Naval Air Development Center.

Location: 200 Kirk Road
             Willow Grove, PA 18966
For further information contact:
             Willow Grove Naval Air Development Center.
             (215) 443-1000

Buckingham, Pennsylvania
Mount Gilead A.M.E. Church

Up a winding path, hidden in a grove of trees, stands Mount Gilead African Methodist Episcopal Church. The isolation of this wooded area made Mount Gilead a natural hiding place for fugitive slaves. The church and a nearby cave were used as stops on the Underground Railroad and as places of worship. The original church was built of logs in 1835. Later, in 1852, it was rebuilt from fieldstone. Situated atop Buckingham Mountain, it commands an impressive view of the township. The church was the last main station on the Underground Railroad in Bucks County before fugitive slaves crossed the Delaware River into New Jersey.

Buried in a small cemetery in front of the church along with other former slaves is "Big Ben" Jones, who served as Mount Gilead's first minister. He stood six feet ten inches tall. Ben had made his escape on the Underground Railroad from Baltimore, Maryland, and survived a bloody attack when his former master attempted to return him to slavery. Although it has had no congregation for more than 55 years, services are still held each year on Easter and Memorial Day at Mount Gilead, and it is marked as a historic place by the Bucks County Conservancy.

Location: on Buckingham Mtn., on Holicong Road
For further information contact:

Bucks County Historical Society
84 S. Pine Street
Doylestown, PA 18901
(215) 345-0210

Fleetwood, Pennsylvania
Kirbyville Inn

Built in 1790, the old Kirbyville Inn is reported to have been a station stop on the Underground Railroad. Discovery of a long-sealed attic during extensive renovations has led to the theory that the hotel was an overnight slave haven. The only visible entrance to the attic was through two outside windows by means of ladder. In what was the attic area, a rough-hewn wooden partition was found to extend the length of the floorspace which gave rise to the Underground Railroad theory. Fugitive slaves apparently were taken to the attic through a trapdoor in the ceiling of the kitchen on the first floor. The opening in the partition is a doorway leading to the portion of the attic where the guest stayed. The partition was erected to prevent light from escaping, or the guests from being seen from the two windows. A man's moccasin was one of the many items found in the attic area. Other items include: two latches, a piece of clothing and an old label from a bottle with these words, "Dr. J.R. Miller, Universal Magnetic Balm."

Location: Ten miles north of Reading on Route 222, at Rich
             Maiden Road.
             (610) 944-7296
             The inn is open from 4p.m. to 10p.m. and is
             closed on Mondays.

Birdsboro, Pennsylvania
Hopewell Furnace National Historic Site
(formerly Hopewell Village)

Berks County is one of Pennsylvania's oldest "interior" counties and has been of interest to historians because it was the home of Abraham Lincoln's ancestors. Berks County also was the scene of substantial Underground Railroad activity. Many fugitive slaves found safety in the wooded area at the Joanna Furnace. Here, a small colony of African-American charcoal workers and their employer, Princeton graduate Levi Smith, aided fugitive slaves. By the mid-1800s, the black community at Six Penny Creek had established the African Methodist Episcopal Church. The church was founded in 1856, served as a station on the Underground Railroad and was the site of the oldest African-American cemetery in Berks County. The names on some of the tombstones are still legible.

The forge has been recently restored by the National Park Service. Hopewell Village is a restored iron-making community that has been re-created as it was in Revolutionary days, when cannon balls were made here for General George Washington's army.

Location: Route 345, north of Elverson
For further information contact:
National Park Service
Hopewell Furnace National Historic Site
#2 Mark Bird Lane
Elverson, PA 19520
(610) 582-8773
TDD# (610) 582-2093

Reading, Pennsylvania
Bethel A.M.E. Church

Only Bethel African Methodist Episcopal Church survives of the three African-American churches that served Reading in 1840. By 1820, 90 African-Americans were counted in the Reading census and many were indentured servants. Rewards, ranging from one cent to five dollars, were offered for runaways' capture and return.

Fugitives who came to Reading were often forwarded to designated points along the Reading and Pennsylvania Railroads and placed on trains traveling to Philadelphia or New York state. Others were assisted by African Methodist Episcopal circuit preachers who traveled from church to church. The Reverend Solomon Porter Hood, who was connected with the Underground Railroad in Lancaster and Chester Counties, was one of these preachers. The artful stained glass windows set in the once elegant Romanesque Revival facade of this church can still be seen. The church is listed on the National Register of Historic Places.

Location: Bethel A.M.E. Church
119 North 10th Street
Reading, PA 19601
(610) 376-7555

Pine Forge, Pennsylvania
Pine Forge

This large stone house was built by Thomas Rutter, a pioneer ironmaster and opponent of slavery. Rutter built Pennsylvania's first ironworks nearby in 1716. In ensuing decades he erected Pine Forge and built this mansion. A system of tunnels underneath the Manor House was used during attacks by Native Americans. Since the Rutters had a strong anti-slavery conviction, they readily offered employment to African-Americans at Pine Forge, whether or not these African-Americans were freed persons or fugitive slaves. Pine Forge was remote from the cities, where slave hunters usually prowled, and those runaways just passing through the area could hide in the Manor House tunnels to elude the slave hunters who pursued them. African-Americans own the Manor House today; it is a building of the

Seventh Day Adventists' secondary boarding school, Pine Forge Academy.

Location: Pine Forge Road, Douglass Township
P.O. Box 338
Pine Forge, PA 19548
(610) 326-5800

Harrisburg, Pennsylvania
Thomas Morris Chester

Born in Harrisburg in 1834, this illustrious African-American distinguished himself as a journalist, pamphleteer, attorney and educator. He recruited African-American soldiers in the Civil War, served as a noted war correspondent, represented the Freedmen's Aid in Europe, was admitted to the English bar in 1870 and held a major post in Louisiana.

Thomas Morris Chester's parents were former slaves. His father was transported to America from Haiti, and his mother escaped from slavery in Maryland to New York City and finally to Harrisburg. In Harrisburg, Chester's parents opened a popular restaurant that became an important station on the Railroad. The Chesters had six children, who assisted their parents with their Underground activities. Harrisburg was the central rendezvous point on Pennsylvania's Underground Railroad. The conductors and station keepers who were connected with the Chester family included Dr. William Rutherford, the Reverend William Jones of the Wesley A.M.E. Church, the McClintock sisters (Harriet, Mary Ann and Elizabeth), and Joseph Bustill, a member of the Philadelphia Underground who taught school in Harrisburg. A Pennsylvania Historical and Museum Commission marker notes the site of the Chester home.

Location: Market Square near Third Street
For further information contact:
Pennsylvania Historical and Museum
Commission

The Christiana Rebellion, Lancaster County, Pennsylvania, September 11, 1851.

William Penn Memorial Museum Building
P.O. Box 1026
Harrisburg, PA 17108
(717) 787-2891

Christiana, Pennsylvania
The Christiana Resistance Monument

Some historians believe that the Christiana Resistance ranks with the Nat Turner uprising as a major episode in African-American history. Alongside John Brown's riot, it was a harbinger of the Civil War. Blood was first shed in the resistance to the Fugitive Slave Law of 1850, when slaves of Edward Gorsuch, a prominent Maryland farmer, were discovered in Christiana in 1851 in the home of fugitive William Parker. They had fled to Lancaster County by means of the Underground Railroad. Gorsuch expressed his intention of "getting his property, or breakfast in hell." On September

11, 1851 threats were exchanged, shots were fired, the cry of "kidnappers" was raised against Parker and neighbors arrived in numbers.

Gorsuch was killed in an exchange of bullets and his son was wounded. Parker and thirty others were tried for treason, but Thaddeus Stevens so ably defended them in court that the jury returned a "not guilty" verdict in fifteen minutes. Parker, the subject of a national manhunt, made his daring escape to Canada while disguised as a Quaker woman. One of the persons who assisted Parker was his boyhood friend Frederick Douglass.

Location: A large granite monument on High Street in downtown Christiana commemorates this event. It is inscribed with all names of those tried for treason.

For further information contact:
Lancaster County Historical Society
230 N. President Ave.
Lancaster, PA 17603-3125
(717) 392-4633

Columbia, Pennsylvania
Wright's Ferry Mansion

Escaping slaves were duly cared for by abolitionist William Wright, who began assisting runaway slaves as early as 1804. From Columbia in Lancaster County Wright forwarded his passengers to the home of his sister, Hannah Gibbons, and her husband, Daniel. The Gibbons, who kept an accurate record of their long Underground experience, destroyed their documentation with the passage of the Fugitive Slave Law of 1850. William Wright also worked with his well-known African-American neighbors, stationmasters Stephen Smith and William Whipper. Some years ago, when Wright's home was restored, an 1829 anti-slavery pamphlet was found in a wall, and slave manacles were discovered in the attic. Dating from 1738, the mansion is open May through October only.

Location: Second and Cherry Streets
                    Columbia, Pennsylvania
                    (717) 684-4325

York, Pennsylvania
William C. Goodridge Marker and House

York County shares with its neighbor, Lancaster County, the distinction of bordering the Susquehanna River and Maryland. Therefore, escaping slaves made their way north through York County as early as 1810. Certainly, the brutal and sinister tactics of slave hunters combined with the courage and determination of runaways and free-born African-Americans to remain free turned most citizens of the area against both slave hunters and slavery.

Born in 1805, William C. Goodridge, a former slave who became a prominent York businessman in 1824, used his home on Philadelphia Street as a station on the Railroad. His house was always under close surveillance by slave hunters. Goodridge maintained a secret straw-covered trench as a hiding place for fugitive slaves. In 1863, Goodridge fled York when Confederate troops threatened the city and were bent on catching him. Although he had built York's first five-story building and held 13 rail cars operated commercially (which were used in his work on the Underground Railroad), Goodridge never returned to his York home. He died in Minnesota in 1873. A Pennsylvania Historical and Museum Commission marker was dedicated on December 16, 1987 in honor of William C. Goodridge.

Location: East Philadelphia Street
For further information contact:
                    Pennsylvania Historical and Museum
                    Commission
                    William Penn Memorial Musuem Building
                    P.O. Box 1026

Harrisburg, PA 17108
(717) 787-2891

Gettysburg, Pennsylvania
The Dobbin House

Prior to the 1820s, runaways were crossing the Mason-Dixon line into Adams County, and were directly aided by anti-slavery friends, both black and white. Mag Palm, a former slave of enormous notoriety, was fondly remembered as "Maggie Bluecoat" (because she wore a sky-blue broadcloth uniform coat of an officer of the War of 1812). She actively aided escaping slaves and protected them herself with a musket she had acquired to deter slave hunters. Mag Palm operated her Underground Railroad activities with the Dobbin family. Built in 1776, the Dobbin House is the oldest house still standing in Gettysburg. The Reverend Alexander Dobbin, the original builder of the large stone house, was one of Gettysburg's most prominent citizens. His descendants were connected with the Underground Railroad. Now a restaurant, the home has sliding shelves in the wall of an addition to conceal a crawl space large enough to hide several adults. During the Civil War the house sustained minor damage from gunfire. The story of the Underground Railroad is interpreted to restaurant visitors by the restaurant manager, when asked.

Location: 89 Steinwehr Avenue
            Gettysburg, PA 17325
            (717) 334-2100

Valley Forge, Pennsylvania
Valley Forge Monument Honoring
Revolutionary War Patriots of African Descent

The bravery of African-American soldiers and sailors was impressive during the era of the Revolutionary War. Crispus Attucks, who in 1750 was advertised as a runaway slave from Framingham, Massachusetts, on March 5, 1770, became the first American to die for freedom in Boston. The war offered many oppurtunities to run away from bondage. A number of escaped slaves served in George Washington's Continental Army at Valley Forge. At least 500 African-Americans suffered terribly along with other soldiers from cold, poor provisions and inadequate clothing during the encampment of the long, harsh winter of 1777-78. Now more than two hundred years later, a ten-foot granite monument entitled "Patriots of African Descent" honors them.

During the antebellum era of the Underground Railroad, Valley Forge was once again connected to freedom and independence. Visitors today will have the oppurtunity to see the monument honoring Patriots of African Descent and can travel as well the same Underground Railroad route that passed through Valley Forge during the 1840s and 1850s.

The major reason for the prominence of the area was its proximity to the Schuykill River. From the former site of Elijah Pennypacker's home in Phoenixville, visitors can follow the trail of escaped slaves past the Patriots of African Descent monument to the former home of Lewis Pert, a station on the Underground that is now a private residence in Valley Forge. Continuing along Pawling Road, they will see Mill Grove the first American home of famed naturalist and artist John James Audubon, which is said by tradition to have been a station in the hands of Quaker Dr. Herbert Wetherill. From there, along the present Route 422, the runaways continued through Norristown, Plymouth Meeting, Whitemarsh and Germantown in Philadelphia to the safety of the Mennomite Johnson home and the free African-American community, a trail of approximately 15 miles from Valley Forge.

Location: Valley Forge Monument, honoring Patriots
        of African Descent, some 150 yards east of
        Valley Forge Memorial Chapel.

For further information contact:
        Valley Forge Convention and Visitors Bureau
        P.O. Box 311

Norristown, PA 19404
(610) 278-3558

Valley Forge National Historic Park
P.O. Box 953
Valley Forge, PA 19481
(610) 783-1077

Chaneyville, Pennsylvania
Murder on the Freedom Train

There were very few Underground Railroad stations in Bedford County. The whole county was dangerous for escaping slaves and their conspirators, as slave hunters often crossed the Pennsylvania-Maryland border here. About four miles north of this border line, on the outskirts of Bedford County, is the town of Chaneyville. Here, according to David Bradley, a Bedford County African-American native who wrote the prize winning book *The Chaneyville Incident*, there are 13 graves marked only by grey rough-cut fieldstones. Bradley explains that no one knows the names of the people or how the bodies got there. What we do know is that they were fugitive slaves. They are buried on the Imes farm, just beyond the family cemetery. According to several Bradford County historical sources, Lester Imes and his neighbors attempted to protect a group of fugitive slaves who had escaped over the Cumberland Mountains with slave catchers closely pursuing them. The fugitive slaves are reported to have told Imes that they would rather die in freedom than return to slavery in Cumberland, Maryland. Although the natural protection afforded by the mountainous terrain and heavy foliage were excellent camouflage for the Underground Railroad, those 13 graves can still be seen at the Imes family burial grounds.

Did they commit the ultimate act of rebellion or did the Maryland slave hunters catch and kill them? The answer is not known.

For more information contact:

Pioneer Historical Society
242 East John Street
Bedford, PA 15522
(814) 623-2011

Mercersburg, Pennslyvania
Little Africa

Mercersburg's proximity to the Mason-Dixon Line made it an ideal theater for Underground Railroad activities during the mid-1800s. Centering here and extending through the small settlements of Rouzerville to Dickey's Mountain, a hazardous area of one hundred miles contained the most secretive, tangled lines of the Underground Railroad. Here, too, agents of slave hunters operated by ruse or by violence. On one occasion, when a fugitive slave chose to fight for freedom, one Mercersburg area officer of the law was killed and two were wounded.

Though many fugitive slaves made Canada their destination, others established small communities in the Mercersburg area. During the 1820s, African-Americans, some of whom were escaped slaves, sought refuge along Fayette Street. By the 1840s, almost 20 percent of the 33 property owners on Fayette Street were African-Americans. The community was called "Little Africa." After the passage of the infamous Fugitive Slave Law of 1850, many former slaves fled to other areas and to Canada. Of the families who remained in Mercersburg, 33 men joined the famous 54th Colored Massachusetts Volunteer Regiment during the Civil War.

Many homes on South Fayette Street that were stations on the Underground Railroad still stand today, as well as the Bethel African Methodist Episcopal Church, which was also a station. These homes are not open to the public.

Location: Four-block radius of South Fayette Street,
            between East California Street and Fourth
            Alley South
For further information contact:

117

Thaddeus Stevens of Pennsylvania elected to Congress in 1848, became an Underground Railroad Stationkeeper and a major anti-slavery spokesperson.

Mercersburg Chamber of Commerce
P.O. Box 161
Mercerburg, PA 17236
(717) 328-5827

Franklin, Pennsylvania
Caledonia State Park

Perhaps no Pennsylvania county outside of the state's urban areas had communities with as wide a range of pro-slavery and anti-slavery citizens. Bounded by Maryland on the south, Franklin County counted both cold-blooded slave-hunters and armed anti-slavery renegades in its heritage. One of the most prominent of the latter was United States Congressman Thaddeus Stevens, who erected Caledonia Furnace here in the early nineteenth century. The "Old Commoner," as he was called, employed freed African-Americans in his ironworks and used his forge as a station on the Underground Railroad. Carl Sandburg described Stevens in his classic work *Abraham Lincoln: The War Years* accordingly:

> Scholar, wit, zealot of liberty, part fanatic, part gambler, at his worst, a clubfooted wrangler possessed of endless javelins, at his best a majestic and isolated figure wandering in an ancient wilderness thick with thorns, seeking to bring justice between man and man —who could read the heart of limping, poker-faced on Thaddeus Stevens?

"Give the Negroes forty acres and a mule," said Stevens, considered by African-Americans to be one of the best friends they ever had.

Others felt differently. During the Civil War, Confederate cavalry raiders led by Major Jubal A. Early sacked Stevens' ironworks. Early subsequently remarked that he was sorry that he had not found Stevens there: "I would hang him on the spot and divide his bones and send them to several states as curiosities."

Location: Junction of U.S. 30 and State Route 233,
            Caledonia State Park
For further information contact:
            Caledonia State Park Office
            40 Rocky Mountain Road
            Fayetteville, PA 17222
            (717) 352-2161

Chambersburg, Pennsylvania
John Brown's Headquarters

Captain Brown, the "Old Man," Osawatomie Brown, Brown of Kansas—called by whatever name, John Brown was known by all of his time. Among the abolitionists, some of whom supported him with money, Brown was revered as a righteous warrior and martyr. Others, including those in the government, regarded him as a murderous insurgent. Son of an Underground Railroad stationmaster, John Brown brooded about the evils of bondage, becoming increasingly obsessed with the idea that God had chosen him to liberate the slaves by force.

John Brown came to Chambersburg in the summer of 1859, describing himself as a prospector. At his headquarters on King Street he received large boxes marked "tools," which really contained carbines. These were moved to a small farm in Maryland, where he had assembled twenty-one followers. His preparations for the infamous attack on Harpers Ferry included a meeting with Frederick Douglass and Shield Green, also an African-American, at an old stone quarry to discuss his plans to raid Harpers Ferry; the assignation was arranged by Harry Watson, an African-American Underground Railroad operator in Chambersburg. On October 16, 1859, John Brown's raiders seized Harpers Ferry, but two days later, after thirteen of Brown's men, including two of his sons, had been killed, they surrendered to a company of U.S. Marines and Virginia militia under the command of Colonel Robert E. Lee. Convicted of treason, John Brown was hanged on December 2, 1859.

Today, the two-and-a-half-story building that housed his headquarters in Chambersburg still stands. Perhaps because Brown lived in Chambersburg prior to his attack on Harpers Ferry, the town was later pillaged and burned thoroughly by the Confederate Army during the Civil War in 1864.

Location: 225 King Street, Chambersburg
For more information contact:

> Chamber of Commerce
> 75 South Second Street
> Chambersburg, PA 17201
> (717) 264-7101
> or
> Kittochtinny (County) Historical Society
> 175 E. King Street
> Chambersburg, PA 17201
> (717) 264-1667

Bellefonte, Pennsylvania
The Linn House

Centre County has a rich heritage of social activism, and African-Americans played a leading role in that history. Many fugitive slaves escaping from southeastern states, after reaching Centre County, settled in Bellefonte. The country's largest African-American community was located here, and included William Mills, grandfather of the internationally recognized singing group, the Mills Brothers. Hugh Manchester, a Bellefonte historian, recorded in his publication *The Linn Home*,

> The Civil War period of the house recalls a tradition long associated with it, that it was once a stop on the famous "Underground Railroad." A 'secret' compartment on the third floor is generally attributed to the place where they were hidden en route to Canada.

Also located in Bellefonte is the small, red-brick African Methodist Episcopal church, which was likewise involved in Underground Railroad activities. Circuit riders, African-American ministers who went from church to church, carried news from Harrisburg to Mifflintown, through Lewistown and Altoona, to this church.

Location: 100 North Allegheny Street
For more information contact:
> Centre County Historical Society
> 1001 E. College Avenue
> State College, PA 16801
> (814) 234-4779

Milroy, Pennsylvania
Milroy Presbyterian Church

The Reverend James Nourse of Milroy, previously called Perryville, was pastor of this Presbyterian church from 1834 to 1849. A strong and able man, he denounced the pro-slavery forces in the county. Nourse was a scholar who once undertook the task of translating the entire New Testament into English from Greek. Under his leadership, an anti-slavery society was organized. Pastor Nourse was assisted by Dr. Samuel Maclay, John Thompson and Samuel Thompson, who transported fugitive slaves over the Seven Mountains from Milroy to Centre County. This church, which still stands today, was an important station in central Pennsylvania.

Perhaps the most famous of the escaped slaves to have lived in Mifflin County was Charles Ball, who escaped to Lewistown. Ball, a Maryland slave, was the subject of an important book, *A Narrative of the Life and Adventures of Charles Ball, A Black Man*, published in 1836 and reprinted in a new edition with the title *Fifty Years in Chains, or the Life of an American Slave*. In his narrative, Ball traces his life as a slave in South Carolina, Georgia, Maryland and as a fugitive escaping on the Underground Railroad to Lewistown, using his adopted name of Richard Barnes. Ball died in Lewistown at the age of 104.

Location: Lower Main Street, Milroy
For further information contact:
> Centre County Historical Society
> 1001 E. College Avenue
> State College, PA 16801
> (814) 234-4779

Lewisburg, Pennsylvania
The Old Stable

On University Avenue in Lewisburg, the Pennsylvania Historical and Museum Commission has erected a historical marker with the following information:

> *Underground Railroad*
>
> *This old stable was a station on the Underground Railroad. Here fugitive slaves were hidden, fed and aided in reaching the next station on their journey.*

From this meager account one gets an idea of the extent of the Underground Railroad as it developed in Union County. Only by piecing together the scattered historical information and that information gleaned from oral tradition can one trace stations and routes.

Location: University Avenue
For further information contact:
Union County Historical Society
Union County Courthouse
2nd & St. Louis Street
Lewisburg, PA 17837
(717) 524-8666

Pottsville, Pennsylvania
The Gillingham's House

Pottsville in Schuylkill County proved to have no coal, yet the tracks of the Underground Railroad ran through the area. James Gillingham was one of the first Quakers in Schuylkill County. According to "Schuylkill County in the Civil War," a pamphlet published by the Historical Society of Schuylkill County in 1961, African-Americans were frequently seen around Gillingham's red brick home on Mahantango Street doing chores. "On at least one occasion, Gillingham's daughter, Phoebe, begged a neighbor not to tell anyone about a strange colored man in the Gillingham yard," the publication states. The interior of the house, now owned by John and Louise Vernosky, has two marble fireplaces. Along with Quaker James Gillingham two African-Americans, John Lee and Nicholas Biddle counted as the main conductors on Pottsville's Underground Railroad. While the city was not a major route for fugitive slave transit, some members of this African-American community can trace their origins to involvement with the Underground Railroad.

Location: James Gillingham's House
            622 Mahantango Street

Pottsville, PA 17901
For further information contact:
The Historical Society of Schuylkill County
(717) 622-7540

Williamsport, Pennsylvania
Thomas Lightfoote Inn

Williamsport had another ardent Underground Railroad stationmaster, Thomas Updegraff, a Quaker who originally settled on the stretch of the Susquehanna River known as "The Long Reach" at the invitation of the prominent surveyer, Thomas Lightfoote. Updegraff and his son Abraham sheltered and gave directions to escaping slaves, most of whom arrived on packet boats at the port by the old Exchange Hotel. The fugitives were sequestered in a barn belonging to the Updegraffs in nearby Black Horse Alley, at the corner of River Alley and State Street. Already old when Thomas Updegraff ran his Underground Railroad station from it, the inn was built over two hundred years ago, and has served as a stop on the Pennsylvania Canal as well as a refuge for runaway slaves. In 1986 it was restored by the Chilson family and is now run under the name of the well-known colonial gentleman surveyor who did so much to promote the area's settlement. The Chilson family is proud to inform the public of the inn's history as an Underground Railroad site.
Location: 2887 South Reach Road
         Williamsport, PA 17701
         (717) 326-6396

Pennsdale, Pennsylvania
The House of Many Stairs

Probably no house in the Quaker village of Pennsdale has been the subject of more fantastic tales than the House of Many Stairs. Built of limestone and fossil, with a red tin roof, the house was known for years as Bull's Tavern. Although

The House of Many Stairs, Pennsdale, Lycoming County, Pennsylvania still stands today.

it is only two stories high, it is an imposing place that once served as a stagecoach stop. Edward Morris, the owner of Bull's Tavern, offered many sleeping rooms, food and drink to his customers. Because people were always coming and going to and from the tavern it helped Morris, a station-master on the Underground Railroad, to shield fugitive slaves. If any customers were slave hunters, the slaves who were resting or eating could exit into various stairways. There are a total of seven staircases in the home, with five steps leading into and out of each room. The slaves were hidden in a small room in back of a concealed panel at the top of one of the many stairways; the house's complexity often caused confusion to those seeking fugitives.

A stone's throw beyond the House of Many Stairs is a small 200-year-old Quaker cemetery, where buried among the dead are Native Americans and African-Americans in unmarked graves.

Location: Still standing today on Village Road, the
              property is now privately owned.
For further information contact:
              Lycoming County Historical Society and
              Museum
              858 West Fourth Street
              Williamsport, PA 17701
              (717) 326-3326

Muncy, Pennsylvania
McCarty-Wertman House

Constructed of logs in 1779, the McCarty-Wertman house
was at one time for fugitive slaves. Toward the end of the
Underground Railroad period, this house stood as a two-sto-
ried clapboard building where runaway slaves were concealed in the large stone cellar. Although the McCarty-
Wertman House today is a charming inn, there is no evidence
that would show that this house once served as an important
stop on Lycoming County's Underground Railroad.
Location: 34 North Main Street
For further information contact:
              Lycoming County Historical Society and
              Museum
              858 West Fourth Street
              Williamsport, PA 17701
              (717) 326-3326

Williamsport, Pennsylvania
Freedom Road Cemetery

Williamsport was one of the prominent stops on Pennsylvania's Underground Railroad. The first station was the
home and caves on the property owned by Daniel Hughes
on Freedom Road. Hughes, a large full-blooded Native
American from the Mohawk tribe, and his African-American wife Annie transported fugitive slaves by boat in the

concealment of night to their home. For almost a century, this road on Williamsport's northern outskirts bore the name of "Nigger Hollow." In 1936, however, at the request of Williamsport's African-American community, the name was changed to "Freedom Road." Although Hughes' large home no longer stands, a state historical marker was erected at the former site. Hughes gave part of his land for a cemetery, and among those buried here are nine known African-American veterans of the Civil War. The cemetery has borne the name of Freedom Road Cemetery since 1936. A Pennsylvania State Historical Marker is located at the cemetary today.

Location: A quarter of a mile beyond the north end of
               Market Street

For further information contact:

    Lycoming County Historical Society
    and Museum
    858 West Fourth Street
    Williamsport, PA 17701
    (717) 326-3326

Smithport, Pennsylvania
Medbury House

Formed in 1804 out of Lycoming County and named for Governor Thomas McKean, this county was a stopping place on the ancient Indian trail which crossed the Big Level when traveling south. The trail was once the main route from Onondaga, the Iroquois capital, to the Ohio River and the Carolinas. Smithport, the county seat, was incorporated in 1853. In 1827, Smithport became a way station on the Underground Railroad. Fugitive slaves passed through Smithport, Eldred, Olean and on to Buffalo and Canada. Documented evidence points to the Medbury House as an important station. A hiding place for fugitive slaves can still be seen in the cellar of the Medbury House, however the house is now a private residence.

Location: 604 East Main Street (at Nelson Street)
             Smithport, PA 16749

Susquehanna, Pennsylvania
Galusha Grow: Father of the Homestead Act

A Pennsylvania Historical and Museum Commission marker dedicated July 5, 1982, reads:

> Susquehanna County was the home of Galusha Grow, sponsor of the 1862 Homestead Act. Montrose County seat was an early abolitionist center and stop on the Underground Railroad. Grow died in 1907 and is buried in the Hartford Cemetery.

Location: Monument Square adjacent to the county
             courthouse.

Sandy Lake, Pennsylvania
Freedom Road Cemetery (II)

In Sandy Lake, there stands a marker erected by the Pennsylvania Historical and Museum Commission inscribed "Freedom Road." The inscription reads:

> In search of freedom, men and women brought from the South by the Underground Railroad settled near here about 1850 and later, after 1850, most of them went to Canada. The cemetery, still in use, lies a short distance above the road.

The members of the community once called "Liberia" fled en masse due to the enactment of the Fugitive Slave Law of 1850. Few laws of Congress have ever produced more bitterness and widespread disobedience than this law. No other was held by the people to be so flagrantly unconstitutional. The Law of 1850 gave slave holders, or those hunting their runaway slaves, the power to organize a posse at any point in the United States to aid them in running down their slaves. It provided for the delivery of fugitive slaves without allowing them a trail by jury. African-Americans in northern cities organized groups armed with weapons to protect their families and friends. Hundreds of lawfully free African-Americans were unlawfully shackled and dragged off in slave coffles to be sold in slavery. Many vowed that they would die before being taken back into slavery.

Location: United States Route 62 in Sandy Lake, Mercer County

Darlington, Pennsylvania
Markers Dedicated to Underground Railroad Sites

In 1979 the Little Beaver Historical Society dedicated two markers commemorating the Underground Railroad. The first dedication was held at the Reformed Presbyterian Church and the second was held at the former home of the Reverend Arthur B. Bradford. Protecting the slave-holding decree of 1845, the Free Presbyterian church was formed and its followers, led by the Reverend Arthur B. Bradford, erected a church in 1847. After the Fugitive Slave Law of 1850 was passed, the congregation declared that the law was un-christian and vowed that they would not respect it. About this time, members of this church became involved with the Underground Railroad. The points where these supporters most often rallied seem to have been the homes of Evan Townsend, with his ingenious trapdoor to the cellar; Benjamin Townsend, with his famous cave at Penn Avenue and Allegheny Road; and David Townsend, with his friendly island in the Beaver River. Milo Louis Townsend, James Irvin, Timothy White, Ellwood Thomas and others were untiring in their assistance to fugitive slaves. Among the noted anti-slavery lecturers who spoke at the Presbyterian Church and "Shuster's Abolition Hall" were Frederick Douglass, Abby Kelly and Steven Foster. Buttonwood, the home of the Reverend Bradford, also welcomed abolitionists and served as a safe-house on the Underground.

Location: Free Presbyterian Church, Plum Street. The second marker is erected at Bradford Road off

Route 551 between Darlington and Enon
Valley.
For more information contact:
Little Beaver Historical Society

Beaver Falls, Pennsylvania
Geneva College

Geneva College was deeply involved with the Underground Railroad and took a strong stance against the issue of human slavery. Founded in 1848 by the Reformed and United Presbyterian Church in Northwood, Ohio, it was moved to Beaver Falls in 1880. While it is well known that Quakers and other Presbyterians received credit for their involvement with the Underground Railroad, the Convenanters, as they were called, did their work as silent sentinels, making significant contributions toward the immediate emancipation of African-Americans held in bondage.

Fugitive slaves were hidden in caves that surrounded the college, which stands a short distance from the Miami River. Wilbur Siebert, an Ohio Underground Railroad historian, notes,

> Family ties, church fellowship, and aggressive anti-slavery leadership, journalistic and political, were the leavening influence of institutions like Oberlin College, Western Reserve College and Geneva College. All contributed to propagate a sentiment that was ready to support the fleeing slave.

The college library houses a major collection of archival materials related to Geneva's involvement with the Underground Railroad.

Location: The campus occupies a wooded bluff
            overlooking the town of Geneva.
For further information contact:
            McCartyney Library
            Geneva College
            Beaver Falls, PA 15016
            (412) 847-6685

Meadville, Pennsylvania
Richard Henderson

Richard Henderson, a friend of John Brown, was probably the most active Underground Railroad agent in northwestern Pennsylvania. He was born in 1801 in Hagerstown, Maryland, of slave parents. At the age of fifteen, he and his brothers Edward and Robert, and a sister whose name is not known, ran away from their Maryland slave owner. They followed a branch of the Underground Railroad known as Jefferson's Route. This route began near the Mason-Dixon line and extended through Bellefonte, the Grampian Hills, Punxsutawny, Brookville and points west. Due to difficulties in crossing a stream of water, the sister died of pneumonia. Although saddended by the death of their sister, the brothers continued on to safety. Upon settling in Meadville, Henderson became a barber. His Arch Street house, since torn down, is estimated to have harbored some five hundred runaway slaves prior to the Civil War. The Pennsylvania Historical and Museum Commission erected a marker to commemorate Richard Henderson's Underground Railroad activities on June 1, 1980.

Location: The marker stands at Liberty and Arch Streets

New Richmond Township, Pennsylvania
John Brown's Tannery

> *Throughout the Underground Railroad, up an down,*
> *traveled Harriet Tubman and Old John Brown*
>   —Lyrics of a period song

Although John Brown was born in Torrington, Connecticut, in 1800, everywhere he traveled and lived he was connected with the Underground Railroad. In 1825, John Brown moved to Randolph, later called Richmond, in Crawford County, not far below Lake Erie. On a side road a short distance south are the remains of the tannery and his home. Here he lived and worked from 1825 to 1835 employing as many as 15 men in producing leather. The tannery and barn had a trapdoor leading into a partial cellar where fugitive slaves were hidden. The tannery has been rebuilt on its original location and is now a museum run by the John Brown Society. Brown also operated the local post office while living in the township. His first wife and son are buried in a cemetery a short distance from the tannery. John Brown was the father of 20 children; several of them died at birth.

Location: Township Road (former LR 20118) south of
             Pennsylvania Route 77, New Richmond
             Township

For further information contact:
             Crawford County Historical Society
             848 N. Main Street
             Maryville, PA 16335
             (814) 724-6080

Erie, Pennsylvania
Commodore Perry Memorial House

Dominated in the north by the urban mass of Erie and the south by the gravitational pull of metropolitan Pittsburgh, Erie City became a major port for Underground Railroad activities. Her fugitives could reach Canada by crossing Lake Erie.

The Perry Memorial House, made of modest gray clapboard, was an important station stop. Fugitive slaves were hidden in the basement. Double fireplaces with secret openings led into stone-walled tunnels, which led to the bay, where runaways could board ships to take them to Canada. A false-walled tunnel can still be seen.

Admiral Oliver Perry, naval hero of the War of 1812, lived in this house while waiting for the final construction of six ships of his nine-vessel fleet built on the lake shore.

Within Erie County itself, abolitionist and Underground activity was considerable, particularly from 1835 to 1853. Other fugitive slave networks ran north from Townsville,

Cambridge Springs, Crawford County, taking their course in northeast, Albion, Branchville, Union City, Waterford, and connecting with Girard.

Location: Commodore Perry Memorial House, Second and
             French Streets

For further information contact:

City of Erie Department of Parks and
Public Works
Municipal Building
626 State Street
Erie, PA 16501
(814) 870-1450

Brownsville, Pennsylvania
Nemacolin Castle

Located in Fayette County, Brownsville is a small community situated on the slope above the Monongahela River. An anti-slavery society was formed here on August 19, 1826, and an account of the meeting was recorded in the Washington County *Examiner*.

The Bowman family members were known abolitionists. Their large stone house was built in 1786 by Jacob Bowman as a residence and trading post. In 1847 it was renovated and enlarged. Its present location is on the same site as Ole Fort Burd. The Bowman's home served as a haven for fugitive slaves who stopped in Brownsville. A secret room in the rear of the mansion was used as a look-out for approaching slave hunters. The African-American conductor, Howard Wallace, wrote in his pamphlet the, "Historical Sketch of the Underground Railroad from Uniontown to Pittsburgh:"

> The main route from William Wallace was Maple Creek, but sometimes we went by the way of Ginger Hill. When fugitive slaves were taken to Maple Creek they were kept by George Norris, also the Bowmans from their house to the river someplace near Belle Vernon, where a small settlement of Colored People lived.

Canadian Osborn Anderson

Martin R. Delaney

Location: The house and grounds occupy an entire block at
             Second Avenue and Front Streets. In later
             years, the Bowman's family homestead name
             was changed to Nemacolin Castle which is
             now a public museum.
For further information contact:
             Nemacolin Castle Tour informantion
             (412) 785-6882
             Brownsville Historical Society
             Brownsville, PA 15417
             (412) 785-6308

Pittsburgh, Pennsylvania
Martin R. Delaney

Probably the most affluent of the blacks who lived in
Pittsburgh during this time was Martin R. Delaney. Born in

Charlestown, West Virginia in 1812, Delaney grew up in Chambersburg and settled in Pittsburgh with his family in 1831. He did his preparatory work in Pittsburgh and applied to Harvard Medical School, where he was accepted. After a year, Delany and two other blacks were dismissed from the school because of a petition signed by bigoted white fellow-students. Returning to Pittsburgh, he founded a black newspaper, *The Mystery*, and completed his professional medical work. Delany defended his views of black re-colonization in Africa, and from 1847 to 1849, he served as editor of Frederick Douglass' famous newspaper, the *North Star*. On September 30, 1850, the *Pittsburgh Gazette* reported that Delany delivered a speech on the topic of the Fugitive Slave Law before a group of prominent white citizens in Allegheny City (now Pittsburgh). Delany stated:

> Honorable mayor, whatever ideas of liberty I have, have been received from reading the lives of your revolutionary fathers. I have therein learned that a man has a right to defend his castle with his life, even unto the taking of life. Sir, my home is my castle, in that castle are none but my wife and my children, as free as the angels of heaven, and whose liberty is as sacred as the pillars of God. If any man approaches that house in search of a slave—I care not who he may be, whether constable, or sheriff, magistrate or even judge of the Supreme Court—nay, let it be he who sanctioned this act to become law, surrounded by his body-guard, with the Declaration of Independence waving above his head as his banner, and the Constitution of this country upon his breast, as a shield—if he crosses the threshold of my door, and I do not lay him a lifeless corpse at my feet, I hope the grave may refuse my body a resting-place and righteous Haven my spirit a home. No! he cannot enter that house and we both live.

Delany's former home was a major stop on the Underground Railroad. Martin R. Delaney was commissioned as a Major in the Civil War. A Pennsylvania Historical and Museum Commission marker was erected on the site of his former home on May 11, 1991.

Location: Third Avenue and Market Street
For further information contact:
                    Pennsylvania Historical Society
                    1300 Locust Street
                    Pittsburgh, PA 15222

Pittsburgh, Pennsylvania
Jane Swisshelm

The name of Jane Swisshelm is frequently mentioned in Pittsburgh's Underground Railroad lore as her former home was a station on the Railroad. Here fugitives were welcomed and assisted. Her sharp and witty writing style carried her to Washington, D.C. as correspondent for Horace Greeley's *Tribune*. Swisshelm edited the *Saturday Visitor*, an abolitionist weekly that uncompromisingly opposed the Fugitive Slave Law and called for total resistance to its implementation. Associated with Jane Swisshelm in Pittsburgh were the Reverend Lewis Woodson, Martin R. Delany, George Vashon, John Peck, George Gardner, Samuel Bruce and Benjamin Tanner, the father of noted African-American Henry O. Tanner, who is portrayed on a U.S. postal stamp. Jane Swisshelm also was a steadfast advocate of women's rights and temperance. Although her former home no longer stands, a Pennsylvania Historical and Museum Commission marker is dedicated to her.
Location: The historical marker stands at Braddock and
                    Greendale Avenues in Edgewood

Pittsburgh, Pennsylvania
Avery College and Church

A blue-and-gold Pennsylvania Historical and Museum Commission marker records the deeds of the Reverend Charles Avery at this location. Avery was an abolitionist, preacher and philanthropist whose wealth came from the production of pharmaceuticals and cotton mills. A member of the Pennsylvania Abolition Society, he gave large sums of money in support of African-Americans, he aided in promoting African-American intellectual equality. In 1849 he founded a college for African-Americans known as the Allegheny Institute and Mission Church. Later this mission church was renamed Avery Memorial African Methodist Episcopal Church during the days of the Underground Railroad. This church became a major center for anti-slavery activities. Avery died on January 17, 1858 and was buried in the God's Acre section of Pittsburgh's Allegheny Cemetery. There is a marble statue of Avery on his grave; on one side there is a figure of Charity and on the other a figure of Justice. Today only a marker testifies to the church's existence.

Location: The marker stands on the south side of the intersection at Nash and Avery Streets

New Castle, Pennsylvania
The Neshannock United Presbyterian Church

In 1851, the General Assembly, which was the highest governing body of the First Presbyterian Church, declared that one could own slaves and still remain a Christian. However, 27 members of the church felt so strongly that the laws of God were higher than those of man that they separated from the larger body and founded the Old Central Church. They purchased property on the northeast side of Diamond (now Kennedy) Square and formed a church with no racial distinctions. During the pre-Civil War period, this church served as a station on the Underground Railroad. The church's minister was jailed at one time for harboring fugitive slaves. In 1949 the church building was destroyed by fire, and in 1950 the property was purchased in Neshannock Township and the church renamed Northminster United Presbyterian Church.

Location: Neshannock Township and Wilmington Road
For further information contact:
            Lawrence County Historical Society

P.O. Box 1745
New Castle, PA 16103-1745
(412) 658-4022

New Castle, Pennsylvania
The White Homestead

Built in 1840 by notorious abolitionist Joseph White, this two-story brick house was one of the most important stops on the Underground Railroad. A large Dutch oven and fireplace were constructed to feed and warm the fugitive slaves who stayed there before they were taken to the next station. The old home still standing is now owned by St. Paul's Lutheran Church.
Location: 305 North Jefferson Street
For further information contact:
                    Lawrence County Historical Society
                    (412) 658-4022

Washington, Pennsylvania
The Le Moyne House

Dr. John Julius Le Moyne was a revolutionist in his native France and took part in the storming of the Bastille in Paris. He became disillusioned with the outcome of the French Revolution and came to America. In 1812, he built the home still standing at 49 East Maiden Street. It was also used by his son, Doctor Frances Julius Le Moyne, who was known as the "Fighting Advocate for Rights." He hated the "peculiar institution of slavery" from his youth and worked vigorously during his adult life to overthrow it. The young Le Moyne also ran for president on the abolitionist ticket and founded an abolition society in Washington.

With the assistance of his family, he operated an Underground Railroad station at this site. At one time the family concealed twenty-five slaves in a secret room on the third floor. Le Moyne's other activities included serving on the board of Washington College and building the first crematorium in the United States. His last surviving granddaughter bequeathed the Le Moyne House to the Washington County Historical Society after her death in 1913 at 101 years of age. Original furniture and other items from the Le Moyne family can be seen here. Visitors are welcome.

Location: 49 East Maiden Street
             Washington, PA 15301
For further information contact:
             Bureau of Travel
             453 Forum Building
             Harrisburg, PA 17120
             (717) 787-5453
             or
             Washington County Historical Society
             49 East Maiden Street
             Washington, PA 15301
             (412) 225-6740

Nat Turner

John Brown, who was connected with the Underground Railroad, wherever he lived. From the Blockson Afro-American Collection.

Virginia

Courtland, Virginia
Nat Turner Historic District

Courtland, or Jerusalem as it was called in 1831, is the site of the most famous slave revolt in American history. Nat Turner, who interpreted the Bible quite literally, believed that God had chosen him to lead his people out of bondage. In 1831 he began his work of destruction.

Turner, a 31-year-old slave belonging to Joseph Travis, was also a preacher of tremendous will and intelligence, and became known as "The Prophet" among his fellow slaves. After laying his plans carefully, in August of 1831 he led an insurrection against white slave-owners as part of his campaign to free enslaved African-Americans. Turner and a large number of his followers attacked various plantations in the area of Southampton County, killing 51 whites. At Courtland, Turner and the insurrectionists had planned to seize the arsenal stabled there before escaping into the Dismal Swamp.

But by October of 1831 most of his followers had been caught. He was unrepentant to the end, entering a plea of "not guilty" at his trial. Regardless, Turner was found guilty of treason, hanged, his body skinned and the flesh boiled down to grease. Gruesome legends maintain that one man had a purse made from the skin. In fact, Turner's skeleton was exhibited to the public for years.

The South became a powder keg as the result of his revolt. More stringent slave laws were enacted, and for years the tenor of life in Southampton and surrounding counties was so deeply affected that slaves were obliged to flee the unbearable conditions there. Self-appointed and irresponsible posses roamed the countryside killing innocent African-Americans at will. The name of Nat Turner remains a controversial one even to the present day.

The Southampton Historical Society has erected two monuments as a reminder of the revolt. One pays tribute to Nat Turner, an the other honors the loyal slaves who aided the whites in their capture of the insurrectionist.

Location: Courtland and vicinity in Southampton County is about 55 miles west of Norfolk on U.S. 58.
From Courtland follow Virginia Route 35 south towards the plantation area that was the site of Nat Turner's revolt.

For further information about Nat Turner and the Courtland Historic District contact:
Virginia Division of Tourism
1021 East Vary Street
Richmond, VA 23219
(804) 786-4484

Hampton, Virginia
The Emancipation Oak Marker

The Emancipation Oak, named by the National Geographic Society as one of The Great Trees of the world, commemorates the granting of freedom to enslaved Americans at the height of the Civil War. Mary Peake, a free African-American teacher, taught children of former slaves under the Emancipation Oak in 1861. The idea of emancipation and its implementation matured slowly in the minds of Congress and President Abraham Lincoln himself; Lincoln was convinced that it was an essential but very delicate act that had to be with the utmost forethought. A preliminary proclamation of September 22, 1862, gave warning that the president would free the slaves in the South, and was followed in January of 1863 by the Emancipation Proclamation itself. Despite the document's conservative stance, it was recognized as a momentous step for the country, and illustrated copies of the Emancipation Proclamation, historical and allegorical prints, and many lesser mementos of Lincoln's actions poured from presses all over the nation.

The Underground Railroad, the movement to break the manacles of slavery, virtually came to a halt when the final version of Lincoln's Emancipation Proclamation was issued on January 1, 1863. The Emancipation Oak, a majestic tree with a limb-spread of 100 feet, still stands on the campus of Hampton Institute to remind visitors of the slow growth of the ideal of freedom in this country.

Location: Emancipation Oak Marker, on U.S. 60 near the entrance of the Hampton Institute, off exit 68 of I-64. Guided tours of the campus are offered.
(804) 727-5000

Virginia
The Great Dismal Swamp

The vast Dismal Swamp on the Virginia-North Carolina border was a refuge for many slaves and a magnet for slave-hunters. Slaves were hunted by men with dogs and guns; hunters disabled their human quarry with bird shot so as not to damage such valuable flesh with heavier ammunition.

Interesting to note is the runaway slave belonging to Augustus Holly of Bertie County, North Carolina. When he was recaptured in the swamp, he was found to be wearing "a coat that was impervious to shot, it being thickly wadded with turkey feathers." The swamp also became the home of a large community of African-Americans whose lives were spent in its dark recesses and whose families were reared

Osman, a fugitive slave who was found living in the Dismal Swamps of Virginia in 1856. Hundreds of escaped slaves lived in maroon communities in this swamp.

This representation of Longfellow's poem, "The Hunted Slave," graphically depicts the anger faced by a fugitive slave and his wife, who are seen fending off a pack of bloodhounds.

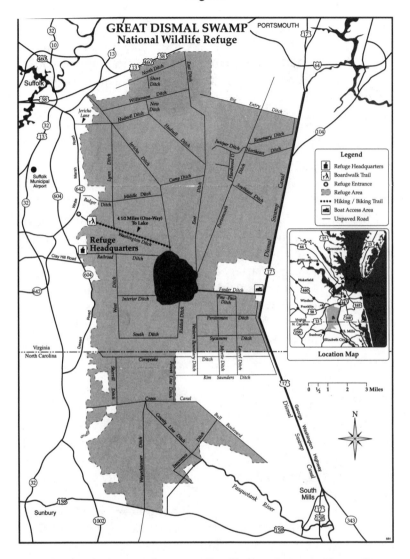

and buried there, despite deadly snakes, yellow flies, mosquitos and ticks.

If it took great courage for fugitives to live in the wilds of the Dismal Swamp, one can imagine the bravery of the slaves who escaped as stowaways or fled on horse or foot at night. The Virginia roads were especially dangerous; they were heavily patrolled by slaveholders and bounty hunters.

Nat Turner had planned his slave revolt in August of 1831, first to kill all white people within reach and then find refuge in the Dismal Swamp.

For further information contact:

> Virginia Division of Tourism
> 1021 East Cary Street
> Richmond, V/. 23219
> (804) 786-4484
> or

For information regarding hiking and biking tours through was is now the Great Dismal Swamp National Wildlife Refuge contact:

> Refuge Manager
> Great Dismal Swamp National Wildlife Refuge
> P.O. Box 349
> Suffolk, VA 23439-0349
> (804) 986-3705

Hampton, Virginia
Fort Monroe

Before the Civil War, large numbers of slaves escaped from Hampton by themselves or through Underground Railroad connections. Many of these desperate slaves made their escape in small boats or with the assistance of friendly sea captains.

During the Civil War, Major General Benjamin F. Butler, a fiery self-confident former attorney and citizen-soldier from Massachusetts was commander of Fort Monroe. An ardent abolitionist, Butler declared runaway slaves "contraband," or legitimate spoils of war in rebellion of federal authority. His bold decision in effect liberated thousands of slaves within fort limits 18 months before President Abraham Lincoln's Emancipation Proclamation. The news spread like wildfire throughout Virginia and surrounding

A wagonload of fugitive slaves arrives at Levi Coffin's. Details from the Underground Railroad, by Charles T. Webbs, courtesy of Cincinnati Art Museum.

Fleeing from the Land of Bondage, arriving at Fort Monroe, Virginia.

states. Soon Fort Monroe was inundated by men, women and children seeking admission to the "freedom fort," as it very shortly became known. Butler ordered food and clothing for the fugitives and employed the able-bodied in work.

Butler's command was challenged in 1861 when the owners of three fugitive slaves who had made their way into Fort Monroe alleged that the general's actions were in violation of the Fugitive Slave Law of 1850. Yet, despite the efforts of Butler, some of his officers turned the slaves away and allowed their owners to repossess their property.

Location: Fort Monroe is three miles south of downtown
              Hampton, off I-64 at eastbound Virginia exit 143.

For further information contact:
              The Casemate Museum
              P.O. Box 341
              Fort Monroe, VA 23651

Charlottesville, Virginia
Monticello

Built largely by slave artisans, Monticello, Thomas Jefferson's "house on the little mountain," was constructed from 1769 to 1801. The house of red brick originally rested upon 5,000 acres of land. Life within Monticello and its surroundings was strongly influenced by the presence of Jefferson's slaves. Oral tradition and written information states that Jefferson had a relationship with his attractive quadroon slave Sally Hemings and sired five children. In this setting of intrigue and revolutionary passion, Jefferson never supported nor denied the accusations regarding his alleged slave children. Woven into this complex history is evidence that several of Jefferson's alleged children ran away, and he did not pursue them.

It was a common practice during this period that the letter 'R' for runaway was branded on the captured slave's cheeks. It was not an uncommon punishment for some slave owners to fasten bells and horns weighing from 12-14

Abraham Lincoln as a young man witnessing a slave auction in New Orleans.

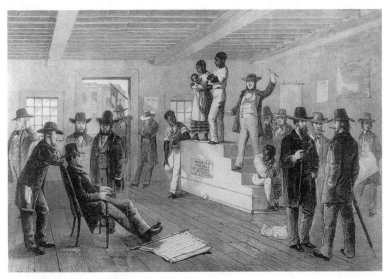

A slave auction in Richmond, Virginia.

Escape of Henry Box Brown.

pounds around the head and necks of slaves who frequently ran away.

Two of Jefferson's alleged sons lived in the state of Ohio for several years, one, according to oral tradition, assisted escaped slaves on the Underground Railroad.
For further information on Monticello contact:

> Thomas Jefferson Visitors Bureau
> Charlottesville, VA 22902
> (804) 293-6789

Richmond, Virginia
The Jackson Ward Historic District,
Where Slaves Were Sold

Slave dealers stood by in every southern town to trade in human flesh. They operated recognized businesses, advertising openly that they had "slaves of all classes constantly on hand ... paying the highest market prices." Their human merchandise, often transported in chains, was washed and

Virginia

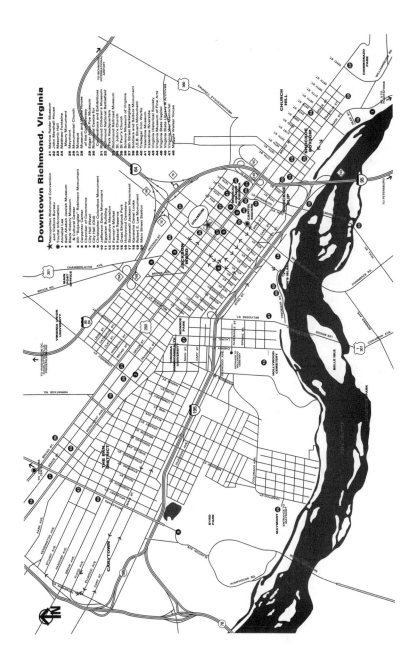

Downtown Richmond, Virginia

★ Metropolitan Richmond Convention and Visitors Bureau
1 Tourist Information
2 Arnold Lee
3 Black History Museum & Cultural Center
4 Bill "Bojangles" Robinson Monument
5 Carpenter Center
6 Chamber of Commerce
7 City Hall (New)
8 City Hall (Old)
9 Edgar Allan Poe Museum
10 Christopher Columbus Monument
11 Egyptian Building
12 Farmer's Market
13 Federal Reserve
14 Great Shiplock Park
15 Hollywood Cemetery
16 Jefferson Davis Monument
17 Stonewall Jackson Monument
18 Kanawha Canal Locks
19 Robert E. Lee Monument
20 Main Street Station

21 Marine Raider House
22 John Marshall House
23 Masonic Hall
24 Matthew Fontaine Maury Monument
25 Maymont
26 Monumental Church
27 Mosque
28 Museum and White House of the Confederacy
29 Richmond Children's Museum
30 Richmond Centre for Conventions and Exhibitions
31 Richmond National Battlefield Park Headquarters
32 Richmond National Battlefield Park Headquarters
35 Richmond Railroad Museum
36 Science Museum of Virginia
37 St. John's Church
38 St. Paul's Church
39 Soldiers and Sailors Monument
40 Tredegar Iron Works
41 Valentine Museum
42 Valentine Riverside
43 Virginia Historical Society
44 Virginia Museum of Fine Arts
45 Virginia State Capitol
46 Virginia State Library & Archives
47 Virginia War Memorial
48 Maggie Walker House

groomed for display like prize horses. The prospect of the auction block frequently triggered flight on the Underground Railroad. Richmond was no different from any other southern city in this respect. Underground Railroad agent and author William Still records the names of 13 fugitive slaves, among them Henry "Box" Brown, who escaped from Richmond.

The Jackson Ward Historic District is a 20-block area of restored 19th century homes. Located in the district were several of the largest slave-trading firms in the South, including Dickerson, Hill and Company, Betts and Company, Davis, and others. The Richmond Directory of 1852 contained the names of 28 persons designated as slave traders, auctioneers and general agents.

One of the busiest slave-marts was in the basement of Old Odd-Fellows Hall. Ironically, a large number of free African-Americans lived in this district among this activity from as early as the 1700s.

The district has been designated a national historic landmark.

After the battle in which Richmond was overtaken by Union forces, an African-American newspaper correspondent sat at the desk of Jefferson Davis, president of the Confederacy, and wrote about the fall of Richmond for his newspaper *The Philadelphia Ledger*. The reporter, Thomas Morris Chester, had assisted his parents in harboring fugitive slaves in their home in Harrisburg, Pennsylvania.

Location: The Jackson Ward is bordered by 4th Street, Marshall Street and Smith Street.

For more information contact:
            Richmond Visitor Information Center
            1710 Robin Hood Road
            Richmond, VA 23220
            (Provides information and maps
            of the Jackson Ward area.)
            (804) 358-5511
            or

The Valentine Museum
1015 East Calay Street
Richmond, VA 23219
(804) 649-0711

Mount Vernon, Virginia
Mount Vernon, Home of George Washington

The flight to freedom actually began long before the Underground Railroad was known as such.

George Washington wrote in 1786 about fugitive slaves in Philadelphia "which a Society of Quakers in the city formed for such purpose has attempted to liberate." Washington, a slaveholder himself, was probably referring to the Pennsylvania Abolition Society, which included among its members at various times such non-Quakers as Benjamin Franklin, Thomas Paine, Dr. Benjamin Rush and the Marquis de Lafayette. Lafayette, who had served as a general under Washington during the Revolutionary War, once asked Washington to join with him in a plan to free all slaves. The proposition was written in a letter from France on February 5, 1783. Washington replied to Lafayette on April 5, 1783, writing, "I shall be happy to join in so laudable a work, but will defer going into a detail of the business till I have the pleasure of seeing you."

The plan never became a reality. Many of Washington's 317 slaves worked on his large plantation as field hands, house slaves, carpenters, gardeners, shoemakers, blacksmiths, brickmakers, coachmen, spinners and weavers. He was sympathetic to their education and recognized marriage between his slaves, unlike most slaveholders. In his will, Washington provided for the manumission of his slaves.

Located about 50 yards southwest of George Washington's grave is the site of an old Mount Vernon burial ground for slaves. William (Billy) Lee, his personal valet, is buried there.

THE UNDERGROUND RAILROAD

Location: Mount Vernon is at the southern end of the
             George Washington Memorial Parkway
             overlooking the Potomac River, 16 miles south
             of Alexandria.
             (703) 780-2000

West Virginia

Harpers Ferry, West Virginia
John Brown's Raid

Taking up arms to free slaves seemed to be the only solution to single-minded abolitionists like John Brown. Early in 1858, Captain Brown, as he was sometimes called, asserted that "what we need is action—action!" He plotted actively to collect a group of devoted followers, seize and fortify a position in the mountains of Virginia and from it make a raid on Harpers Ferry.

"Men, get on your arms; we will proceed to the Ferry." With these bold words, John Brown, commander-in-chief of his own provisional army, set in motion his troop of liberators on a peaceful Sunday, October 16, 1859, and began his march to Harpers Ferry. Brown was 59 years old, and triumphantly wore a long, white, messianic beard. With his band of 21 men of both races, he began his famous raid on the federal arsenal.

Brown was eventually captured, tried for treason and hanged. After his death, John Brown became a martyr and his career was made the subject of numerous books and films. His abolitionist and Underground Railroad activities are marked by monuments throughout the nation.

Location: Harpers Ferry (the town) is situated on a point
              of land at the confluence of the Shenandoah
              and Potomac Rivers about 70 miles northwest of

Washington, D.C., and may be reached by
I-270 and U.S. 340.

Hours: The park is open daily, 8:00 a.m. - 5:00 p.m.
(304) 535-6223

Charlestown, West Virginia
Site of the Wagon that Carried John Brown to His Execution

The Jefferson County Museum is located in the Old Charlestown Civic Center. Among the several thousand artifacts on display is the wagon that conveyed John Brown to his execution. Originally owned by the Sadler brothers of Charlestown, it was used both as a furniture and undertakers' wagon. On what was described as an unusually warm day, December 2, 1859, it conveyed Brown, sitting atop his coffin, from the Jefferson County jail to the site of his execution. Displaying no outward fear, Brown ascended the scaffold calmly, momentarily pausing to remark on the picturesque scenery and the "beautiful country" of Virginia. After a 15-minute wait while the militia surveyed the crowd in an effort to avert any final rescue attempt, the hangman released the trap door below John Brown and he fell to his death, a martyr to slavery.

Fourteen months later, Northern and Southern men found themselves fighting the great Civil War, a bloody conflict predicted by John Brown.

Location: Samuel and Washington Streets
The Jefferson County Museum
P.O. Box 992
Charlestown, WV 25414
(304) 725-8628

West Union, West Virginia
Jacko Cave

Located in Doddridge County, Jacko Cave is strongly

identified by oral tradition as a hiding place for fugitive slaves. Named after Luke Jacko, the innkeeper who used the cave, it lies near a well-traveled road. Jacko's inn, according to tradition, was a notorious rendezvous for men whose comings and goings mystified the neighborhood. Prominent guests at the inn are said to have disappeared, and many skeletons were later found in the cave. Luke Jacko is reported to have been a conductor on the Underground Railroad and to have worked with Ephraim Bee, the Western Union postmaster. Bee later became a member of the first West Virginia legislature. The public can still visit this cave.

Location: The entrance to Jacko Cave is above the old
             northwestern turnpike, which is a part of U.S.
             Route 50.

For further information contact:
             Division of Tourism
             State Capitol Complex Bldg. 6
             Room 564
             2101 Washington Street E.
             Charlestown, WV 25303
             1-800-225-5982

Charlestown, West Virginia
The Site of the Old Jail

John Brown, the embodiment of the larger-than-life Connecticut Yankee, came to national prominence when he was a militant Free Soldier in Kansas and fought pitched battles with the pro-slavery forces in the territory in 1856. Brown and several of his men were confined in 1859 in the Charlestown jail after the raid on Harpers Ferry. The old jail, built of brick and stone, stood on this site from about 1803 until 1933, when it was demolished to make way for the present U.S. Postal Office building.

On the morning of his execution, on his way out of jail, Brown handed his last written words to a guard. They were: "I, John Brown, now am quite certain that the crimes of this guilty land will never be washed away except with blood. I had, as I now think, vainly flattered myself that without much bloodshed, it might be done." Only four years later, at the height of the Civil War, African-Americans were urged to take up arms and join the Union Army.

Location: Southwest corner of George and Washington Streets

For further information on John Brown, and to see more artifacts visit or contact:

Jefferson County Museum
P.O. Box 992
Charlestown, WV 25414
(304) 725-8628

Charlestown, West Virginia
The Site of John Brown's Gallows

Early on the morning of December 2, 1859, the date set for John Brown's execution, he was awake and reading his Bible. Brown wrote a brief note to his wife, enclosing a description of his will and the epitaphs of his dead sons and himself, which he wished chiseled on the old tombstone of his grandfather, after whom he was named. Brown gave his blessing as he said good-bye to four of the five men also held there who had been with him in the Harpers Ferry raid.

To the fifth, John Cook, who had given damaging testimony against him, Brown said, "You have made false statements that I sent you to Harpers Ferry." As "Old John Brown" walked to the gallows on that bright and clear Friday morning, he was surrounded by fifteen hundred federal troops under the command of Colonel Robert E. Lee. As Brown was led to the gallows, a slave woman said, "God bless you, old man; if I could help you I would." Seven of Brown's men had escaped and ten were killed; two of the slain were his own sons.

Brown's exploits inspired many to verse. The song, "John Brown's Body Lies A-Mouldering in the Grave" originated at a camp meeting in Martinsburg and was sung all over the country. The poetic imagination of Stephen Vincent Benet transformed it into an epic poem written in both rhyme and blank verse, "John Brown's Body;" while Julia Ward Howe, moved by the tune as it was sung by a company of African-American soldiers while visiting Washington, D.C., added new verses to it that became "The Battle Hymn of the Republic."

Location: Samuel Street between McCurdy and Beckwith
             Alleys

For further information contact:

The Jefferson County Museum
P.O. Box 992
Charlestown, WV 25414
(304) 725-8628

Charlestown, West Virginia
The Jefferson County Courthouse

The Jefferson County Courthouse is a red brick Georgian colonial building set on a high stone foundation and separated from the street by a small yard. Extending across the front is a tall portico with four Doric columns. In these imposing surroundings, John Brown was arraigned for preliminary examinaiton one week after his capture. Cannons were trained on the courthouse, a threat to those who had ideas of rescuing him and or of lynching him.

In fact, there had been numerous plans to rescue him made by northern followers, but Brown discouraged every attempt. His trial was the subject of national and international discussion and debate. His last speech was made on November 2, 1859, during the court proceedings:

> I have, may it please the Court, a few words to say. In the first place, I deny everything but what I have all along admitted—the design on my part to free the slaves. I intended certainly to have made a clean thing of that matter, as I did last winter when I went into Missouri and there took slaves without the snap-

ping of a gun on either side, moved them through the country, and finally left them in Canada. I designed to have done the same thing again, on a larger scale.

Location: Northeast corner of George and
              East Washington

Wheeling, West Virginia
The Wheeling House Hotel

Most of the official historic sites of the state are silent with regard to the Underground Railroad's history of operation within West Virginia. Still, it is documented that hundreds of escaped slaves used the Appalachian Trail while passing through the cities of Wheeling and other small towns before crossing into the free states of Ohio and Pennsylvania. Although it is closed to the public today, The Old Wheeling House Hotel still has the atmosphere and charm of the antebellum period. It also has a historical connection with the Underground Railroad. Eber Pettit a conductor from Fredonia, New York, had written warmly about The Wheeling House Hotel's landlord, who gave assistance to escaped slaves by sending them to nearby safe-houses. The hotel nomination to become a historic site is under consideration by the National Park Service. Another old historic landmark, of a vastly different nature, was the auction block that once stood near the Wheeling House Hotel.

Location: The Wheeling House Hotel is located at 10th and
              Main Streets, Northeast Corner (not open to
              the public.)

For further information about the Wheeling House Hotel
              and Slave Auction Block contact:
              Oglebay Institution Madison Museum
              Ogebay Park
              Wheeling, WV 26003
              (304) 242-7272

NEW ENGLAND

Connecticut

James W.C. Pennington,
Pastor of the African Congregation Church

Hartford was the home of the most distinguished fugitive slaves in America. Pennington was born a slave in Maryland in 1809, but fled and escaped via the Underground Railroad.

Trained as a blacksmith, he eventually received a divinity doctorate from the University of Heidelberg, Germany and preached against slavery from New England to Europe. He frequently wrote about the inhuman conditions of his people; his narrative, *The Fugitive Blacksmith or Events in the History of James W.C. Pennington, Formerly Slave in the State of Maryland*, was published in 1849. Early in his career he served as pastor of the African Congregation Church in Hartford. He later became the first minister of the First Shiloh Presbyterian Church in New York, performing the marriage ceremony of another Maryland fugitive slave, Frederick Douglass. The Congregational Church on Talcott Street in Hartford where Pennington preached was destroyed in the 1950s, but a plaque marking the site is at the corner of Talcott and Market Streets in downtown Hartford.
Location: Talcott and Market Streets
For further information contact:
> Greater Hartford Tourism District
> One Civic Center Plaza

Hartford, CT 06103
(204) 258-4286
or
(800) 793-4480

Bloomfield, Connecticut
The Francis Gillette House

Most prominent among the Underground Railroad workers in Connecticut was Francis Gillette, who lived in Bloomfield and Hartford. He was trained in the law but never practiced before the bar, instead devoting himself to working at his ancestral farm for social causes such as abolition, temperance and educational reform. When at his Bloomfield residence, which was a station on the Underground Railroad, he warmed and cheered himself by the fire listening to his fugitive guests, whose stories and songs made a lifelong impression on him. Related by marriage to Harriet Beecher Stowe, Gillette and another relative by marriage, John Hooker, purchased a 100-acre farm just west of Hartford in 1853. Among his famous houseguests was Mark Twain. Gillette used this home as a station on the Underground as well; the barn, which no longer stands, was a safe house for fugitives. In 1854 Gillette was elected to the United States Senate, where he voted against the Kansas-Nebraska Act, which would have permitted slavery in the territory.
Location: 511 Bloomfield Avenue
           Bloomfield, CT 06002
For further information contact:
           Wintonbusy Historical Society
           (203) 242-7175

Canterbury, Connecticut
Prudence Crandall Museum

Prudence Crandall, a Quaker schoolmistress, was imprisoned because she admitted African-American students to her boarding school for girls from Boston, New York and Philadelphia.

In 1833 Sarah Harris, an African-American, applied for admission as a non-resident student, and was accepted. However, most of the white parents withdrew their children from the boarding school in protest. Crandall stood her ground, even though she was warned by a prominent minister's wife that if she did not dismiss the young African-American girl, her school would fail. "Let it fail then," Crandall replied, "for I should not turn her out." She boldly declared that she would open a school exclusively for African-Americans. Her neighbors attempted to burn the school down, and threw manure into the well; the village doctors refused to treat her students and the grocers refused to sell her food. Prudence Crandall was eventually arrested and served a night in jail. Abolitionists throughout the nation came to her defense, and after her case was presented, Connecticut's highest court dismissed her on a technicality. However, to protect her students, she closed the school after a mob broke all of its windows. A short time later she moved away from the sea.

Although Canterbury was located on an important Underground Railroad route, there is no documented evidence that slaves were harbored in Prudence Crandall's school. Oral tradition suggests that they were probably hidden on her father's farm. Today, her school has been turned into a museum.

Location: Prudence Crandall Museum (corner of Routes 14 and 169) Canterbury, CT 06331
(203) 546-9916

Farmington, Connecticut
The Grand Central Station of Connecticut Underground Railroad Lines

The town of Farmington has been called the Grand Central Station of the Underground Railroad by African-American historian Horatio T. Strother in his book, *The Underground Railroad in Connecticut*. Strother cited several reasons for this. One was geographical: Farmington was located on the turnpike system that lined New Haven and Hartford. Another Underground Railroad source has postulated a more personal incentive, stating that

> when the beloved Farmington minister Dr. Noah Porter invited the African-American scholar Reverend James W.C. Pennington of Hartford to exchange pulpits, the intellect and eloquence of the former slave broke down prejudice and paved the way for Underground Railroad activities in Farmington.

Certainly, a number of the town's leading citizens were involved in the Underground. At least eight stations have been recorded, including Timothy Wadsworth's house at 340 Main Street, the Smith-Cowles House (now the home of the headmaster of Miss Porter's School), Lyman Hurlburt's home on High Street, Elijah Lewis' home on Hartford Road and Horace Cowles' house on Main Street.

Another Farmington stationmaster was Austin F. Williams; his home still stands today at 127 Main Street. Williams made provisions for receiving African slaves who were involved in the famous Amistad case, and later used his home as a station on the Underground Railroad, hiding fugitives in a cellar under the carriage house. The house is registered as a national historic landmark.

For further information contact:

Greater Hartford Tourism District
One Civic Center Plaza
Hartford, CT 06103
(800) 793-4480

Hartford, Connecticut
Harriet Beecher Stowe House

"In the midst of those fugitive slaves troubles," wrote Frederick Douglass, "came the book *Uncle Tom's Cabin*, a work of marvelous depth and power." Although Harriet

Beecher Stowe wrote most of her famous novel in Brunswick, Maine, she lived for a time in Hartford in a home adjacent to that of Mark Twain. The restored Stowe home contains original furniture and other items of the internationally known author.

Location:　71 Forest Street
　　　　　　Hartford, CT 06105
　　　　　　(203) 525-9317

New Haven, Connecticut
United Church-on-the Green

Among the most vigorous of anti-slavery workers and Underground Railroad agents were Reverend Simeon S. Jocelyn and Reverend Samuel W. Dutton, pastors of the United Church-on-the Green. Jocelyn was one of the founders of the New Haven Anti-Slavery Society, established a church for African-Americans. He was also the brother of Nathaniel Jocelyn the artist, who painted the portrait of Cinque, celebrated hero of the Armistad Slave Muntiny Case.

Reverend Dutton sheltered escaped slaves in his home on College Street, at the time when Reverend Henry Ward Beecher delivered his lecture in Dutton's church. Dutton and his sister assisted in raising funds for a company of men to protect Kansas from pro-slavery forces. Another African-American minister, Reverend Amos G. Beman, was also active in New Haven's Underground Railroad activities; with the assistance of his congregation Berman aided hundreds of escaped slaves.

Location:　The Green is in the center of New Haven,
　　　　　　adjoining Yale University. United
　　　　　　Church-on-the Green stands at the corner of
　　　　　　Temple and Elm Streets. Tours by
　　　　　　appointment only.
　　　　　　323 Temple Street
　　　　　　New Haven, CT 06511
　　　　　　203-787-4195

Joseph Cinque, leader of the Amistad Mutiny painted from life by Nathaniel Jocelyn. "What a Master Spirit is his" wrote Whittier of Cinque, "what a soul for the tyrant to crush down in bondage."

New Haven, Connecticut
Monument of Cinque, Leader of the Famous *Amistad* Slave Mutiny

Plotted escapes and revolts among enslaved Africans, even before they docked in America, were many.

On August 22, 1839, a low-lying, mysterious schooner lay off the shores of Montauk, New York. Her topsail gone, her remaining sails tattered, and carrying no flag of nationality, she drifted as a vagabond. The schooner was called the *Amistad*, a Spanish slaver whose human cargo of 53 Africans had, under the leadership of the forceful Cinque, killed all but two of the crew and taken over the vessel, bringing her into the harbor at Montauk.

Upon landing, the African slaves were charged with piracy and murder, while Spain claimed ownership of both the slaves and the ship. As the slave trade was an explosive issue, the *Amistad* case became a national sensation. Joseph Cinque electrified this bitter feud with his bearing and commanding presence, inspiring former President John Quincy Adams himself to come to Cinque's defense. The wealthy Tappan brothers of New York, staunch opponents of slavery and notable Underground Railroad agents, gave large sums to support the case of the Africans.

The case with its web of international complications, went through a legal labyrinth from court to court, and finally appeared before the United States Supreme Court, the first civil case in its history. The elderly Adams carried the day defending the Africans, and they were declared free men by the court.

Herman Melville took this incident for the plot of his novelette, *Benito Cereno*.

Location: In front of City Hall on Church Street
For further information contact:

> Greater New Haven Convention
> & Visitors Bureau
> One Long Wharf Drive
> Suite 7
> New Haven, CT 06511
> (203) 777-8550

Maine

Augusta, Maine
The Nason and the Williams Houses

When fugitive slaves managed to avoid the danger of passing through the New England states and arrived in Augusta, they were assisted by the Nason and the Williams families. Behind a large bookcase in the Nason House is a removable panel that opens to a hidden room large enough to hide two slaves. This room led to the cellar, through which the fugitives could exit.

Although the fourteen-roomed Williams House is no longer standing, it once was used as a station stop on the Underground. The house was located along the waterfront on Cony Street. Local historians believe that the main center of Underground Railroad activity was situated along the river between the Nason, Weeks and Williams families, who finally smuggled fugitives onto vessels bound for Canada. It was not unusual for escaping slaves who traveled through Maine to receive Underground Railroad assistance in China, Dirigo, Brunswick, Bangor, Brewer and Portland. The Nason House is a private home.

Location: Nason House
              12 Sumner Street
              Augusta, ME 04330
For further information contact:

Kennebec Historic Society,
c/o Special Collections
University of Maine At Augusta
University Avenue
Augusta, ME 04330
(207) 621-3355

Gardiner, Maine
Episcopal Parish House

Fugitive slaves who had survived the dangerous trek of the Underground Railroad from the South into Maine were welcomed by the congregation of the Episcopal Parish House.

In this church there are several places of concealment. A large brick room with a small entrance served as a secret chamber. In another portion of the basement is a section of stonework against which is built another room with an open doorway. Located in the church's attic is a small cubicle without windows, large enough to conceal several people. Entry is made by a pull-down stairway. Unwelcome visitors such as slave hunters were treated as trespassers on the church's property, which is located on the west bank of the river.

Location: 83 Dreden Avenue
Gardiner, ME 04345
(207) 582-9830

Brunswick, Maine
Harriet Beecher Stowe Home

Harriet Beecher Stowe is reported to have begun to write her powerful novel *Uncle Tom's Cabin* while her husband taught at Bowdoin College. It is recorded that her inspiration for the book came from an anti-slavery sermon delivered at the First Parish Church on Main Street. Abolitionist sentiment exploded with a force that shook the world when

Uncle Tom's Cabin was published in 1852. The book sold over 3,000 copies in 24 hours, 100,000 in eleven weeks. More than 1,000,000 copies were sold in the then British Empire. Southerners were livid, and banned the book. In slave states, those caught reading it were fined or sentenced to a jail term.

This was the case with Samuel Green, a black minister and Underground Railroad conductor, who was sentenced by the Maryland courts to serve ten years in jail for having in his possession a copy of *Uncle Tom's Cabin*. It's now understood that the book inspired men who had not read a book in years to read it; women neglected their washing to sewing and read it.

Harriet Tubman, working as a cook in a large hotel to earn money for her Underground Railroad excursions, stated to a fellow servant that she did not want to see the play *Uncle Tom's Cabin* that was appearing in Philadelphia. "I've heard *Uncle Tom's Cabin* read, and I tell you Mrs. Stowe's pen has not begun to paint the picture of what slavery is at the far South. I've seen the real thing." The home is run as a gift shop, inn and restaurant.

Location: 63 Federal Street
             Brunswick, ME 04011
             (207) 725-5543

Vassalboro, Maine
The Farwell Mansion

A short way beyond Vassalboro township is a historic and stately dwelling built in 1842 that remains in use as a private residence to this day. It was well patronized by northbound fugitive slaves seeking freedom on the Underground Railroad. Neither the original owner of this large house, Captain Ebenezer Farwell, nor his family ever lived in this house. Farwell was a slave trader and was killed on a voyage to Africa. His widow sold the home to Israel Weeks, who gave sanctuary to fugitive slaves who, according to family tradition, were hidden in the cellar. The home is not open to the public.

Location: Riverside Drive, Vassalboro
For further information contact:
                 Maine Publicity Bureau
                 Box 2300
                 Hallowell, ME 04347
                 1-800-533-9595
                 or:
                 The Vassalboro Historical Society
                 (207) 923-3505

Massachusetts

Boston, Massachusetts
Statues of Abolitionists Charles Sumner and Wendell Phillips

Foremost among 19th-century champions of abolition and equal rights for African-Americans were Charles Sumner and Wendell Phillips. Sumner, a Harvard graduate and United States Senator, was extremely outspoken in his attack on the South and was an ardent advocate of immediate freedom for slaves. When William Still published his book *Underground Railroad* in 1872, Sumner said in his endorsement, "I always hesitated which to honor most, the fugitive slave or the citizens who help him, in defiance of unjust laws. Your book will teach us to honor both." On his deathbed among his last words was a plea to Frederick Douglass to see that the Civil Rights Bill was carried through. Sumner's funeral procession was headed by African-American mourners.

Wendell Phillips, also a Harvard graduate and noted orator, gave up flourishing law practice in Boston in 1837 to join with the anti-slavery movement of William Lloyd Garrison. Phillips was connected with the Underground Railroad as an attorney representing fugitive slaves in court. He was uncompromising in his stand and unceasing in his demands that slavery be eliminated even if it meant the end

of the Union. The bronze statue of Phillips bears the inscription, "Champion of the Slave."
Location: The statues of Sumner and Phillips are on
            Boylston Street at the Mall
For more information contact:
            Massachusetts Historical Society
            1154 Boylston Street
            Boston, MA 02215
            (617) 536-1608

Boston, Massachusetts
The Emancipation Group Monument

Located on Park Square in Boston is a duplicate casting by sculptor Thomas Ball called "Emancipation Group," donated by Moses Kimball. The model for the kneeling slave was Ascher Alexander, a fugitive slave from Missouri.
Location: Park Square
            Boston, MA

Boston Massachusetts
Twelfth Street Baptist Church

Sometimes called "The Second African Meeting House,"the Twelfth Street Baptist Church under the leadership of its popular pastor Reverend Leonard Grimes became a major station, on Boston's Underground Railroad. Though he was born of free parents in Leesburg, Virginia, Grimes was arrested in 1815, tried and found guilty for his earlier Underground Railroad activities in Washington, DC. After his release from prison, he moved to Boston. His church became the center of attention during the arrest of two famous fugitive slave cases, Shadrach and Anthony Burns (who were members of his church). Shadrach, as he was called, was rescued and sent to Canada, while Burns was returned to slavery in Virginia. Grimes and other concerned

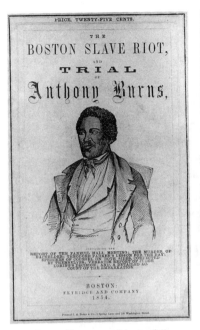

The Reverend Leonard Grimes. He was arrested in Washington, D.C. for Underground Railroad activities. Later, in Boston, his church became a haven for escaped slaves.

Anthony Burns, subject of the famous Boston Fugitive Slave Case of 1854.

African-Americans, with the assistance of white abolitionists purchased Burns' freedom.

Location: Twelfth Street Baptist Church
              150 Warren Street
              Roxbury, MA
              (617) 442-7855

Amesbury, Massachusetts
John Greenleaf Whittier House

Although his Quaker coat had been spattered with eggs and the office of his anti-slavery newspaper, *The Pennsylvania Freeman*, burned, John Greenleaf Whittier displayed a passion for the abolition of slavery. He lived in Amesbury for 56 years, operating an Underground Railroad station stop in his house; most of his poems were written here, and the desk he worked at as well as other interesting memorabilia are still to be seen in the home.

As Poet Laureate of New England and the author of "Snowbound," Whittier remarked near the end of his life to visitors in his home, "Oak Knoll," in Danver, Massachusetts, "I set a higher value on my name as appended to the Declaration of Anti-Slavery Sentiment in 1833 than on the title page of any book." Whittier came to Philadelphia in December of 1833 as a delegate from Massachusetts to organize the American Anti-Slavery Society. The Declaration of Anti-Slavery Sentiment was written principally at night in the attic of African-American Underground Railroad agent James McCrummel. The Whittier House is open to the public and tours are available.

Location: 86 Friend Street
             Amesbury, MA 01913

Boston, Massachusetts
The Farwell Mansion

The property of the Farwell Mansion currently owned and maintained by the League of Women for Community Service was a former station on the Underground Railroad. Built by William Rice Carne, this old Mansion sheltered fugitive slaves, who were kept total darkness until it was safe to move them to distant safe houses.

Location: 558 Massachusetts Avenue
             Boston, MA 02167
             (617) 720-1713

Boston, Massachusetts
Faneuil Hall

Often called the "Cradle of Liberty," Faneuil Hall Market today is a complex of historic buildings filled with vendors and restaurants. Built by Peter Faneuil in 1761, the original hall was destroyed by fire, but was rebuilt in 1761. By the mid-1840s, the rhetoric of abolitionists was to echo and re-echo from these walls. William Lloyd Garrison, Senator Charles Sumner, Thomas Wentworth Higginson and Wendell Phillips, unquestionably one of the greatest orators of his day, spoke here. Frederick Douglass, Charles Lenox Remond and William C. Nell demanded immediate slave emancipation, and the Boston Vigilance Committee, composed of African-Americans, was organized in this hall. Leonard Grimes, a prominent Boston Underground Railroad agent, was part of the huge crowd that gathered when Anthony Burns was jailed, soon to be taken back to captivity in Virginia by a ship sent by the President of the United States. Despite the consultations of Bronson Alcott and the Reverend Theodore Parker with Richard H. Dana Jr., Burn's attorney, he was indeed removed to Virginia, and 50,000 citizens cried "Shame!"

Later, Burns returned to Boston; $1,300 had been paid for his freedom. He settled in St. Catherine, Canada, and was ordained a Baptist Minister. He had refused an offer to exhibit himself in a museum made by the circus promoter P.T. Barnum.

It is ironic that the hall was a gift to the city by Faneuil who gained great wealth from the slave trade. A century later, the hall was the site of speeches by anti-slavery lecturers.

Location: Faneuil Hall stands in Faneuil Hall Square,
                Merchant Row.

Nantucket, Massachusetts
The African Meeting House

Nantucket is the ancestral home of two prominent Quaker anti-slavery and Underground Railroad personalities, Levi Coffin and Lucretia Coffin Mott; the Jethro Coffin House is the oldest one on the island, built in 1686. Lucretia

Mott's former home is located at 15 Fair Street and also still stands. Africans, slave and free, worked as Mariners in Nantucket's whaling industry, some used their vessels to transport fugitive slaves escaping on the Underground Railroad. During the 19th century Nantucket's African community was located in an area called "New Guinea."

Still standing, The African Meeting House was built around 1820, and served as a church and meeting house for the New Guinea community. Frederick Douglass, several years after his Underground Railroad journey, delivered his first public address here on August 12, 1841, in Athenalum Hall.

The African Meeting House was purchased by the Museum of Afro-American History in Boston. Presently this organization is soliciting funds to restore the African Meeting House.

Location: The African Meeting House is at York and
             Pleasant Street
For more information contact:
             The Museum of Afro-American History
             46 Joy Street (Beacon Hill)
             Boston, MA 02114
             (617) 742-1854

Nantucket, Massachusetts
The African Baptist Church

The island of Nantucket's history dates back to 1659, when it was bought by Thomas Macy, a Puritan landowner living on the mainland, for 30 pounds and two beaver hats from Native Americans. They called it "Nanticut," meaning "the far away land." Nantucket is the ancestral home of two prominent Quaker anti-slavery personalities, Levi Coffin and Lucretia Coffin; the Jethro Coffin house is the oldest one on the island, built in 1686. Frederick Douglass visited Nantucket and delivered a lecture at the African Baptist Church, one of the oldest surviving African-American sanctuaries in

New England. The Whaling Museum, located at 18 Johnny Cake Hill, was built in 1847 as a sperm-candle factory, and now contains many relics of the whaling era. Many African-Americans worked on whaling ships, including Peter Green, second mate of the *John Adams*. During a violent storm at sea he piloted the vessel safely home. A number of seamen who were involved in the whaling industry used their vessels to transport fugitive slaves on the Underground.

Location: The African Meeting Church at York and
             Pleasant Streets
             Nantucket, MA 02554

New Bedford, Massachusetts
The Whaling Museum

New Bedford, an important port, welcomed many runaways, and the sea had its own story of the Underground Railroad. Located at the mouth of the Acushmet River, Westport, near New Bedford, was the home of wealthy African-American sea captain Paul Cuffe. Shortly after the end of the War of 1812, Cuffe took 38 African-Americans aboard his famous ship *The Traveller* and set sail to Sierra Leone in Africa. He provided for all of the expenses of the emigrants out of his own pocket, hoping that his passengers would find a better life for themselves.

Ironically, within a few years of Cuffe's philanthropic effort, the American Colonization Society was formed, much to the outrage of freed African-Americans.

Cuffe was a close friend of two prominent Philadelphia abolitionists, James Forten and Cyrus Bustill, the latter an African-American Quaker whose great-grand-daughter Louisa was Paul Robeson's mother. Cuffe made his fortune as a shipbuilder, and today his compass as well as a collection of "toggle harpoons" designed by Lewis Temple, the African-American metalsmith, are on display in the Whal-

Paul Cuffee and his brig, **The Traveller.** *He took thirty-eight fellow African-Americans to Sierra Leone in Africa, paying for their expenses.*

Twelfth Baptist Church (Second African). It became known as the "Church of the Fugitive Slaves" in Boston; Pastor Leonard Grimes.

ing Museum. Paul Cuffe is buried in a cemetery next to the Quaker meetinghouse in Westport.

Location: 613 Pleasant Street
             New Bedford, MA 02740

New Bedford, Massachusetts
Nathan Johnson House

As steeped in tradition as any Underground Railroad station in Massachusetts was the home of Nathan Johnson, who operated a general store to cover his activities. In 1838, a slave of about 20 years of age named Frederick Augustus Washington Bailey escaped from his owner in Maryland and journeyed on to the noted African-American conductor Nathan Johnson. Johnson provided shelter for the fleeing slave and his fiance, Anna. He also suggested that the fugitive change his last name to "Douglass" after reading the book *Ivanhoe*. African-American Underground Railroad conductor David Ruggles, who had given assistance to hundreds of fugitive slaves, had sheltered the young runaway for nearly two weeks, made his marriage arrangements and sent the newlyweds on to Bedford through the help of Underground Railroad seamen William C. Tabor and Joseph Rickelson. In later life, Frederick Douglass, a proponent of moderation, would oppose the fiery William Lloyd Garrison's extremist abolition tactics. This house is open to the public.

Location: 21 Seventh Street
             New Bedford, MA 02740

Roxbury, Massachusetts
William Lloyd Garrison House, Residence of the Renowned Abolitionist

A deeply religious man, William Lloyd Garrison was willing to cast away the Church, the Constitution and the Union in the name of immediate emancipation. He devoted

William Lloyd Garrison, prominent anti-slavery agitator, editor of
The Liberator.

his full time to the abolitionist cause, and paid for his convictions in a way that helped further the cause and define his enemies.

In 1835 Garrison was confronted by a pro-slavery mob shouting "Kill him! Lynch him! Hang the abolitionist!" Seized and tied up, he was finally rescued by delegates of the mayor of Boston. By 1841 he was calling upon northern states to secede from the Union; he was burned in effigy in Charleston, South Carolina. Garrison was one of the founders of the New England and the American Anti-Slavery Societies. His famous anti-slavery newspaper, *The Liberator*, appeared in Boston on New Year's Day in 1831 and did not cease publication until 1865. This home is open to the public.

Location: 125 Highland Street
                 Roxbury, MA 02119

Lewis Hayden, escaped slave and well-known agent in the Boston Underground Railroad. Hayden's home still stands today.

Boston, Massachusetts
Lewis Hayden House

The desperate courage that served the Underground Railroad was forcibly demonstrated by Lewis Hayden, a dedicated conductor on the Boston line. Hayden was himself a slave who had escaped from Kentucky in 1816 and settled in Boston. He made his large, four-story home on Beacon Hill a station stop. When William and Ellen Craft made their daring escape in 1848 from Macon, Georgia, they were forwarded to Hayden's home. Upon recovering the Crafts, Hayden placed himself by two kegs of gunpowder and stood with a candle, grimly determined to blow up his home, the Crafts and himself, rather than surrender his guests if slave hunters came to his door.

In 1851, Hayden led a group of Boston African-Americans in liberating, by force, a fugitive slave named Frederick Jenkins (known also as Shadrach) from federal officers.

Hayden operated his station with his wife Harriet, and assisted his friend Harriet Tubman when she passed through Boston. He was elected to serve in the Massachusetts Legislature in 1873. After his death in 1889, a scholarship fund at Harvard University was established by his widow. This house is open to the public.

Location: 66 Phillips Street
            Boston, MA 02114

Boston, Massachusetts
African Meeting House

Boston's African Meeting House was built with money raised by Cato Gardner, a freed slave. Erected in 1806, this venerable African meetinghouse, also referred to as the "Abolition Church," is the site at which William Lloyd Garrison and ten others founded the New England Anti-Slavery Society on December 16, 1832. It was a fancy name for an infant organization, since the constitution published in *The Liberator* of February 18, 1832, boasted only twelve signators. Membership increased very slowly, and after three years the name was changed to the Massachusetts Anti-Slavery Society. The congregation of the meetinghouse provided fugitive slaves with food, clothing and shelter before directing them to other stations. The house is standing and is open to the public.

Location: 8 Smith Court
            Boston, MA 02114

Boston, Massachusetts
African Meeting House, Abiel Smith School

Today this rustic wood-frame building remains relatively unchanged from when it stood centuries ago. Presently this building is the home of the Museum of Afro-American History; it is the site where Boston's first school for African-American children was built in 1834. The museum today

Henry David Thoreau, cele-brated Concord Massachu-setts author and anti-slvery reformer.

houses important historical documents pertaining to African-American life in New England, including a rare copy of Phillis Wheatley's book of poems published in 1773. A portion of the museum's permanent exhibits tells the story of the Underground Railroad. Located around the corner from the museum was the home of William Nell, a prominent African-American attorney and historian, and a major agent on the Underground Railroad.

Location: 46 Joy Street (one block west of the State House)
             Boston, MA 02114

Concord, Massachusetts
Town Hall Bell

Concord is rich with historical, literary and anti-slavery associations. It was home of Ralph Waldo Emerson, Franklin B. Sanborn, Henry David Thoreau and the Alcott family. They were all abolitionists and were connected with the

Underground Railroad. Thoreau's former home and that of his intimate friend Emerson were stations on the Underground; they were both associates of John Brown. Thoreau called Brown "an angel of Light," while Emerson said that the "Old Man" was filled with a "simple artless goodness." In Concord, on October 30, 1859, Thoreau had rung the great Town Hall bell as John Brown was tried for treason before a Charlestown, Virginia (now West Virginia) judge, his feet fettered and his bayonet and saber wounds still bleeding. Thoreau became an accessory after the fact of Harpers Ferry, aiding the flight of the escaping five fugitives to Canada.

Location: Still standing, Town Hall once had a prime
              location, facing the famous green, and is easy
              to find when entering the town

Concord, Massachusetts
"Orchard House," the Bronson Alcott Home

Known as "Orchard House," this two-and-a-half story house with central chimney and small-paned windows was the second home of the Alcotts. In front of the house are great elm trees, and in the rear was an apple orchard. To feed his family, Alcott worked for his neighbors and established his famous Temple School. He believed children must know themselves to escape from the tyranny of custom. Whenever a fugitive slave escaping on the Underground Railroad came along, the Alcotts fed, sheltered and passed him on to the next conductor. Orchard House was the scene of Louisa May Alcott's *Little Women;* she longed to be an actress and novelist and roamed the fields with her friend Henry David Thoreau, studying the birds and the flowers. This house is open to the public.

Location: Lexington Road
              Concord, MA 01742

Concord, Massachusetts
Ralph Waldo Emerson House

Known as the "Sage of Concord," Emerson was an ardent abolitionist. After his visit to Europe that lasted from 1847 to 1848, he became the leader of the philosophical/literary movement, transcendentalism. He not only contributed money to the anti-slavery cause, but was always ready to lend his horses to transport fugitive slaves toward their next destination. With his pen, Emerson wrote several anti-slavery pamphlets, and entertained leading anti-slavery friends in the home that he built himself in 1826 and lived in from 1835 until his death in 1882. This house is open to the public.

Location: Lexington Road and Cambridge Turnpike
             Concord, MA 01742

Concord, Massachusetts
Jonathan Ball House

This house is considered one of the historic houses of Concord, and was erected by Jonathan Ball, a goldsmith, about 1720. The Bartlett family, which owned the house during the era of the Underground Railroad, harbored fugitive slaves here overnight and transported them by stagecoach to West Fechbury. One of the Bartlett's escorts was Henry David Thoerau. Another was neighbor Francis Bigelow, the village Blacksmith, who escorted Shadrach, the famous fugitive slave, to Concord. Bigelow's home stands today at 5 Sudbury Road, directly across the street from the Concord Library. The Jonathan Ball house is now the home of the Concord Art Association, and is open to the public with special arrangement.

Location: 15 Lexington Road (Route 2A)
             Concord, MA 01742

West Upton, Massachusetts
Polly Dean Bradish House

Polly Dean Brandish, wife of town blacksmith Harvey Bradish, was a well-known anti-slavery spokesperson and conducted a station on the Underground Railroad here. Her house can be identified by a plaque commemorating her activities that was placed by the local women's club during the town's bicentennial in 1935. It has a secret stairway leading to the attic, where slaves were hidden. Bradish used not only her home, located at 10 North Main Street, across from the blacksmith shop of her husband, but the South-worth Tavern, which stood on the site of the present Town Hall. During her time Dolly Bradish brought many abolitionists here, including Wendell Phillips, "the proper Bostonian of first rank," and William Lloyd Garrison. The house is owned today by members of the Buddist religious sect, and is not open to the public.

Location: Number 10, North Main Street
            West Upton, MA 01568

Newburyport, Massachusetts
Garrison Statue

In Brown's Park, at the corner of Green and Pleasant Streets, stands the statue of the "Great Liberator" William Lloyd Garrison, abolitionist orator, publisher of *The Liberator* and champion of the cause of the slaves.

Though nothing stands to mark his contributions, the Reverend Thomas Wentworth Higginson, a native of Newburyport, was also an ardent abolitionist who used his pulpit to speak out against slavery and his home as a station on the Underground Railroad. An imposing man of great strength, Higginson was wounded in the rescue of Anthony Burns when he and Lewis Hayden led a group of abolitionists in battering down the door of the Boston courthouse to rescue the fugitive Burns. During the Civil War, Higginson was the colonel of America's first African-American regiment; after the war he edited the *Atlantic Monthly Magazine* and wrote a book entitled *Army Life in a Black Regiment.*

Among the other Underground Railroad stationmasters at Newburyport were the Honorable Richard Plumer, Captain Alexander Graves and William Jackman.

Location: Brown's Park, Green and Pleasant Streets
             Newsburyport, MA 01950

Springfield, Massachussetts
St. John's Congregational Church

Visitors can still view the stained glass window that holds the inscription: "In Memory of John Brown, Hero of Harpers Ferry." Brown lived in Springfield for a short period of his life. St. John's Congregational Church was founded in 1844 by free African-Americans and white abolitionists. Frederick Douglass' name is included among the famous abolitionists who spoke from the church's pulpit.

Location: 643 Union Street
             Springfield, MA
             (413) 734-2283

Stoneham, Massachusetts
Home of Deacon Abijah Bryant

Midway between Reading and Medford lies Stoneham, where the house at Number 307 Main Street bears a tablet with the following inscription.

> Underground Railroad. This house, the home of Deacon Abijah Bryant, harbored many fugitive slaves in the years preceding the Civil War.

The house is not open to the public.

Location: 307 Main Street
             Stoneham, MA 02180

New Hampshire

Canaan, New Hampshire
The Furber-Harris House

Charles Lord wrote in a letter dated July 6, 1896; "My maternal grandfather, James Furber, lived several years in Canaan, where his house was one of the stations on the Underground Railroad. His father-in-law, James Harris, who lived in the same house, had been engaged in helping fugitive slaves on toward Canada since 1830." Furber is said to have transported fugitives to Lyme, New Hampshire. Located across the road from the Furber-Harris home was the Noyes Academy, where 14 African-American students were enrolled. In 1835 an anti-abolitionist mob used 95 yoke of oxen to drag the school into the swamp. Undaunted by the mob's attack, a Canaan resident and abolitionist Dr. Timothy Tilton proudly requested that "The Slave's Friend" be inscribed on his tombstone, which can still be seen in the Canaan Street Cemetery.

This is a private home and is not open to the public.
Location: Corner of Back Bay and Foxhill Roads
                Canaan, NH 03741

Peterborough, New Hampshire
The Cheney House

The Cheney family of Peterborough were ardent abolitionists and conductors on the Underground Railroad. From

1835 to 1845 Deacon Moses Cheney's home served as a station on the Freedom Line. Elias H. Cheney, editor of the *Peterborough Transcript*, recalled in 1915 that as a boy he had accompanied some slaves part of the way to Hancock, New Hampshire. The Cheney family operated its fugitive slave network with three other Peterborough families, the Whitcombs, the Morrisons and the Tuttles. Frederick Douglass was staying with these families and was a house guest in the Cheney home when he visited Peterborough to lecture at the New England Anti-Slavery Society in the Old Town House in 1840. The Reverend Oren Burbank Cheney, later president of Bates College, was, like his father and brother, connected with a branch of the Underground extending from Portland, Maine, to Effingham, New Hampshire.

While president of Bates College, Cheney introduced a policy of admitting African-American students, and assisted in establishing Storer College, an institution for African-Americans, at Harpers Ferry, West Virginia. Several of Storer College's former buildings are maintained by the National Park Service. However, the Cheney house is a private residence and not open to the public.

Location: Upper Union Street
             Peterborough, NH 03458

Littleton, New Hampshire
The Carleton House

Edmund Carleton, an attorney and lumber merchant, abandoned his legal profession and, with the assistance of his wife Mary, founded the Littleton Anti-Slavery Society in 1837 and operated an Underground Railroad station in his home. As a station keeper, Carleton was bold and tireless, taking his passengers to distant stations on the Underground. When the Library of Congress purchased his collection of William Lloyd Garrison's famous anti-slavery newspapers, *The Liberator*, it called the collection "one of the most perfect obtainable."

This home is not open to the public.
Location: 32 Carleton Street
             Littleton, NH 03561

Canterbury, New Hampshire
Chamberlain Farm

Anti-slavery sentiment was more widespread in New England than in any other section of the country, and hatred of slavery was particularly deep-seated in John Abbot Chamberlain. One of New Hampshire's leading abolitionists, he was a relative of Stephen Symond Foster, the celebrated anti-slavery lecturer. Chamberlain's property was located on the Underground Railroad route that ran from Salem, Massachusetts, and Concord, New Hampshire, into Meredith Ridge, NH. On two occasions his nephew Mellen Chamberlain led slaves from Concord to his uncle's home.

The Chamberlain Farm is not open to the public.
Location: West Road, Canterbury
             Canterbury, NH 03224

Weare, New Hampshire
Moses Sawyer House

Frederick Douglass had several Underground Railroad friends in New Hampshire during the time he was fugitive slave. Recorded in the history of New London, New Hampshire, is a reference that Douglass was entertained in the home of Hugh B. Clough in 1842. Another source, the history of Weare County, recorded that Douglass commenced writing his autobiography while visiting Moses Sawyer's home. A dedicated friend of the Underground, Sawyer hid fugitive slaves in his cellar. This is still preserved and open to the public. Sawyer maintained close ties with John Greenleaf Whittier and William Lloyd Garrison. His cousin, Robert Brown of West Newbury, Massachusetts, with the assistance of Thomas Folsom operated stations that connected with Sawyer's fugitive slave network.

The Moses Sawyer House is not open to the public.

Location: Route 77
                 Weare, NH 03281

Concord, New Hampshire
Nathaniel White: Founder of the American Express Company

The entire story of the Underground Railroad will never be known because of the very nature of the movement. Oral tradition in many cases is all that we have to record the events as they actually occurred. A surviving granddaughter of the White family recalls her grandmother's stories of fugitive slaves arriving at her grandparent's farm. She recalled that some slaves arrived on horseback and were hidden in the attic or the haymow. Her grandparents, Nathaniel and Armenia White, were prominent citizens of Concord's anti-slavery society and were friends of anti-slavery poet John Greenleaf Whittier, who once experienced mob violence for his words in Concord. Nathaniel White controlled vast rail and stagecoach properties in New Hampshire and Canada; this transportation empire ultimately became the American Express Company. Although the Whites were involved in the anti-slavery movement, there is no documentation that their transportation interests were ever used for the Underground Railroad.

This is a private home not open to the public.

Location: The former residence of Nathaniel and Armenia White still stands on Clinton Street, Concord, NH 03301.

Lee, New Hampshire
The Cartland Homestead

Built in 1745 on 20 acres of land, the Cartland homestead,

called by some "the poor man's retreat," was an important station on the Underground Railroad. The Cartlands belonged to the Society of Friends, and were relatives of John Greenleaf Whittier. The poet is said to have carved his initials alongside others' on a beech tree located on the Cartland's property. Frederick Douglass was also a welcome visitor in the years that he was a fugitive slave. Runaways were hidden in a small room in the cellar. In 1902, one of these former slaves, Oliver Gilbert, returned to the Cartland homestead with his son, a student at the University of Pennsylvania, and recalled that he had helped to build the stone wall in front of the home.

Location: Open House Number 4. Contact the Lee, New
             Hampshire Historical Society or the Chamber
             of Commerce
             Lee, NH 03824
             (603) 659-2964

Jaffrey, New Hampshire
Amos Fortune

Although Amos Fortune was not connected with New Hampshire's Underground Railroad, no history of the African-American presence in the state would be complete without including his name. He was still a boy when he was brought to the United States. After serving several masters, Fortune saved enough money to purchase his freedom when he was 60 years old. In 1781 he moved from Woburn, Massachusetts, to Jaffrey an established a tannery business. By the age of 70 Fortune had become one of Jaffrey's leading citizens. He was chosen as an attorney for some of the townspeople, and both African-American and white apprentices served under him. In 1795 Fortune founded the Jaffrey Social Library. A New Hampshire state historical marker reads: "Buried behind Jaffrey's colonial meetinghouse nearby are Aunt Hannah Davis, 1784-1863, resourceful and beloved spinster who made bandboxes, and Amos For-

tune, 1710-1801, African-born slave who purchased his freedom, established a tannery and left funds for Jaffrey's
church and schools."

Location: South side of route 124 in Jaffrey Center, about
              two miles west of the junction of Routes 124
              and 202.
              Jaffrey, NH 03452

Milford, New Hampshire
Leonard Chase House

Sometimes the opposition to anti-slavery speakers expressed itself in a vicious manner. Milford and other towns
in the 1840s were of divided mind, and an anti-slavery
speaker might find the opposition as well as sympathizers
among the members of his audience. Thomas Parnell Beach,
a Milford printer, was jailed for making a public statement
against slavery in Newburyport, Massachusetts, during a
widely-publicized anti-slavery gathering held in 1843.
Leonard Chase, a Milford Underground Railroad stationmaster, was not slow to express his outrage at Beach's
imprisonment. Local history records that Chase's home was
a documented station on the Road to Freedom, as was the
home of his business partner and next-door neighbor,
Daniel Putnam. The two men shared views on slavery and
temperance. Another Milford family was also connected
with the anti-slavery movement and the Underground Railroad. The Hutchinson family, internationally known African-American singers, included anti-slavery songs in their
repertoire, along with the customary religious hymns and
ballads. Jesse Hutchinson, Jr., composed "The Bereaved
Slave Mother" and also one of the most famous anti-slavery
songs, "Get Off the Track." The family often appeared with
Frederick Douglass and sang after his lectures.

The house is not open to the public.

Location: 15 High Street
              Milford, NH 03055

For further information about New Hamsphire's Underground Railroad, contact:

> New Hampshire Office of Vacation Travel
> 105 London Road, Prescott Park
> Concord, NH 03301

Rhode Island

Providence, Rhode Island
**Brown University's Slave Trade and Underground
Railroad Connection**

Quaker Moses Brown, one of the most prominent philan-
thropists of his time, inherited a vast fortune built largely
on his family's involvement in the lucrative slave trade.
Brown's family was instrumental in establishing the Ivy
League university that bears their name. Historical documents record that the family interest in the slave trade
passed from Captain James Brown to his brother Obadiah,
then to his four nephews: Nicholas, Joseph, Moses and
John. On one fateful voyage in 1765, more than 100 of the 196
slaves on the Brown's vessel were lost as the result of a slave
mutiny.

Moses Brown and his brothers Nicholas and Joseph never
participated in the sale of human cargo again. Like John
Newton, the former slave trader who wrote the soul-stirring
words of "Amazing Grace" and became a noted abolitionist,
Moses Brown actively worked against his former means of
livelihood. References in his correspondence suggest that
Brown played a vital role in the New England anti-slavery
movement. His former home, located on Wayland and
Humbolt Avenues, became a major station on the Underground Railroad, lying on the route that ran from New
Bedford to inland Massachusetts. His magnificent mansion,

built in 1786, is no longer standing. As early as 1819, Moses Brown helped a group of Providence African-Americans to select a lot on Meeting Street, which he purchased and deeded to them. Brown's brother John, however became one of the leading supporters of the African slave trade of his day.

Location: A former property of Moses Brown, now called the Seril Dodge House, is located at number 10 Thomas Street in Providence. The Rhode Island Historical Society holds a vast amount of Moses Brown papers relating to slavery and his involvement with African-Americans.

For further information contact:

Rhode Island Historical Society
121 Hope Street
Providence, RI 02906
(401) 331-8575

Providence, Rhode Island
Bethel A.M.E. Church

According to local tradition, Harriet Tubman visited this church, a known station on the Underground Railroad. Founded in 1795, the African Freedmen's Society, which became the Bethel A.M.E. Church, was located on Meeting Street. After serving as a place of worship for 96 years, its last sermon was preached in September 1961. The building was then sold to Brown University. A second home for the historic congregation was purchased.

Originally located on Pond and Angel Street, the Pond Street Baptist Church began as a part of the African Union Society Meeting and School House, which was founded in 1821. According to the local tradition, the original church was a station stop on the Underground Railroad. Another church, the First Baptist Church, is mentioned as a station stop; however, there is no written documentation to this effect.

Location: Bethel A.M.E. Church

38 Rochambeau Avenue
Providence, RI 02903
(401) 272-9186

Westerly, Rhode Island
The Charles Perry House

Active abolitionists in Westerly were comparatively few, but Charles Perry, because of his moral convictions, operated a line of the Emancipation Train in this town. It has been written that the Perrys were as numerous as blackberries. His neighbors despised him because of his anti-slavery activities. On one occasion, Perry was greeted with scorn and mockery as he escorted Frederick Douglass to an anti-slavery meeting. A number of the mean-spirited citizens in the gallery threw eggs and pails of water at Perry. Nevertheless, loyal to the cause, he maintained one of the most unusual stations of the Underground Railroad. In a wooded area between King Tom's Farm and Shumuncanoc, fugitive slaves lived and waited in stone huts topped with saplings and a sod roof until it was safe to continue their journey northward towards Canada.

Location: 4 Margin Street
               Westerly, RI 02891

Pawtucket, Rhode Island
The Daggetts

The Daggetts were slaveholders. The present house was built in 1685 and remodeled in 1790; it replaced the original edifice built by John Daggett in 1644 when the earlier one had burned down during King Philip's War. On the wooden beams of the house there is a ring from which a slave's hammock had hung. Although the story of the Underground Railroad is filled with tales of secret compartments sliding doors, the Daggetts used an attic with a secret closet to hide from the Indians during the Colonial period.

Location: Slater Park, Off U.S. 1A
Pawtucket, RI 02860
Open June to mid-September on Sundays from
2:00 to 5:00; by appointment during the rest of
the year by appointment with the Pawtucket
Chapter of the DAR.
(401) 728-8670

Pawtuket, Rhode Island
Pidge Farm

Although Ira Pidge's farmhouse no longer stands in Pawtucket, fugitive slaves were sheltered in the family's large barn, once located on the present site of the Outlet Service Center. A mural in Pawtucket City Hall is reported to be a copy of Ira Pidge's homestead.

Underground Railroad conductor Jacob Babcock, born near Hopkinton, was an active member of Rhode Island's network. Ostracized by his friends and neighbors, Babcock lived to see African-Americans once held in captivity freed, and was congratulated for his dedication to the cause by people who had previously scorned him.

Location: The old farmhouse was once located on Ridge
Avenue.

Newport, Rhode Island
George T. Downing Block

In his monumental *Directory of the Names of Underground Railroad Operators* embracing some 3,200 entries, Wilbur Siebert designates 143 names as those of African-Americans. However, his listing did not identify George T. Downing among them, nor did he mention hundreds of other African-Americans who contributed to the movement.

George T. Downing was born in New York City in 1819 and died in Newport on July 21, 1903. During his lifetime he was one of the most respected and prosperous African-

Effects of the Fugitive Slave Law of 1850. From the Blockson Afro-American Collection.

George T. Downing Block. Born in New York City, where he operated an Underground Station, he later became Newport, Rhode Island's most prosperous African-American.

Americans in the United States. He was acquainted with all of the celebrated African-American abolitionists and Underground Railroad agents. He was an intimate friend of Frederick Douglass and Senator Charles Sumner of Massachusetts, and knew five U.S. presidents during his lifetime. Downing once refused the offer of an introduction to President Millard Fillmore because, as he said, he was unwilling to touch the hand that had signed the Fugitive Slave Law of 1850. While operating his famous oyster house at 690 Broadway in New York City, he willingly contributed large sums of money to the anti-slavery cause. Upon settling in Newport in 1855, he quickly established himself as the friend of any fugitive slave alighting there. Although his home is no longer standing, a section of the city between Bellevue and Downing Streets is called the "George T. Downing Block." For further information contact:

> The Newport Historical Society
> 82 Touro Street
> Providence, RI 02840
> (401) 846-0813

Newport, Rhode Island
Isaac Rice House

Much of the success of Newport's Underground Railroad could be credited to Isaac Rice. Born free in Narragansett in 1793, Rice was brought to Newport at an early age and lived there until his death. Rice became the most prominent African-American in the state of Rhode Island. His home was a haven for journeying fugitive slaves; Harriet Tubman and Frederick Douglass also found shelter there. Rice conducted his clandestine activities with the help of his African-American friends, George T. Downing of Newport, and Nathan Johnson of New Bedford, Massachusetts. For many years prior to his death in 1866, Rice was a gardener for Governor Gibbs and planted trees that now grow in Touro Park. His wood frame house is still in the possession of his descendants, but is not open to the public.

Location: 54 Williams Street
             Newport, RI 02903

Newport, Rhode Island
Touro Synagogue

According to oral tradition, early members of Touro's congregation are reported to have sheltered escaped slaves in the synagogue. Often called the oldest synagogue in America, Touro Synagogue had an early association with African-Americans, since a number of slaves and former slaves played a major role in the construction of the stately colonial edifice. Newport was one of the leading slavetrading centers in colonial America, rivaling Boston in the number of slave ships departing from its shores. The old slave Market was located on Long Wharf and Washington Street. Division Street separated slaveholding from freedom; on the freedom side of the street fiery abolitionists called for slave liberation and supported a school that provided education for freed African-Americans. Some Jews bought, sold and enslaved Africans from the colonial period until the end of the Civil War, while others were actively involved in the anti-slavery movement and served as agents and conductors on the Underground Railroad.

Location: Touro Synagogue
             72 Touro Street
             Newport, RI 02840
             (401) 847-4794

Central Falls, Rhode Island
Elizabeth Buffum Chace House

When Elizabeth Buffum Chace welcomed fugitive slaves in her house in Central Falls, the village was called Valley Falls. Elizabeth and her sister, Lucy Buffum Lovell, were daughters of Arnold Chace, who became the first president of the Massachusetts Anti-Slavery Society when it was formed by William Lloyd Garrison in the 1830s. Due largely to the anti-slavery sentiment of the Buffum and Lovell family women, the Female Anti-Slavery Society of Rhode Island was organized in 1835. The two sisters on numerous occasions forwarded their fugitive slaves to the Reverend Joshua Young, the Unitarian minister in Burlington, Vermont.

In their book, *Two Quaker Sisters*, Elizabeth Chace wrote, "I am ashamed to say that my early Quaker ancestors in Newport, Rhode Island, were interested in the slave trade and ships came into the harbor direct from Africa and most of the human cargo was dispersed in that village and redistributed to other sections." Her sister Lucy wrote, "We were few in number and the great body of Quakerism in the country was against us. Our lips were sealed in the meetings and out of the meetings we were disgraced, despised and rejected."

The Chace, Buffum and Lovell families made major contributions in banking, manufacturing, politics and education to American life. The Elizabeth Buffum Chace House was demolished many years ago, however in 1994, she will be inducted into the Central Falls Hall of Fame that has been established at the Central Falls High School.

Location: The house once stood at the corner of Sunmer and Illinois Streets

For further information about Rhode Island, contact:

Rhode Island Black Heritage Society
1 Hilton Street
Providence, RI 02903
(401) 751-3490/3491 or (401) 846-0813

Vermont

Burlington, Vermont
The Reverend Joshua Young House

The Reverend Joshua Young was a man who substantially contributed to the anti-slavery cause. In 1854 he preached in the Unitarian church at Burlington a week after the famous Anthony Burns fugitive riot in Boston. His sermon was entitled "God Greater Than Man," and was published in Burlington. Young was a graduate of Bowdoin College with Phi Beta Kappa honors, and pursued his studies at Harvard. Having repeatedly harbored fugitive slaves in Boston, he joined his Underground Railroad friends in the same service in Burlington. Fugitive slaves whom he aided told him stories of the cruelties practiced upon them and their fellow slaves. He saw on the backs of the fugitives the livid scars of the slave driver's lash. Though he avoided hiding slaves in his house, he provided refuge for some of them in his barn or in various cellars, garrets, homes and offices in the area. In 1859 the Reverend Young attended the funeral of John Brown at North Elba, New York, and preached the sermon. The next day the Burlington Newspaper denounced him, and shortly thereafter, six of the most prominent families in his congregation withdrew from his church. At the age of 36 he found himself socially ostracized, and resigned within a year. He later filled pastorates in Massachusetts.

This house is not open to the public.

Location: 98 South Willard Street
             Burlington, VT 05401

Bennington, Vermont
The First African-American Minister of the Congregational Church in America

Although the Reverend Lemuel Haynes was not connected with the Underground Railroad, no complete history
of Vermont can be written without mentioning his name. He
was born in 1753 in West Hartford, Connecticut, and died in
Granville, New York. When he was 21 years old, Haynes
joined the minutemen as a Continental solider, accompany-
ing the Massachusetts army under Benedict Arnold, and
marched with Ethan Allen against Fort Ticonderoga. After
he was ordained as a minister in 1785, the Reverend Haynes
traveled throughout Vermont. Between 1787 and 1833 he
preached and held permanent pastorates in other Vermont
towns, including Clardendon, Dorset, Mancaster, Pawlet,
Rutland, Tinmouth and Bennington. The Reverend Lemuel
Haynes became one of the first African-Americans in the
United States to serve as pastor for a white congregation.
Although he was minister for fifty years, he mentioned the
subjects of race and slavery only once in his sermons. Ironi-
cally, his first call to fill a pulpit came from Torrington,
Connecticut, the town where the notorious abolitionist John
Brown would be born five years later in 1800.

Location: The old First Church on Monument Avenue in
             Old Bennington Village where Haynes
             preached is one of the most attractive
             churches in New England. In the Bennington
             Museum, located on West Main Street, is a
             painting of Haynes preaching to a white
             congregation.
             Bennington, VT 05201
             (802) 447-1571

Bennington, Vermont
William Lloyd Garrison's Marker

Garrison's marker is located on Old Bennington Commons 50 feet west of the site where he founded his first newspaper, *The Journal of the Times.* Garrison was later persuaded by Benjamin Lundy, publisher of the anti-slavery newspaper *The Genius of Universal Emancipation,* to go to Boston. In that city he published his famous anti-slavery newspaper, *The Liberator,* in 1831. His paper was committed to the immediate emancipation of all humans held in bondage and was vitriolic in the abuse that it heaped on slaveholders.

Location: Old Bennington Commons
               Bennington, VT 05201

Burlington, Vermont
The Wheeler House

In 1859 the president of Vermont's Colonization Society was the Reverend John Wheeler. He also served as the sixth president of the University of Vermont. Earlier in his career, he had lived in Charleston and Cambridge, South Carolina, and had established religious services for slaves in those cities. According to local tradition, the Reverend Wheeler was so outraged when the infamous Fugitive Slave Law was enacted that he assisted fugitive slaves as they traveled through Burlington. The former Wheeler home is now owned by the University of Vermont.

Location: Corner of Main and South Prospect Streets
For further information contact:
               Historic Preservation Office
               University of Vermont
               Burlington, VT 05401
               (802) 656-4006

Burlington, Vermont
The Salmon Wires House

The home of Salmon Wires was a minor station on the Underground Railroad. Wires was an insurance agent who sometimes concealed fugitive slaves in his inner office. Although his wife and daughter occasionally objected to having slaves in their home, according to local tradition, they actually coordinated their Underground Railroad activities with the Reverend Joshua Young's wife, who lived across the street from the Wires. The family's former two-story wood frame house still stands today but is a private residence not open to the public.

Location: 118 South Willard Street
Burlington, VT 05401

Ferrisburg, Vermont
Rowland T. Robinson: Vermont's Famous Underground Railroad Stationmaster

The Rowland T. Robinson House, known also as "Rokeby," was an important station on the Underground Railroad. Robinson was a blind writer of Vermont Folklore and a noted anti-slavery advocate. A birthright Quaker whose family had moved to Vermont from Rhode Island in 1793, Robinson was a friend of Isaac T. Hopper, William Lloyd Garrison, Lucretia Mott, the Reverend Samuel J. May and Frederick Douglass, as well as other anti-slavery leaders. He also issued the call for "The Great Anti-Slavery Convention," which was held in Ferrisburg on July 17th and 18th in 1843.

The family reserved a room in Rokeby for fugitive slaves called the east room or "slave room." The Robinson children were not permitted to ask questions about meals that were delivered to fugitive slaves. The runaway slaves were driven at night to distant stations, which might include North Ferrisburg, Charlotte, St. Albans, East Montpelier, and on into Canada. The house contains a vast archival collection of anti-slavery items, furnishings and personal memorabilia belonging to the Robinson family.

Location: Robinson (Rokeby) House Museum
U.S. Route 7, R.D. 1, Box 1540
Ferrisburg, VT 05456
(802) 877-3406

Woodstock, Vermont
Chief Justice Titus Hutchinson House

"Every age teaches its own lesson," said William Ellery Channing, the celebrated anti-slavery minister. "The lesson of this age is that of sympathy with the suffering, and of devotion to the progress of the whole human race." Titus Hutchinson, a former chief justice of the Vermont supreme court, exhibited his sympathy for the suffering as an active stationmaster on the Underground Railroad. Justice Hutchinson operated his station cunningly for years and was known for his indifference to danger. In 1976, during the construction of a bridge, an Underground Railroad tunnel was discovered extending from the Hutchinson home to the Kedron River. Running for approximately four-tenths of a mile, according to a local newspaper, the tunnel is now closed, and, although the Hutchinson house still stands, it is currently used as a place of business.

Location: On the green in Woodstock
26 Elm Street
Woodstock, VT 05091

For further information contact:
The Woodstock Historical Society
(802) 457-1822

MIDWEST

Illinois

Jacksonville: Key Site in Underground Railroad Activities

While most escaping slaves made their way to Canada, where they were assured of freedom, some remained in Illinois. One of these was Benjamin Henderson, a multi-talented craftsman who bought his freedom and moved to Jacksonville. Henderson became a conductor on the Underground, and directed his passengers to other free African-Americans and to white station keepers who took them on to Springfield. The Asa Talcott home, located today at 859 Grove Street, was a station on the fugitive slave network; local tradition says that it is connected to a tunnel that was used by slaves seeking freedom. Another Jacksonville resident, the Reverend D. Pat Henderson published *The Statesman*, believed to be the first anti-slavery newspaper west of the Allegheny Mountains. A stone marks the location in Jacksonville of the home of Jonathan Turner, an Illinois College professor and abolitionist who boasted of his arrest for harboring escaped slaves. Illinois College and the Congregational church in Jacksonville were founded by New Englanders who ardently opposed slavery. The college's first president was Harriet Beecher Stowe's brother Edward, while the Congregational church was called the "Abolition Church" by Jacksonville's Southern sympathizers.

Owen Lovejoy Homestead, Princeton, Illinois. An importnat Underground Railroad station, courtesy Owen Lovejoy Homestead.

For further information about Jacksonville and the Asa
Talcott house, contact:
Illinois State Historical Society
Springfield, IL
(212) 782-4836

Princeton, Illinois
Owen Lovejoy Homestead

Although there were several families in Bureau County who were station keepers on the Underground Railroad, which was commonly known as the "John Brown Trail" in many sections of Illinois, it was Owen Lovejoy, fiery abolitionist preacher and brother of Elijah Lovejoy, who is remembered most vividly. Lovejoy and his wife Eunice were always open to harboring escaped slaves; he was finally indicted in 1843 by a grand jury for sheltering two slave women in his home, but was acquitted at his trial. Despite, or perhaps because of, his abolitionist leanings, Lovejoy was elected to serve in the United States Congress, and it is believed by historians that he assisted Abraham Lincoln in drafting the Emancipation Proclamation.

In 1837, before Bureau County was even organized, an escaped slave named C. Reign Beau (better known as "Rainbow Johnson") fled to Princeton and was befriended by Owen Lovejoy. For some time he assisted Lovejoy in his Underground Railroad operation. Johnson later became a lecturer, preacher and politician, and during the early 1860s organized the "Rainbow Society," to which most of the prominent men in Princeton belonged. Rainbow Johnson would be called an "Uncle Tom" by many African-Americans today, for his society was exclusive in its membership and one of its amendments prohibited all "colored persons" from fellowship in the organization or witnessing any of its proceedings.

Location: The Owen Lovejoy homestead is on State Route 61 on east edge of Princeton. It is open to the public by appointment with a small admission charge, with special group rates. Call (815) 879-9151 to arrange a visit.

Alton, Illinois
Rock House

Another well known site in Alton is the Rock House. It was in this building that an anti-slavery association was organized with the assistance of the Reverend Elijah P. Lovely shortly before his death. The house was also station on the Underground Railroad.

Location: College and Clawson Streets

Alton, Illinois
Elijah P. Lovejoy Monument and Gravesite

Of all the methods used to support the Underground

Railroad, none was more powerful than the anti-slavery press. Elijah Lovejoy, a transplanted New England abolitionist, minister and school teacher, had in 1833 become editor of *The Observer*, a Presbyterian weekly in St. Louis. His anti-slavery views became extremely unpopular, and in 1836 he moved to Alton, Illinois, near the Missouri border. Lovejoy continued to advocate immediate abolition in his new paper, *The Alton Observer*. Mobs destroyed three of his presses, and on November 7, 1837, while he was guarding another new press, Lovejoy was killed. His martyrdom helped advance the cause of the abolitionists and the Underground Railroad in the North, arousing hundreds of citizens throughout the region who had previously been indifferent on the subject of slavery. Lovejoy was 35 years old when he was murdered. His grave is located about 75 yards behind this monument. The remains of one of his presses, salvaged from the Mississippi River where it was hurled in the mob attack, are on display in the lobby of the office of the Telegraph Building, 111 East Broadway.

Location: The Lovejoy Monument is located at Fifth and Monument Streets.

Junction, Illinois
Hickory Hill: Old Slave House

Hickory Hill, known today as the "Old Slave House," stands in Junction, Illinois. It was built in 1834 by John Crenshaw, the wealthy grandson of John Hart of New Jersey, who was one of the signers of the Declaration of Independence. The Old Slave House has become a mecca for those who are interested in slavery in Illinois; much like the notorious slave kidnapper Patty Cannon in Delaware, Crenshaw seized slaves and free African-Americans alike to run an Underground Railroad in reverse. Oral tradition has it that kidnapped slaves were kept on the third floor, which had narrow doorways leading into small rooms that were used as slave pens.

There are many tales of horror about what went on in these pens. Severe punishment was meted out to unruly slaves, and two whipping posts to which slaves were tied by their thumbs still remain. It was rumored that Crenshaw used one of the rooms for breeding purposes. In fact he purchased a slave named Bob whose sole purpose was to sire as many slaves as possible. One can still see the "breeding room" or "Uncle Bob's room," a den that reeks of the degradation of slavery, the "single most painful episode" in American slavery.

Location: Hickory Hill still stands 9 miles west of Shawneetown, near the intersection of Illinois 13 and Illinois 1.

Hours: April through October, open daily 9a.m.-5p.m. November, weekends only from 9a.m.-5p.m.

Quincy, Illinois
Friends of Dr. Richard Eells House

Dr. Richard Eells' home was known as the most important Underground Railroad station in Quincy. Fugitive slaves escaping from Missouri were told to go there when they reached the town. In 1837, Eells attended the Illinois Anti-Slavery Convention and was elected to the board of managers. In 1842 he was charged with harboring and assisting a slave named Chauncey Durkee of Missouri, and was convicted and sentenced to pay a fine of $400 and the cost of the prosecution. The case was taken on writ of error first to the Supreme Court of Illinois and, after Eells' death, to the Supreme Court of the United States, which upheld the judgment of the original court in 1852. Presently the Friends of Dr. Richard Eells House are touring students through, to acquaint them with early Quincy architecture as well as the abolitionist movement.

For further information about Eells House contact:

Friends of The Dr. Richard Eells House

c/o of Gardner Museum of Architecture
and Design
322 Maine Street
Quincy, IL 62301
(217) 224-6873

Quincy, Illinois
The Grau Mill and Museum

The Grau Mill is on the site of one of the most widely recognized former stations on the Underground Railroad in northern Illinois. The United States Post Office acknowledged its importance by selecting the Grau Mill and Museum for the first day of issue ceremonies for the Harriet Tubman stamp. The mill was located on the old stagecoach road from Quincy to Chicago; its owner, Miller F. Grau, was a German immigrant who was an ardent abolitionist and operated a station at his homestead along the road to freedom for escaping slaves.

Location: Spring and York Roads
             Quincy, IL 62301

Springfield, Illinois
President Abraham Lincoln's Home and National Historic Site

Abraham Lincoln lived in this home from 1844 to 1861. It was the only home he ever owned. While he lived in Springfield, "Billy the Barber's" shop was a favorite haunt for the future president. Lincoln had befriended William de Fleurville, a Haitian who had arrived in Springfield virtually penniless in 1831, and became his lawyer as well as his customer. Before he left for Washington, the president-elect visited Billy the Barber's shop one more time to bid him goodbye.

Although many African-Americans of the time considered John Brown to be their liberator and best white friend,

President Abraham Lincoln took the step of inviting Frederick Douglass, Sojourner Truth and Martin R. Delaney to the White House. He commissioned Delaney as the first African-American to hold the rank of major during the Civil War; in return, Delaney proposed to Lincoln a plan by which the routes of the Underground Railroad could be used to infiltrate the South with Union soldiers.

Lincoln had strong personal feeling against the "peculiar institution" of slavery, but his political intentions in the beginning were not so much to abolish slavery as to prevent its spread. On June 16, 1868, he delivered his famous "house divided against itself" speech, in which he declared, "I believe the government cannot permanently endure half slave and half free," but he disavowed extreme abolitionist doctrines and stressed a conservative route of change. He was what can best be described as an anti-slavery moderate who favored gradual abolition. Indeed, his Emancipation Proclamation did not free all the slaves, but left untouched several slave states and territories that supported the Union during the Civil War.

Recently, scholars located early legal documents that chronicled Lincoln as a workaholic young attorney from 1837 to 1861. He represented a diverse clientele that included slaveowners and abolitionists. Scholars associated with the Lincoln legal papers research project discovered that Lincoln had a prosperous law practice that permitted him to support a wealthy lifestyle and a political career.

For more information contact:

Illinois Tourist Information Center
310 South Michigan, Suite 108
Chicago, IL 60604
(312) 793-2094 or
President Abraham Lincoln House
Eighth & Jackson Streets
Springfield, IL
(217) 529-4586

Springfield, Illinois
Zion Baptist Missionary Church

Thomas Jefferson Houston, progenitor of the noted Houston family (not to be confused with Sam Houston), was born a slave on August 10, 1829, in Kentucky as Thomas Jefferson Hunn. He was later sold to a cruel owner in Missouri and repeatedly attempted to escape, for which he was beaten severely. When he finally made his way to freedom he changed his surname to Houston. Upon settling in Springfield, he became a conductor on the Underground Railroad, guiding fugitive slaves from Missouri into Illinois and other free states. On one occasion, Houston freed his brother Joseph from captivity and later helped his brother free his wife and children.

During the Civil War, Thomas Jefferson Houston served with the Union forces. After the war he married Katherine Kirkpatrick, a former slave who had fled from a cruel owner in Paducah, Kentucky. The Houstons, who have lived in Springfield for seven generations, are included among the leading African-American families in the nation. They have achieved recognition as physicians, bankers, teachers, librarians, nurses, firemen, social workers, administrators and attorneys. One of their descendants, Charles Hamilton Houston, taught law at Howard University in Washington, D.C., and was recognized as one of the most respected attorneys of his time. Among those in his classroom was Supreme Court Justice Thurgood Marshall who laid much of the groundwork for the landmark civil rights decisions of the 1950s.

Descendants of Thomas Jefferson Houston still worship at Zion Baptist Missionary Church, which was founded by Houston and his wife and other African-American families.
Location: 1601 East Laurel Street
             Springfield, IL

John Jones, a successful African American businessman and agent on the Underground Railroad in Chicago, Illinois, courtesy Chicago Historical Society.

Chicago, Illinois
Wealthy African-American Underground Railroad Agent: The Portrait of John Jones and His Wife

John Jones was born free in North Carolina in 1817, and became one of the nation's wealthiest African-Americans, making a small fortune in the tailoring trade. He taught himself to read and write and his tailoring establishment at 119 Dearborn Street in Chicago prospered, enabling him and his wife Mary to expand the abolitionist activities they had begun in Alton, Illinois. They established an Underground Railroad station in their spacious home where scores of escaped slaves were sheltered. Jones' mansion also served as a meeting place for local and national abolitionist leaders; he numbered Alan Pinkerton, Frederick Douglass and John Brown among his many friends. Douglass generally stayed with the Jones family when he visited Chicago. Although the large and impressive home is no longer standing, a portrait of Jones and his wife is on view at the Chicago Historical Society.

Location: Chicago Historical Society
Pat Kramer, Public Relations
1601 North Clark Street, Lincoln Park
Chicago, IL 60614
(312) 642-4600

Chicago, Illinois
**Plaque Commemorating Chicago's Role in The
Underground Railroad**

Chicago was the great terminus, the point where most of the lines of the Underground Railroad converged. Here escaped slaves were virtually safe, for they were not only assured of the protection by white people, but also by the African-American community, protectionn strong enough to prevent their capture. Chicago epitomized the allure of the Underground Railroad, which held the excitement of privacy, the secrecy of burglary and provided opportunity for the bold and adventurous. Before he went on to found his famous detective agency, Alan Pinkerton ran an Underground depot near Chicago in his cooper shop, which has since been torn down.

When John Brown arrived in Chicago in December of 1858 with his guerilla fighters and caravan of eleven slaves rescued from Missouri, fresh from one of the boldest adventures in American history, it was to Pinkerton that he went. Inviting the notorious abolitionist and the little army into his home, Pinkerton sat with his pistol under his coat while his wife fed them. He then took the caravan to the home of John Jones, the noted African-American stationmaster. Later the slaves were sent on to Detroit, where they boarded a ferry to Canada.

Location: A plaque commemorating the role that Chicago played in the Underground Railroad may be seen at 9955 Beverely Avenue. It reads,

Refuge for slaves. On this site, then in the midst of the prarie, stood the Gardiner home and tavern, built in 1836, it was bought by William Wilcox in 1844 and became a refuge for slaves during the Civil War. Erected by Chicago Charter Jubilee, authenticated by the Chicago Historical Society, 1937.

Galesburg, Illinois
Knox College

Numerous passengers on the Freedom Line were harbored by Galesburg conductors, Knox College students among them. George Davis and Samuel Hitchcock forwarded escaped slaves to Endeavor and on to Ontario with the assistance of the Blanchards and other families. It was at Knox College that Abraham Lincoln and Stephen Douglas held the famous debate in which Lincoln declared: "A house divided against itself cannot stand." Because it is the only site of the Lincoln and Douglass debates still standing, the Old Main Building at Knox College has been named among the National Register of Historical Sites.

Along a line more than 100 miles long from Quincy to Galesburg there were villages and neighborhoods that helped escaping slaves travel north through Hancock, McDonough and Fulton Counties. Among the stations that are remembered are Mendon, Round Prairie, Plymouth, Roseville, Canton and Farmington. The Reverend William B. Dodge, minister of the Milburn Congregational Church, is reported to have opened his church to fugitive slaves. At a meeting of the congregation on December 2, 1859, a resolution that encouraged the work of the Underground Railroad and set aside a day of remembrance for John Brown, martyr to abolition, was written into the records.

Location: Old Main Building, Knox College
             Galesburg, Illinois
             (309) 343-0112

Levi Coffin's Indiana Fountain City home.

Indiana

The Levi Coffin Homestead, the "Grand Central Station"
of the Underground Railroad

Among Indiana's most famous residents was Levi Coffin, the reputed president of the Underground Railroad. Born in Guilford, North Carolina, Coffin made his home in Newport, as Fountain City was formerly named. This was probably the most famous home in Indiana, called the "Grand Central Station of the Underground Railroad." From 1826 to 1846, over 2,000 fugitive slaves are reported to have stopped there for food, medical attention, clothing and shelter. Coffin and his wife Catherine, both strong Quakers, hid slaves in a garret off an upstairs room over the dining room, and in a basement spring room.

Harriet Beecher Stowe's characters Simeon and Rachel Halliday were based on Levi and Catherine Coffin. In her novel *Uncle Tom's Cabin* Stowe also described a station stop on Eliza's journey as "a Quaker settlement in Indiana." The Coffins had helped the real-life model for Stowe's Eliza during her flight to freedom. Their house was on a direct line between Canada and Cincinnati, where possibly the greatest number of fugitives crossed the Ohio River from bordering slave states.

Among the reported 2,000 fugitive slaves assisted by Levi Coffin was William Bush, who reached the Coffin's home

229

Eliza Harris, immortalized, as a fictional character in Harriet Beecher Stowe's Uncle Tom's Cabin, springing from one ice floe to another on the Ohio River.

Margaret Garner, resisting capture by slave hunters, kills her child rather than let her be taken back to slavery.

wearing wooden shoes he had carved for himself. Settling in Newport, Bush became a conductor for other fugitive slaves while following the blacksmith's trade. He won the town's gratitude during an epidemic when he dared to bury the dead.

Location: Fountain City is nine miles north of Richmond on U.S. 27

Pennville, Indiana
Eliza Harris Marker

A stone cairn and bronze plaque commemorate the escape of Eliza Harris, the prototype for the character Eliza in *Uncle Tom's Cabin*. Her daring escape is a remarkable story, one of the best of the Underground Railroad. Faced with the threat of being separated from her only child, Eliza planned their flight to freedom beyond the far side of the river. But when she reached its banks she discovered that the ice had broken up and was drifting in large cakes and floes. In desperation as her persuers closed in, Eliza darted onto the ice, holding her child in her arms. Springing from one floe to another, she lost her shoes in the icy waters but struggled on with bleeding feet to the opposite shore and the safety of the Ohio Underground Railroad.

Location: One mile north of Pennville
For further information contact:

> Kosciusco County Historical Society
> PO Box 1071
> Warsaw, IN 46581-1071
> (219) 269-1078

The society has information on the marker.

Parke County, Indiana
Underground Railroad Marker

Alfred and Rhoda Hadley were ardent anti-slavery activists who used their farm as a station on the Underground.

When local residents decided to commemorate the farm-house in 1926, the owners did not wish to have a marker erected on their land so it was placed in a nearby grove of maple trees on another property. The marker is constructed of boulders from old farms in the area, some of which also sheltered fugitive slaves. Its text reads as follows:

> *Memorial to Alfred and Rhode Hadley*
> *and others of Bloomingdale*
> *who maintained an*
> *to assist Fugitive Slaves to Freedom*
> *Parke County and Penn Township Historical Societies*
> *1926*

Location: One mile northeast on U.S. 41

Terre Haute, Indiana
Allen Chapel African Methodist Episcopal Church

Runaway slaves felt reasonably safe once they arrived at Allen Chapel African Methodist Episcopal Church in Terre Haute, a busy station on the Underground Railroad. Frequently, wagonloads of fugitive slaves from different routes, with as few as one or as many as ten passengers, arrived at the church with no previous knowledge of each other. Since they usually came destitute, supplies of clothing and food were kept on hand by members of the congregation. The church was at one time pastored by Hiram Revels, who was during the period of Reconstruction one of the United States' first African-American senators and an appointee to a post formerly held by Jefferson Davis. The original structure that at one time housed the Underground Railroad station was demolished in the early 1900s to make way for a new church building. Today, Allen A.M.E. Church has a small museum and exhibition hall in its lower level displaying material relating to slavery and the Underground.
For further information contact:

Vigo County Historical Society

1411 South Sixth St.
Terre Haute, IN 47802
(812) 235-9717
Location: Third and Crawford Streets
Terre Haute, IN 47802

Mt. Pleasant, Indiana
Mt. Pleasant Beech African Methodist Episcopal Church

Mt. Pleasant Beech Church is preserved as the site where Indiana's first African Methodist Episcopal Conference was held in 1840. Descendants and friends of those who once attended this church return annually from throughout the United States on the last Sunday in August to hold services and enjoy a day of reunion. Founded in 1837, the original church was built of logs cut from trees that stood nearby. In 1840, two nationally known African-American ministers and Underground Railroad agents, Bishop Morris Brown and the Reverend William Paul Quinn, visited this church. Quinn was a circuit rider who preached in several other churches in the area. A marker on the front of the church tells its history.

Free colored people form North Caroling settled here in 1828. On June 16th, 1832, by resolution adopted by a vote of the church members, they chose the A.M.E. Church as their religious denomination. On October 2nd, 1840, the Indiana Annual Conference of the A.M.E. Church was organized here.

Location: One mile north of Carthage, Indiana, on a plot of ground surrounded on all sides by farm fields.
For further information contact:
Vigo County Historical Society
(812) 235-9717

Iowa

Iowa was settled as a free state primarily by easterners who were naturally connected to the anti-slavery cause.

The Underground Railroad began in southwest Iowa and ran in a northeasterly direction across Adair County to what is now the town of Stuart, then east down the Raccoon River Valley to Adel or Redfield, thence to Des Moines and through Grinnell to Muscatine. It is reported that John Brown supervised this section of the railroad. Cherry Place, east of the present Iowa Historical Building, was one of the main stations in Des Moines, but the original building no longer exists.

Runaways were also hauled by night to Columbus City in Lewis County or to Iowa City in Johnson County, where the conductors were William Penn and Dr. Jesse Bowen. John Brown was concealed during his last night in Iowa City in Bowen's home. From here Brown and his men were forwarded to West Liberty and harbored at an old grist mill.

The Underground entered Cedar County from Iowa City. Stations were approximately 12 miles apart—the distance a team of horses could travel at night without tiring or attracting attention. A station might not be used twice in succession, also to avoid attention. Some of the station buildings still exist in West Branch, others have been lost during the past 130 years.

All Quakers were suspect because of their opposition to slavery, but many non-Quakers were also involved in the

system. United States Congressman Josiah B. Grinnell, John Brown's friend, is considered the most prominent station-master among Iowa's Underground Railroad workers. Like Brown, Grinnell was an ardent abolitionist. (Grinnell College is named in his honor.)
For further information contact:

> Iowa Tourism Commission
> 200 E. Grand Avenue
> Des Moines, IA 50309
> 1-800-345-4692

Springdale, Iowa
John Brown's Headquarters

Today in the town of Springdale is a large granite boulder with a bronze tablet marking the site of an old farmhouse where John Brown quartered men in the winter of 1857-58. The inscription reads:

> Here was the home of William Maxon, a station on the Underground Railroad where John Brown of Osawatomie recruited and trained eleven men for the raid on Harper's Ferry. —Let some poor slave mother whom I have striven to free with her children from gallows stair put up a prayer for me.
> —Whittier

John Brown made a deep impression upon the Quakers in the community. A blacksmith shop produced one thousand metal pikes, a weapon approximately fifteen inches long and very similar to a knife or sword. They were later taken by Brown and his men to Harper's Ferry. When he left Springdale to go to Chicago, the citizens joined at the Friends meetinghouse to offer a prayer for his success.
Location: The marker stands three miles northeast of Springdale.

Grinnell, Iowa
Josiah B. Grinnell, Founder of Grinnell College

United States Congressman Josiah B. Grinnell, John Brown's friend, is considered the most prominent station-master among Iowa's Underground Railroad workers. Like Brown, Grinnell was an ardent abolitionist. When Brown introduced himself to Grinnell, he quietly explained that he was the "awful Brown" and that he needed a place to stay Sunday because he would not "travel on the Sabbath." Grinnell had a chamber in his home that he called the "liberty room." John Brown, while on his way to Canada in the winter of 1858-59, stacked his arms there; along with his company of fugitive slaves who slept there. "They came at night, and were the darkest, saddest specimens of humanity I have ever seen, glad to camp on the floor, while the veteran was a night guard, with his dog and miniature arsenal ready for use on alarm," Grinnell later explained. Although Grinnell's home was demolished, articles relating to the history of Grinnell and his home can be viewed at the Grinnell Historical Museum.

Location: Grinnell Historical Museum
             1125 Broad Street
             Grinnell, IA 50112
             Near Grinnell College
             (which is named in honor of him)

Salem, Iowa
The Lewelling Quaker House

Twelve miles south of Mt. Pleasant, in Salem, stands the Lewelling House. Built in 1840 by Quaker Henderson Lewelling, this large stone house served as a major safe house, called the "ticket office," on the Underground Railroad. Fugitive slaves were concealed in a tunnel under the house. This house also served as an office for Justice of the Peace Nelson Gibbs, an ardent anti-slavery worker. In 1848, Gibbs ruled against a group of armed men led by a slave owner

who threatened damage to the house and to staunch anti-slavery citizens if they did not release the slaves held under Lewelling's protection. The slave owner and his associates left Salem without their property, though later he sued the citizens for their participation in the flight of his "chattel."
Location: Off Highway 218, about 8 miles to Salem
For further information contact:
>Salem City Hall
>(319) 258-4531

Keosauqua, Iowa
The Pearson House

Built in a modified Georgian design in the 1840s by Benjamin F. Pearson and restored by the Van Buren County Historical Society, the Pearson House was a stop on the Underground Railroad line that extended from northeast Missouri into southeast Iowa. This house has two cellars, one with an entrance from the outside, the other with an inside entrance. This arrangement made it possible to admit slaves into the house by night and hide them in the inner cellar, which could not be seen from the outside. The Pearson House still contains the trapdoor that was concealed by a rug. Fugitive slaves were often transported from Keosauqua to Winchester, Birmingham and Fairfield, Iowa. Other important routes on Iowa's Underground Railroad included Des Moines, Salem, Denmark, Lewis, Nebraska City, Clinton, Iowa City, Richland, West Liberty, Earlam, Newton, West Branch, Columbus City and Oskaloosa. The Pearson House is open to tourists in the summer.
Location: At the corner of County Road and Dodge Street

Tabor, Iowa
John Todd House

When John Todd, a former Oberlin College student, moved from Ohio to Tabor, he became the moving spirit in

John Brown (Todd) house, Tabor, Iowa. Sketch by William Wagner, courtesy Tabor Historical Society.

the Underground Railroad. Todd made his home a prominent station. Two small oval windows in the house are positioned under the eaves at the front and mark the area where fugitive slaves were sometimes hidden. Most often slaves were hidden in Todd's barn. Todd was associated with John Brown in the movement to Kansas and Nebraska.

Although Brown and his followers were not men of peace, to the Quakers they embodied the violent struggle against human slavery in which the Quakers so firmly believed. John Brown used the Todd house as his headquarters between 1854 and 1856. A historical marker in the town's park states that the site was once John Brown's campground.

Although most of Tabor's citizens were connected with the Underground Railroad, others were alarmed at possible retaliation from Missouri slave owners, and held a public meeting condemning John Brown for his Underground Railroad activities.

Tours of the Todd House are by appointment only through the Tabor Historical Society.

Location: On Park Street. Tabor is ten miles south of Glenwood on U.S. 275.
Tabor Historical Society
P.O. Box 417
Tabor, IA 51653

Lewis, Iowa
The Reverend George B. Hitchock House

This sandstone house on a hill above the Nishnabotna River was a station stop on the Underground Railroad. John Brown visited the home many times and is said to have led fugitive slaves in singing spirituals. The home was built by Reverend George B. Hitchock, a Frontier Congregationalist circuit rider who came to Lewis in 1853. In the cellar was a secret room where slaves were sheltered until they could be conveyed to the next station. The Reverend Hitchcock's house was a popular stopping place for travelers, trappers and government officials, in addition to serving as a church meeting place and anti-slavery headquarters. It is reported that Hitchcock dressed fugitive slaves in the clothing of his wife and daughter and transported them over the river under the eager eyes of slave hunters who were pursuing them.

Location: The Hitchcock House is located a mile west of Lewis, Iowa.

For further information about the Hitchock House contact:
Iowa Tourism Commission
200 E. Grand Avenue
Des Moines, IA 50309
1-800-345-4692

Michigan

Detroit, Michigan
Windsor, Ontario, Canada

As the southern most tip of Canada, Windsor, Ontario was a particularly favorable place of crossing by fugitive slaves into the "promised land." The trail of African-Americans ran through the large city of Detroit, where many abolitionists and anti-slavery activists found much work to do.

There are a number of groups involved with the preservation of African-American history and heritage in the area, a few of them are listed below. These places can provide further inforamtion for the sites listed on the following pages.

Detroit Chamber of Commerce
600 West Lafeyette Boulevard
Detroit, MI 48226
(313) 964-4000

Detroit Visitor Information Center
100 Renaissence Center, Suite 1900
Detroit, MI 48243-1056
(313) 259-4333

Museum of African-American History
301 Frederick Douglass
Detroit, MI 48202
Contact: Patrina Chapman, (313) 833-9800

Detroit Upbeat Tours
18430 Fairway Drive
Detroit, MI 48221
Contact: Tim Dagg, (313) 341-6810
For more information on Michigan's Historical Markers:
Michigan Bureau of History
Department of State
717 West Allegan Street
Lansing, MI 48918
(518) 373-1668

Detroit, Michigan
William Webb House and the Frederick Douglass and John Brown Marker

There is considerable evidence that John Brown was in Detroit with the 12 slaves that he and his men rescued from their Missouri owners in 1859. It was in Detroit that Brown first discussed his plans for the raid in March of 1859 on Harper's Ferry while he was visiting the home of William Webb, a prominent African-American grocer and Underground Railroad agent. With them were Frederick Douglass, George de Baptiste, William Lambert, Dr. Joseph Ferguson, John Jackson, the Reverend William Monroe and Willis Wilson. John Brown told the gathering of abolitionists his scheme to emancipate the slave. Although Douglass and the other Underground Railroad agents were equally determined to end slavery, Brown was the only one to choose the route of force.
Location: 185 Congress Street

Detroit, Michigan
George de Baptiste House and the Second Baptist Church

Among the most ingenious of the Michigan Underground Railroad agents were George de Baptiste and William Lambert, who created the Order of the African Mysteries, with

William Lambert, co-founder of the African Mysteries and a leading agent on the Detroit, Michigan, Underground Railroad. Courtesy of the Lambert family.

its system of secret signs. These signs-handshakes, passwords and other signals—were known and used by agents throughout the Underground Railroad system. Fugitives slaves reaching Detroit could find safety at the residence of de Baptiste, who had worn out his welcome in Madison, Indiana, because of his Underground activities. William Lambert, who was born in Trenton, New Jersey, became a leader of the Michigan African-American Underground with de Baptiste's assistance. Lambert devoted 32 years to the Freedom Train. Both men were intimate friends of Frederick Douglass and John Brown.

Organized in 1836, Second Baptist Church in Detroit is the oldest African American Church in Michigan and has been documented as a major station on The Underground Railroad members of this church worked cooperatively with black and white abolitionists, including George de Baptiste and William Lambert. Located in front of the Church Commemorating the first celebration of the Emancipation Proclamation in Detroit which was held at Second Baptist on January 6, 1863. The exhibits, organized by the curator of the church, documents the history of the Underground Railroad, documents the history of the Underground Railroad in Detroit and surrounding communities. The Curator gives an informative and well researched tour of the Church. For further information about George de Baptiste House

and Second Baptist Church contact:
Dr. Nathaniel Leach
Wednesdays and Fridays
10:00 a.m. - 3:00 p.m.

Location: 441 Monroe, corner of Beaubien
Second Baptist Church
The George de Baptiste House is located on the south side of the 800 Block of East Larned Street

Muskegon, Michigan
Memorial of Jonathan Walker: The Man With the Branded Hand

Born in Harwich, Massachusetts, on March 22, 1799, Jonathan Walker grew up on a Cape Cod farm and eventually became a sea captain. After many years at his trade, he went to Florida to salvage a wreck in 1844. One torrid day he departed from Pensacola with seven slaves in his open boat, bound through the Gulf of Mexico for a Bahamian Island. As the craft approached Cape Florida, it was overtajen by another vessel and Walker was forced to give the fugitive slaves back to their owners. He was sent back to Pensacola in chains, where he was placed in a pillory and pelted with rotten eggs. By order of a federal court, his right hand was branded with the letters "SS" for "Slave Stealer."

Eventually his fines were paid by abolitionist friends and he returned to New England, where he attracted large audiences on the anti-slavery circuit as "the man with the branded hand." A tall, large-framed man, double-jointed and exceedingly strong, Walker emigrated to Muskegon in 1862 to manage a small fruit farm. When he died, Frederick When, who was unable to attend his funeral, sent his condolences describing Walker as the "Slave Saviour." Two stanzas by poet John Greenleaf Whittier are inscribed on the ten-foot obelisk at the entrance to Evergreen Cemetery in Muskegon, where he is buried.

His gravestone was placed by another abolitionist, Photius Fisk. Muskegon's Urban League gives an annual Jonathan Walker Award to a citizen who has worked to improve race relations.

Location: Evergreen Cemetery

For further information about the memorial of Johathan Walker contact:
Michigan Travel Bureau
PO Box 30226
Lansing, MI 48909
1-800-543-2937

Battle Creek, Michigan

Sojourner Truth Gravesite

Sojourner Truth, an unlettered African-American woman born a slave in New York State is memorialized by a statue in the Oakhill Cemetery in Battle Creek. Alone and in company with her friend Frederick Douglass and other leading abolitionists, always in the plainest clothes, she wandered the land speaking with an orator's eloquence and a victim's rage against the institution of slavery. Frequent efforts were made to silence her, and she was stoned and beaten for her words. Unlike Harriet Tubman, who was a small woman, Sojourner stood over six feet tall; there is some evidence that she, like Tubman, gave help to escaping slaves through the Underground Railroad, but the only slave she is documented to have freed was her son, liberated through court action. Sojourner had escaped from slavery as Isabella, and renamed herself to symbolize her wandering and her message. She was past 50 when she came to Battle Creek and began her mission, and already aged when President Abraham Lincoln invited her to the White House. She was 105 when she died in 1883, having lived to see the day when the slaves were emancipated.

Location: Oakhill Cemetery, South Avenue and Oakhill Drive

Battle Creek, Michigan
Kimball House Museum

Now officially owned by The Battle Creek Historical Society, the Kimball House was once owned by three generations of Kimball family doctors. Located on the second floor of this museum are mementos from the life and times of Sojourner Truth, the first person of any race to bring nationwide fame to the city of Battle Creek, Michigan. Until the present day, no new information has been uncovered that she was directly connected to the Underground Railroad existed, although in fact she did assist many escaped slaves to find new homes. Included in the exhibit are many books that have been written about Sojourner, her dress, and a rare document in which she attempted to write her name. She had the power to capture her audience, and her withering replies to hecklers became legend. She is known for her famous "Ain't I a Woman" speech.

Sojourner Truth's funeral in 1883 was considered one of the largest Battle Creek had ever seen.

Location: Kimball House Museum
             196 Capital Avenue, N.E.
             Battle Creek, MI 49017
             (616) 966-2496

Author Charles L. Blockson standing in front of the Underground Railroad monument in Battle Creek, Michigan.

Battle Creek, Michigan
Underground Railroad Sculpture Marks the former site of Quaker Eratus Hussey's House

In October of 1993, a 14 foot tall, 28 foot long silicone bronze sculpture dedicated to the Underground Railroad weighing over 7 tons was unveiled across the river from the old Erastus Hussey House. Sculpted by renowned African-American artist Ed Dwight,the sculpture was intentionally cast imaging African-American family as a "cohesive unit." On the other side features a wagon train, with Quaker Conductors Erastus Hussey and his wife Sarah led by Harriet Tubman. (The cover photo of this book.)

During his 20 years as a stationmaster on the Underground Railroad, Erastus Hussey assisted hundreds of escaped slaves through Battle Creek, using his home as a waystation. A respected businessman, Hussey made boots and shoes and sold groceries. He was also active in politics, serving as mayor, county clerk and state senator, and was a delegate to the Republican Convention that nominated Abraham Lincoln in 1860. Hussey also edited the abolitionist newspaper *The Liberty Press,* closing his remarks with the message, "Yours in bondage till all oppression ceases beneath the sun".

A grant from the Kellogg Foundation to the United Arts Council help to fund the project. Funding was also provided by the estate of Glenn A. Cross, a Battle Creek businessman and civic leader.

For further information about the Underground Railroad
sculpture contact:
Kellogg Foundation
One Michigan Avenue
Battle Creek, Michigan 4907
(616) 968-1611

Location: South of the Linear Park and north of the Battle Creek River near the Kellogg House, where it is accessible for public viewing.

Adrian, Michigan
Laura Haviland Statue

The statue of Laura Haviland located in front of City Hall in Adrian is one of only a few statues in the United States dedicated to women. Known as Auntie Laura, Haviland was a gentle Quaker woman who, despite her inbred aversion to violence, plunged herself into the boiling turmoil of the anti-slavery conflict. Her home was a station on the Underground Railroad, and she risked her life many times by helping slaves escape. One slave owner offered a $3,000 reward for Haviland's arrest.

In addition to helping fugitive slaves, she organized the first anti-slavery society in Michigan with Elizabeth Chandler. As if this were not enough, she founded a school for white and African-American frontier children, the Raisin

Institute in Raisin, Michigan, as well as the Michigan Girls Training School at Adrian. Laura Haviland and her husband Charles are buried in the Raisin Valley Cemetery in Adrian.

Location: The statue's site is on Main Street in front of City Hall.

Detroit, Michigan
Marker of Seymour Finney's Former House and Barn

In Detroit escaped slaves were hidden in Seymour Finney's livery barn, one block from his hotel, the Temperance House. A plaque on the Detroit Bank and Trust Company marks the hotel's location. Finney was connected with the Underground Railroad for more than 30 years; his station was the last before fugitive slaves were transported across the river to Canada . Among the conductors who assisted Finney were George de Baptiste, William Lambert, William Webb, Joseph Ferguson, William Monroe and John Richards.

Location: Southwest corner of Joseph Campaw and Clinton Streets; the site of Seymour Finney's barn, where many fugitive slaves were sheltered, is at State and Griswold Streets.

Marshall, Michigan
The Crosswhite Boulder

The most famous incident in Michigan's Underground Railroad history involved Adam Crosswhite and his family. Crosswhite, his wife and four of their children were fugitive slaves from Kentucky who had escaped and settled in Marshall in 1846. Fearing that he might be recaptured by his former owner, Crosswhite arranged with his neighbors that he would fire a signal shot in case such a thing happened. One fall morning this shot was heard, and it was discovered that Crosswhite and his family had been arrested.

They were rescued by the neighbors and spirited away to

safety in Canada, but a number of Crosswhite's friends were arrested in the process and heavily fined for assisting a fugitive slave.

Henry Clay of Kentucky used the Crosswhite case as one of his arguments in favor of the Fugitive Slave Law, which was adopted in 1850. The rescue also influenced the Dred Scott court decision stating that a slave was reclaimable even if he lived in free territory.

A boulder with a plaque on it lies at the approximate site of the defense of the Crosswhite family's freedom.

Location: The boulder is located near Triangle Park at the junction of East Michigan and East Mansion Streets.

Nebraska

Nebraska City, Nebraska
Allen B. Mayhew Cabin and John Brown Caves

As Americans moved west, the question of slavery dogged every step of their way. Compromises in Congress only postponed the day of reckoning. Like Kansas, Nebraska became involved in the fierce struggle over slavery. With the passage of the Kansas-Nebraska Act of 1854, Nebraska was established as a territory.

The most notorious escape in the territory occurred in 1858, a year before John Brown's arrival, when a Nebraska City slave owner named Nuckolls was fined $10,000 for crossing the river into Tabor, Iowa and severely injuring a man who had transported Nuckolls' two slave girls to freedom in Chicago.

The Underground Railroad movement in Nebraska was centered in Nebraska City, Camp Creek and Little Nemaha. One Underground Railroad site known as John Brown's Caves consists of a series of caverns connected by an underground passage to a log cabin where fugitives were sheltered. Tradition had credited John Brown, who passed through the area in December 1859, with protecting the runaways, but new evidence provides that Allen B. Mayhew was responsible for maintaining the station. A small museum located on the property displays material relating to the cabin's connection with the Underground Railroad.

THE UNDERGROUND RAILROAD

Location: John Brown's Caves and Museum are located
three miles west of Nebraska City on NE.2

For further information on John Brown's Caves and
Museum contact:
Nebraska Division of Travel and Tourism
P.O. Box 94666
Lincoln, NE 68509
1-800-228-4307

Ohio

Cleveland, Ohio

Cleveland was an important center for Underground Railroad activities. The city became the switching station for several routes. A route ran from Norwalk through Wakeman to Oberlin, through Lakewood to Cleveland. Another route ran northeast through Medina to Berea and at last to Cleveland. A third route ran from New Philadelphia into Massillon and Cuyahoga Falls to Brecksville. Routes also ran from Warren and Portsmouth into Cleveland. Still other escaped slaves were sent by the Columbus and Cincinnati Railroad and the Cleveland and Western Railroads, escaping through Alliance into the city of Cleveland. A number of escaped slaves were delivered by schooners at the foot of Superior Street in the city as early as 1815. Several homes connected with the Underground Railroad still stand in Cleveland today.

For further information about Underground Railroad sites contact:

The African-American Museum
1765 Crawford Road
Cleveland, OH, 44106
(216) 791-1700

Akron, Ohio
John Brown's House

Langston Hughes, the famous African-American poet and author, was fascinated with John Brown. Hughes wrote, "The Civil War that freed the slaves began with John Brown's raid on Harpers Ferry in 1859." According to scholar W.E.B. DuBois, it was Brown's example that "did more to shake the foundation of slavery than any single thing that happened in America." Brown lived in this two-story white frame house for two years during the 1840s. On exhibition are items relating to his life.

Location: 514 Diagonal Road
For further information regarding John Brown's House
            contact the house owner:
            Summit County Historical Society
            550 Copley
            Akron, OH 44321
            (Tours of the home begin at this site)
            (216) 535-1120
For further information regarding John Brown contact:
            Hudson Library and Historical Society
            22 Aurora Street
            Hudson, OH 44236
            (216) 653-6658

Akron, Ohio
Sojourner Truth Monument

Everyone who is versed in the history of the anti-slavery and the women's rights movements knows the name of Sojourner Truth. Few people, however know that there was a time when the only name Sojourner Truth had was her slave name, Isabella. A stone monument marks the site where she gave her famous "Aint I a Woman?" speech in 1851.

Location: The site of Sojourner Truth's speech is now
             occupied by the Donner Press Building, at 37
             North High Street in downtown Akron

Akron, Ohio
John Brown Monument

In Perkins Park in Akron stands a monument to John
Brown. History has bequeathed unto him many titles, and
he fancied himself a latter-day Gideon chosen by God to
strike down slavery. The son of an Underground Railroad
stationmaster, he brooded all his life on the evil of slavery.
His friend, the great orator Wendell Phillips, said of him in
1856, "He stands like a solitary rock in a more mobile society,
a fiery nature, and cold temper, and a cool head—a volcano
beneath a covering of snow."

Cut into his monument are these words: "He died to set
his brothers free and his soul goes marching on."
Location: Perkins Park
For further information on John Brown's monument
             contact:
             Summit County Historical Society
             550 Copley
             Akron, OH 44320
             (216) 535-1120

Jefferson, Ohio
Joshua R. Giddings' Law Office

Joshua R. Giddings was one of Ohio's earliest abolitionist
Congressmen; he was also a colleague of President Abraham Lincoln. Giddings' roar filled the Capitol Chamber in
Washington, D.C., as he vented his fury at Southern pro-
slavery Democrats. His law office in Jefferson was used as

a station on the Underground Railroad, and his son Grotius worked with John Brown to organize secret societies in the county. After the escape of fugitive slave John Price, the subject of the Oberlin-Wellington Rescue of 1859, Giddings led about 2,000 anti-slavery people to Cleveland to protest the arrest of the citizens if Oberlin who had been involved in the rescue. If they would not be released peacefully, the group would try to release the arrested by force. However, better judgement prevailed as tempers cooled.

After John Brown's raid on Harpers Ferry, Congress tried to implicate Giddings in Brown's activities, but he was later exonerated. Both Giddings and United States Senator Benjamin Wade of Ashtabula, Ohio, from time to time aided fugitive slaves. Charley Garlick, an escaped slave, made his home with the Giddings family, and for many years after Gidding's death lived in the rear of the law office. The law office is open for public tours.

Location: ll2 North Chestnut and Jefferson Street
For further information contact:
> Ashtabula Chamber of Commerce
> P.O. Box 96
> 4366 Main St.
> Ashtabula, OH 44004
> (216) 998-6998

Cherry Valley, Ohio
John Brown, Jr.'s House

John Brown had many friends in Ashtabula County. Weapons used in his raid on Harpers Ferry were hidden in King and Brothers Cabinet Shop and in other places of concealment in Cherry Valley. With the aid of Grotius Giddings, Brown organized a number of secret societies here called either the League of Freedom or the Sons of Freedom. When John Brown was captured by federal forces, a large number of his Ashtabula friends made plans to free him, but

Brown persuaded them not to try such a dangerous mission. Ashtabula County became an armed camp. Sentries were posted outside of John Brown Jr.'s home. Sheet iron with portholes was placed on the upper story of the Brown house to protect the defenders.

Another son, Owen Brown, spoke from the courthouse steps the night his father was hanged for the attack on Harpers Ferry. John Brown Jr.'s house still remains.

Location: Dorset Road, Route 307 Southeast of Jefferson, Ohio

For further information on John Brown, Jr.'s House contact:

Ashtabula Chamber of Commerce
P.O. Box 96
4366 Main St.
Ashtabula, OH 44004
(216) 998-6998

Cleveland/Hudson, Ohio
Case Western Reserve University and the Harriet Tubman Museum

Case-Western Reserve, originally located in Hudson, Ohio, was known as an avid abolitionist center. Nestled in the woods on Hines Hill Road in Hudson is a house where John Brown once lived. Only the red chimney is visible from the road. Still in existence under the barn floor is said to be a secret compartment where John Brown's father Owen hid fugitive slaves. In Hudson, Owen Brown taught his son always to respect the rights of the African-Americans and Native Americans who lived in the area. The Western Reserve Historical Society Museum and Library at 19825 East Boulevard has exhibits and documents relating to John Brown as well as materials concerning African-American culture. The present institution was formed in a merger with Case Institute.

The Harriet Tubman Museum is named for the most

widely known Underground Railroad conductor of her time. Named in honor of the woman called "The Moses of Her People," this museum has information on Tubman and over 5,000 artifacts pertaining to African-American culture from the slavery through the Civil Rights periods.

Location: Tubman Museum
9250 Miles Park
Cleveland, OH
(216) 341-1202

Ripley, Ohio
The Rankin House

Built in 1828, this two-story brick house overlooking the Ohio River was residence of the Reverend John Rankin, educator and abolitionist. Many an escaped slave from Kentucky was guided to Rankin's farm by the North Star and the light that each night beamed from an upstairs window. For forty years the outspoken Presbyterian minister passed fugitive slaves north, while his sons stood ready to defend them with guns; Rankin and his family sometimes housed as many as twelve escaped slaves at a time. Slave owners offered rewards, as much as $2,500, for the "abduction or assassination" of Rankin and other conductors. One winter eve, a slave woman carrying her child crossed over on the Ohio River's melting ice to find refuge here. Harriet Beecher Stowe drew on this as well as other episodes in Underground Railroad history to create the story of Eliza Harris in *Uncle Tom's Cabin*.

In 1845, Rankin founded the Free Presbyterian Church of America, which excluded slaveholders and actively opposed the institution of slavery. He also established an academy for African-American students wrote anti-slavery articles for William Lloyd Garrison's *The Liberator*.

The Rankin house is owned by the state of Ohio.

The Rankin House, Ripley, Ohio. For forty years Reverend John Rankin forwarded escaped slaves north from his home.

Location: 1824 Liberty Hill, north of Ohio Route 52, about 55 miles southeast of Cincinnati. The Rankin House is also called Liberty Hill. Visitors are encouraged to follow the route of fugitive slaves by climbing a "staircase to liberty."

For more information, including tour information, contact:

Ripley Heritage
P.O. Box 176
Ripley, OH 45167
(513) 392-1627

The house is open for tours in the summer months; for Fall, Winter and Spring tour information contact Lobina Frost, Curator, c/o Ripley Heritage.

Ripley, Ohio
John Parker's Home

Although John Parker respected the Underground Railroad work of the Reverend John Rankin of Ripley, he did not think it proper to ask white men how to abduct slaves from Kentucky. He had once been a slave in Kentucky himself, and had paid $2,000 for his freedom. Parker, a large, shrewd man of impressive appearance, knew the dangers and difficulties in liberating and assisting slaves, and yet held no reservations liberating them from their owners. It is reported that he took an active role in removing over 1,000 slaves from bondage, transporting them to his home, located in Poke Patch, Ripley's African-American community. Possessed with an inventive mind, Parker was among the limited number of African-Americans who obtained patents in the United States during that period.

He was also the owner and capable manager of a large foundry in Ripley. Parker's former home still stands today.

Location: Last house on Front Street

For further information contact:

> John Parker Home
> 300 Front Street
> Ripley, OH
> or
> Charles Nuckles
> Clerk of City Council
> Room 308
> 801 Plum Street
> Cincinnati, OH 45202

Wilberforce, Ohio
Wilberforce's Proud African-American Tradition

Wilberforce has the distinction of being the first college owned and operated by African-Americans. It was named for William Wilberforce, an early British Abolitionist who, with his countrymen Thomas F. Buxton, Granville Sharpe and former slave trader John Newton, helped end the British slave trade in 1807. (Newton was the ship captain who, after his conversion to Christianity, wrote the soul-stirring words to "Amazing Grace.")

The Reverend Daniel Alexander Payne, who was the university's first president and a former bishop of the African Methodist Episcopal Church, harbored fugitives in churches wherever he pastored. The Maxwell House, today a private home located on Brush Row Road, once served as a stop on the Underground. The Howell Place, located on Wilberforce Switch Road (U.S. Route 42) was also a stop on the fugitive slave network. Located also in Wilberforce today is the National Afro-American Museum and Cultural Center at 1350 Brush Row Road, one-half mile west of U.S. Route 42. Completed in 1988, it is one of the largest African-American museums in the nation. The museum is located on the original campus of Wilberforce University.

Dr. Fleming, the museum's Director, serves on the National Afro-American Museum's first National Park Service Underground Railroad Advisory Committee.

For further information about Wilberforce University and
the National Afro-American Museum call:
(513) 376-4944
or
(513) 376-6011

or write:

National Afro-American Museum
P.O. Box 578
Wilberforce, OH 45384

Xenia, Ohio
The Freedom Train Stopped in Xenia

Fugitive slaves who made their way on the Freedom Train to Xenia were sympathetically received there, especially by the free African-American community. No one will ever know how many escaping slaves were harbored in Xenia, but what we do know is that the Underground Railroad lives on there today, for located throughout the town are a number of private homes that once served as stations on the fugitive slave network. Included among Xenia's Underground Railroad stations are the following homes:
the Reverend Samuel Wilson House, 204 Market Street;
the Ferguson House, 1040 Hilltop Road;
Hilltop Road House, 1351 Hilltop Road;
the Leach House, 713 East Main Street;
the Robin House, 987 U.S. Route 35 East;
the David Monroe House, 246 Market Street;
the Davis Monroe House, 559 East Market Street.

The Davis Monroe House has been included in the National Park Service study of the Underground Railroad in Ohio.

For further information contact:
> Underground Railroad Study Project
> National Park Service
> Denver Service Center
> P.O. Box 25387
> Denver, CO 80225
> 1-800-524-7878

Westerville, Ohio
Benjamin Hanby, Stationmaster and Composer of "My Darling Nellie Gray"

The Reverend William Hanby settled in Westerville in 1854. His main source of income was harness-and-saddle-making, and he built a large barn at the back of his home to house his shop. Both he and his friend the Reverend Lewis

Davis, first president of Otterbein College in Westerville and Hanby's next-door neighbor, harbored fugitive slaves in the haymow of the barn. Hanby's oldest son Benjamin sometimes transported slaves at night through an alley that led to the street. Some fugitives were taken to Alexander's rake factory, where they were covered with garden supplies and transported to the next station keeper at Mount Vernon.

Hanby wrote the first stanza and chorus to "My Darling Nellie Gray" in 1850 after hearing his father describe the romance between a fugitive slave named Joseph Selby and his attractive sweetheart Nellie Gray, who was sold down the river from Kentucky to a plantation in Georgia. Some time later, after he returned home from witnessing a slave auction in Kentucky, he added four more stanzas and a further chorus. Despite the national popularity of the song, Hanby received no royalties.

Location: 160 West Main Street

For further information contact:

> Ohio Division of Travel and Tourism
> P.O. Box 1001
> Columbus, OH 43266-0101
> 1-800-BUCKEYE

Ashtabula, Ohio
"Mother Hubbard's Cupboard"
The Hubbard House

This substantial brick house was built by Colonel William Hubbard, an ardent abolitionist who held a position of authority on the Underground Railroad. It was an important refuge for fugitive slaves. Hubbard had a tunnel dug from the barn to the edge of Lake Erie so that rowboats could deliver fugitives to waiting vessels whose trusted captains could transport their human cargo either on to Buffalo or straight to the Canadian shore. This station was known as "Mother Hubbard's Cupboard" and also as the "Great Emporium" in Underground Railroad codes. It was the boast of the people of Ashtabula County that no slave was ever captured within its borders. The following statement appeared in the *Ashtabula Sentinel* on December 21, 1850: "The voice of the people is, Constitution or no Constitution, law or no law, no fugitive slave can be taken from the soil of Ashtabula County back to slavery. If anyone doubts this real sentiment, they can easily test it." The Hubbard House has recently been restored and is open to the public.

Location: Corner of Walnut Street and Lake Avenue
For further information on The Hubbard House Contact:

> Ashtabula Chamber of Commerce
> P.O. Box 96
> 4366 Main Street
> Ashtabula, OH 44004
> (216) 998-6998

Oberlin, Ohio
Oberlin City Cemetery

Located in City Park is a monument commemorating John Copland, Jr., student at Oberlin College, Lewis Leary, a native of Oberlin, and Shields Green, a fugitive slave from South Carolina. They were associates of John Brown, killed in Brown's raid on Harpers Ferry. Lewis Leary was poet Langston Hughes' maternal grandfather. A cenotap honoring the three African-American freedom fighters was erected in Westwood Cemetery alongside their graves. In October, 1972 the monument was relocated to City Park.

For further information on City Park, contact:

> Oberlin Department of Streets
> (216) 775-7270

Oberlin, Ohio
Oberlin College Underground Railroad Monument

Oberlin has a unique tradition pertaining to African-Americans. John Brown's father Owen was a trustee of Oberlin College, fiery abolitionist Theodore Weld was a teacher there, and the community stood steadfast against slavery. In fact, the whole town was a refuge for the Railroad, and when in 1858 a fugitive slave named John Price was seized on the outskirts of Oberlin, hundreds of citizens followed him and his captors to nearby Wellington, stormed the hotel where Price was confined and freed him. Later they helped him north toward Canada and safety.

When John Brown addressed a massive crowd in the spring of 1859, telling them how proud he was of the Oberlin students for rescuing John Price, the hero-worshippers cheered him ecstatically. The case became known nationally as the Oberlin-Wellington Rescue. When three of John Brown's men at Harpers Ferry were identified as Oberlin African-Americans, Oberlin and abolition became synonymous. A monument commemorating the Underground Railroad is located on campus.

Location: Oberlin College maintains a visitors information
              center in the Student Union, Wilder Hall, on
              West Lorain Street.
For further information contact:
              Oberlin College Library
              (216) 775-8285

Cincinnati, Ohio
Harriet Beecher Stowe's House

Before *Uncle Tom's Cabin* was published, Harriet Beecher Stowe and her husband Calvin lived in this large, white, two-story house situated on a hill in the old Walnut Street section of Cincinnati. Stowe used this home as a station on the Underground Railroad, taking advantage of the woods that formerly surrounded it to bring fugitives in under cover of darkness. In the low-raftered basement where slaves were hidden, a concrete slab covers a tunnel leading outside; runaways slept on straw in small hideaways until the time was right to move on north.

Long known for her anti-slavery sentiments, Harriet Beecher Stowe came from a family notable for its impact on American values; her father was Lyman Beecher, president of Cincinnati's Lane Theological Seminary, while her brother, Henry Ward Beecher, was one of the nation's leading preachers. Her 18 years in Cincinnati gave her the background for her most famous work, *Uncle Tom's Cabin*, a book that helped to change the course of the nation's history.

Location: 2950 Gilbert Street
For further information contact:

The Cincinnati Historical Society
Eden Park
Cincinnati, OH 45202
or

Contact: Harriet Beecher Stowe House
(513) 632-5120

The House is now a Museum.

Mount Pleasant, Ohio
Benjamin Lundy's House

Benjamin Lundy, who was the most widely traveled of the abolitionists, said he had walked 5,000 miles and had ridden 20,000. He had traveled through 19 states, Haiti, Canada, Texas and Mexico, moving rapidly from place to place. It is believed that Lundy was the first to move for the formation of societies to encourage the consumption of goods produced by free labor. In 1821 he began publishing his anti-slavery newspaper, *The Genius of Universal Emancipation*. William Lloyd Garrison worked for Lundy in his Baltimore, Maryland, print shop. Before his death in 1839, Lundy was converted to the doctrine of immediate emancipation of all slaves. His home is registered as a national historic landmark.

Location: Union and Third Streets

For further information about Benjamin Lundy House
                        contact:
                        Division of Travel and Tourism
                        P.O. Box 1001
                        Columbus, OH 43266-0101
                        1-800-BUCKEYE

Wisconsin

Milton, Wisconsin
The Milton House Museum

Before the Civil War, the Milton Inn served as a station on the Underground Railroad. The Emancipation Train went underground literally in the wilderness on the property of staunch abolitionist Joseph Goodrich. In 1844, five years after the founding of the village of Milton, Goodrich built an unusual hexagonal inn of poured concrete and hand-dug a tunnel from it. Slaves had to use a rope to climb out of the tunnel. If any customers were slave hunters, the fugitive slaves resting and eating in Goodrich's basement could exit to a cabin and follow creek beds and lakes north to Canada. Stories are recounted today about Sojourner Truth, the famous abolitionist lecturer, speaking at the inn. A former stagecoach stop, this inn is reported to be the oldest cement building in the United States.

Location: At the intersection of Wisconsin State Highways 59 and 26, in Milton

For further information on the Milton House contact:

      Commons Restoration
      440 North Jackson
      Janesville, WI 53545
      (608) 752-4519

Janesville, Wisconsin
Tallman House

Built in 1855-1857 by William M. Tallman, this large brick house with 20 rooms was a safe house for slaves escaping on the Underground Railroad. Tallman, an abolitionist, had operated an Underground Railroad station in New York State before moving to Wisconsin. Abraham Lincoln was an honored guest in this home when he visited the Tallman family in 1859.

When fugitive slaves approached this house, a bell was rung to warn the servants and a lantern signal was given at the window on the second floor. Fugitives were hidden in servants' bedrooms in the rear wing. When it was safe for fugitives to move to the next station, they left through a secret stairway in the maid's closet. From Janesville they were led to Rock River, where a boat was waiting for them. Their next station stop was the Milton House at Milton. Other important trails on the Underground Railroad in Wisconsin included the following communities: Albion, Beloit, Green Bay, La Porte, Liberty, Prairie (now Pickett), Milwaukee, Kenosha, Ripon and Waukesha.

Location: The Tallman House is located north of
Janesville's business district, on U.S. 14 at
440 N. Jackson Street
(608) 868-7772

Waukesha, Wisconsin
Lyman Goodnow's Grave

When Caroline Quales, a sixteen-year old slave girl, made her daring escape in 1824, she became Wisconsin's first passenger on the Underground Railroad. Caroline was an attractive, fair-skinned girl, fair enough to pass as white. When her mistress, in a fit of anger, punished Caroline by cutting off her long, shining black hair, the proud and educated young woman casually boarded a steamboat in St. Louis to Alton, Illinois. However, she was pursued by slave hunters who were promised a $300 reward, put up by her mistress, for Caroline's return. A free black man, suspecting that she was a fugitive slave, warned her of the danger of remaining in Alton and put her on a stagecoach traveling to Milwaukee. Some time later, after being passed from one station on the Underground to another, Caroline was forwarded to Lyman Goodnow in Waukesha. After a five-week, perilous journey, Goodnow escorted Caroline the last 600 miles to safety in Detroit, Michigan, and from there she crossed the Detroit River to Windsor. Caroline Quales was Wisconsin's first Underground Railroad passenger to reach safety on the Freedom Train in Canada. Lyman Goodnow's grave is marked with a bronze plate honoring him as the first conductor on Wisconsin's Underground Railroad.

Location: Prairie Home Cemetery, Waukesha

For further information about Lymon Goodnow's grave and other Wisconsin Underground Railroad activities contact:

The Wisconsin Historical Society
816 State Street
Madison, WI 53707
(608) 262-3266

SOUTH

Alabama

Plateau, East Mobile, Alabama
Cudjoe Lewis Memorial

At one point in America's antebellum history, forty-five percent of Alabama's population were enchained in slavery. State law permitted up to one hundred lashes on the bare back for such crimes as forging a pass, attempting to run-away or engaging in riots. Yet in spite of the relentless opposition a few Alabama slaves, favored by rare good fortune, escaped into the North.

Over the years, almost all physical evidence pertaining to slavery in Alabama has vanished. Occasionally, one can still find evidence where slavery once existed. Although the importation of slaves had been declared illegal by both Great Britain and the United States in 1807, enforcement of the law was spotty. One of the last to arrive by slave ship, Cudjoe Lewis landed in Mobile Bay in 1859 aboard the *Clothilde*, having been captured and sold by Africans in Dahomey.

After the Civil War he and his shipmates founded Plateau, Alabama, where he lived into his 90s. Descendants of those enslaved Africans who landed on the *Clothilde* erected a monument in a section of Mobile called Africa Town.

Location: Africa Town is reached from central Mobile by
            taking U.S. 43 north to the Bay Bridge turnoff.
            Cudjoe Lewis's monument and the Union

Baptist Church is located at 506 Bay Bridge Road.

Louisiana

Destrehan, Louisiana
Destrehan Plantation

Built in 1787 by Jean D'Estrehan, Destrehan Plantation is the oldest intact plantation in the Mississippi Delta. This simple Caribbean-style manor house rested upon 5,000 acres of land. Jean D'Estrehan owned a large number of slaves who worked in his indigo and sugar cane fields, and two of its original slave quarters have recently been restored.

Solomon Northup, who was lured from his home in New York State, served as a slave for twelve years on a plantation similar to Destrehan near the Red River in northern Louisiana before he regained his freedom. Louisiana permitted a person to shoot a runaway who would not stop when ordered to do so. Nevertheless, a few slaves managed to reach the Promised Land. John Mason, an escaped slave from Kentucky, was recaptured and taken to New Orleans; however fifteen months later he escaped finally to Hamilton, Canada. The Louisiana State Supreme Court cautioned pursuers that they ought to try to avoid giving an escaped slave a "mortal wound," but if he were killed, "the homicide is a consequence of the permission to fire upon him." The court made it a capital offense to encourage insubordination or to use language to entice slaves to escape. If a slave struck his owner, a member of the owner's family or an overseer "so as to cause contusion, or shedding of blood," was permitted to kill the slave.

Location: Destrehan Plantation (on La. 48 at Destrehan.)
            P.O. Box 5
            Destrehan, LA 70047
            (504) 764-9315

Bayou Boeuf, Louisiana
Bayous and Swamps: A Haven for Escaped Slaves

Bayou comes from a Native American word, the Choctaw "bayuk," meaning creek or stream. Along the low, swampy Gulf Coast there are several large bayous, whose waters swarm with fish, alligators and other animals of the forest. The slow-moving waters of southern Louisiana were used by runaway slaves who often found shelter among the Chickasaw, Choctaw and Chitimacha Indians. It was easy to hide in these remote and inaccessible locations that included giant cypresses with Spanish moss and subtropical vegetation. There is evidence to prove that slaves escaped into Bayou Boeuf and planned a slave conspiracy, witnessed by Solomon Northup, who later wrote about it in his popular book, *Twelve Years a Slave*. The conspiracy failed when its leader, Lew Cheney, a shrewd, cunning slave, sacrificed all of his companions and informed his owner of the conspiracy to receive special privileges. The conspirators' original plan was to organize a band of marooned slaves strong enough to fight their way to Mexico, the southern terminal of the Underground Railroad, where slaves were promised freedom by the Mexican government.

For further information about Louisiana bayous and

swamps contact:
Honey Island Swamp Tours
4610 Redwood
New Orleans, LA 70127
(504) 242-5877

Tours by Isabelle:
P.O. Box 74072
New Orleans, PA 70174
(504) 367-3963
The Cotton Blossom:
(The New Orleans Steamboat Company)
2 Canal St., Ste. 1300
New Orleans, LA 70130
(504) 586-8777 (contact Lucille Le'Obia)
Le'Obs Tours and Transportation Service
4635 Touro Street
New Orleans, LA 70122
(504) 288-3478

New Orleans, Louisiana
Congo Square

During the Colonial period, the square was known as "Place Congo" or "Congo Plains." George Washington Cable (1844-1925), the well-known Louisiana author, wrote around the turn of the century that in early years Congo Plains did not attract the house servants as much as it did field hands. The square was known for its blend of dancing and music, a combination of African, Caribbean and contemporary African-American. In 1853, Henry Didimus said that there was a considerable amount of "patting" and "shuffling;" he also stated, "the feet scarce tread wider space than their own length, but rise and fall, turn in and out, touch first the heel and then the toe, rapidly and more rapidly."

The women of the square were gaily dressed and wore golden bracelets, earrings and ornaments of African origin. All joined hands in the singing, together with prayers, and danced uninterruptedly until nine o'clock p.m. Just as the coded spiritual conveyed hidden signals expressing danger, hiding and escape, in truth, the pat and the shuffle dances were used as a medium of communication. Although the Calinda, Chacta, Babouille, Juba, Ring Dance,

The Faithful Groomsman. A hitching post that became a symbol of the Underground Railroad. When lit, the lantern signaled safe haven for the runaway slaves. From the Blockson Afro-American Collection.

Dance was intimately connected with the Underground Railroad.

Congo and Voodoo dances were performed, the Bamboula was the most widely known. Its origin, according to tradition, is said to have come from the African drum bamboula.

The Creole Code played a vital role in Louisiana's Underground Railroad history. The Code was used as a safe guidance for slaves escaping to freedom, way to communicate, to pass notes and letters. A mixture of African Spanish and French, the Code was passed from generation to generation beginning around the early 17th century. The value of the Code lay in its secrecy.

To the white visitor's eyes, the dancing was considered sensational. However, enslaved Africans considered it a form of "Puttin' on Ole Massa," and of survival. It is a historical coincidence that Congo Square is located at Armstrong Park in the heart of New Orleans; the park is named for Louis Armstrong, a native son and world-famous musician whose statue is near the Square entrance.

Location: Congo Square, 1200 Rampart Street
             Armstrong Park
For further information on Congo Square contact:
             Historic Landmark District Preservation
             Resource Center
             605 Julia St.
             New Orleans, LA 70130
             (504) 581-7032

New Orleans, Louisiana
Musee Conti Museum of Wax

Planters from throughout the South during Marie Laveau's lifetime used to visit the slave dealers on Gravier or Bienville Streets to enlarge their plantation with slaves. A number of these planters used the opportunity to visit Marie Laveau, the most famous and most powerful of all the Voodoo Queens of New Orleans. No history of the city would be complete without mentioning her name. She ex-

Marie Laveau, New Orleans' famous Voodoo Queen, courtesy Louisiana State Museum.

ercised great control over her admirers, both rich and poor, slave and freed. Laveau claimed knowledge of the future, the ability to read the mind and the ability to heal the body. She was famous for mixing love potions for people who sought a love, had lost a love, or who wanted to separate from an abusive love mate.

In Maryland, Frederick Douglass learned from an old African that if slaves wore the roots of a certain herb on their right side, no white person could whip them. Some slaves who were connected with the Underground Railroad spoke of using voodoo to "put de mouth" (a curse) on their masters and masters' family members.

Included among the lifesize wax figures in the Musee Conti is a model of Marie Laveau as well as one of Madame Lalaurie, mistress of the "haunted house" located at 1140 Royal Street. According to tradition, Lalaurie was charged with finding such disturbing delight in torturing her slaves that she was asked to leave New Orleans.

Louisiana

Location: Musee Conti Museum of Wax
917 Conti Street
(504) 525-2605

Mississippi

Beauvior, Mississippi
Jefferson Davis Home and Shrine

Senator Jefferson Davis, owner of a large Cotton plantation in Mississippi, declared in the first session of the Thirty-
first Congress:

> Negroes do escape from Mississippi frequently, and the boats
> constantly passing by our long line of frontier furnish great
> facility to get to Ohio, and when they do escape it is with great
> difficulty that they are restored ... those like myself, who live
> on that great highway of the West—the Mississippi River are
> most exposed have a present and increasing interest in this
> matter.

Jefferson Davis had a good cause for concern about his
property, for abolitionists such as Dr. Alexander Ross of
Toronto, Canada were busy in the deep South encouraging
slaves to escape on the Underground Railroad. Ross' profession was that of a physician, but he found time for many
other activities; he was also a distinguished ornithologist
and Canada's most important Underground Railroad Conductor. When Ross visited Vicksburg, he found that slaves
had heard of Canada from other slaves brought from Virginia and the border slave states; but the impression they
had was that Canada was so far away, it would be useless
to try to reach it. Ross made at least five trips into the deep

South, posing as a bird-watcher. John Greenleaf Whittier dedicated one of his poems to him.

Visitors can wander Beauvior, 56 acres, or visit the museum to view exhibits relating to Jefferson Davis' life as President of the Confederacy.

Location: Beauvior
224 West Beach Blvd.
Beauvior, MS 39530
(601) 388-1313

Kentucky

Owensboro, Kentucky
Josiah Henson Trail

The fictional character of Uncle Tom in *Uncle Tom's Cabin* was based partially on the real-life career of an escaped slave named Josiah Henson. Henson had been a Maryland slave whose owner, Isaac Riley, transported him to Riley's brother Amos' plantation in Owensboro. Henson was about 36 years old when he arrived in Kentucky with his family. He became a model slave and served as overseer of the plantation.

However, late in 1830 he gathered his family together and with them escaped to freedom, going first to Indiana, and from there to Canada via the Underground Railroad. He later told his life story to Harriet Beecher Stowe and wrote an autobiography entitled *Father Henson's Story*. Stowe wrote the introduction to the second edition of his book, which was published under the title *Truth Stranger Than Fiction: Father Henson's Story of His Own Life*.

Location: The former site of the Riley plantation is designated by a historical marker on U.S. 60 near the village of Maceo, just west of the Davis County line. No evidence of the plantation remains.

Josiah Henson, a trustworthy Kentucky slave, who later escaped to Canada. He returned to his former owners' plantation to lead other slaves to freedom. Henson served as a role model in Harriet Beecher Stowe's novel Uncle Tom's Cabin.

Berea, Kentucky

Berea College: The First Interracial College in the South

Although Kentucky joined the union as a slave state, it was also inhabited by anti-slavery leaders such as the Reverend David Rice, James B. Birney, Cassius M. Clay, David Barrow, the Reverend John Fee and others who agitated for slave emancipation. John Fee was a former slaveholder who became a highly vocal abolitionist and founded Berea in 1858 as the first college—not only in Kentucky but the South—with the purpose of admitting African-Americans as well as white students. The Reverend Fee also hid runaway slaves in his interracial college.

Those who aided him in establishing it, or who attended his anti-slavery church, were ostracized by the community. Fee was often threatened by angry mobs, and his church meetings broken up. On one occasion a mob dispersed his teachers. This drove several families across the river into Ohio. Fee was among them, and was warned that if he came back to Kentucky he would be hanged.

Like Fee, Cassius M. Clay was a prominent slaveholder

who became an abolitionist. He was driven out of Lexington, Kentucky, by pro-slavery citizens after he expressed anti-slavery sentiments in *The True American*, the local newspaper.

A native of Louisville, former World Heavyweight Boxing Champion Muhammad Ali, had been christened Cassius Marcellus Clay in honor of the abolitionist; he later changed his "slave name" to reflect his adopted Muslim religion.

Location: Berea College is a mile from the Berea exit off I-75, on Chestnut Street.

For more information contact:

Hutchins Library
Berea College
Berea, KY 40404
(606) 986-9341

Washington, Kentucky
Old Slave Market

Although John G. Birney, president, and other members of the Kentucky Society for the Gradual Relief of the State from Slavery called for gradual emancipation, the "peculiar institution" of slavery stood firm in Washington. It was the second largest town in Kentucky, and it was a place where slaves were sold. An auction block may still be seen on the courthouse green. When Harriet Beecher Stowe visited Washington in 1833, she saw slaves sold on the block, and she was so stirred by the abhorrent scene that she recorded the experience in her novel *Uncle Tom's Cabin*.

Also in Washington is a restored building called the Paxton Inn. This building is reported to have been a station stop on the Underground Railroad when it was owned by James A. Paxton, who is said to have hidden escaped slaves in the cellar. A prominent lawyer, Paxton married twice, both times into the Marshall family and was related to Chief Justice John Marshall. Paxton later moved to Ohio because he "would not rear his family in a state that supported slavery."

Location: Washington is just off U.S. 68 about five miles south of Maysville.

For further information contact:

The Washington Visitor Center
(606) 759-7411

North Carolina

Guilford, North Carolina
Guilford College Historic District

Underground Railroad activities developed early in North Carolina, as is implied by the act that the colony passed providing that "any person harboring a runaway shall be prosecuted and compelled to pay a sum of twenty-five pounds or serve the owner of the slave, should he be convicted, and suffer accordingly." Vestal Coffin, a Quaker, organized the Underground Railroad near the site of present-day Guilford College in 1819. Addison Coffin, his son, entered into its service as a conductor. Vestal's cousin, Levi Coffin, became a conductor on the fugitive slave network in early youth and continued his unflinching service through his relocation to Indiana right up to the Civil War. A historical marker identifies his nearby birthplace. Levi Coffin, who was often called the "President of the Underground Railroad," noted in his book *Reminiscences of Levi Coffin*, which was published in 1876, that "runaway slaves used frequently to conceal themselves in the woods and thickets of New Garden [North Carolina], waiting opportunities to make their escape to the North." There were stations in Jamestown, now High Point, and Goldsboro. Mount Jefferson, overlooking Jefferson and West Jefferson in Ashe County, was until recently known as Nigger Mountain because northern sympathizers befriended escaping slaves by hiding them on its slopes, supplying them with food and loaning them horses.

Lunsford Lane, a slave from Raleigh, North Carolina, purchased his freedom and removed his family to Boston, soon after becoming an agent on the Underground Railroad and a speaker for the anti-slavery cause.

Location: Levi Coffin's birthplace is on U.S. 421 at
             Greensboro in Guilford County.
For further information about Levi Coffin's birthplace
             contact: Travel and Tourism Division
             450 North Salisbury Street
             Raleigh, NC 27611
             1-800-847-4862

South Carolina

Charleston, South Carolina
Denmark Vesey House

Slave unrest persisted in America from the early years of the slave trade until John Brown's famous raid on Harpers Ferry. The earliest known rebellion in the colonies occurred in Gloucester County, Virginia, in 1663. In 1739 in Stono, South Carolina, the Spanish governor helped to provoke a rebellion when he told slaves that if they made their way to St. Augustine, Florida, they would be given their liberty. Led by a slave named Cato, a group of fugitives attempted to make their way to Florida and freedom, killing 21 whites as they went. However, they were overtaken and 43 slaves were executed.

One of the largest slave revolts in the United States was set in motion by Telemarque, otherwise known as Denmark Vesey, at the Emmanuel African Methodist Episcopal church in Charleston. The plot reputedly involved hundreds of enslaved African-Americans. Vesey, who in 1799 had won a lottery of $1,500 and with it purchased his freedom, visited Haiti and became obsessed with the concept of liberation that led to that country's independence. He believed something like the Haitians rebellion could take place in South Carolina. His revolt threatened the very fabric of the plantation system there, but before his rebellion was executed he was betrayed by a house slave who informed on his plans.

After a series of trials, 35 insurgents were hanged, among them Denmark Vesey and his dedicated friend Gullah Jack. The plot managed to change the status of slave life in South Carolina, which reverted from the most liberal to the most restrictive conditions.

Location: Denmark Vesey's former residence at 56 Bull Street was declared a National Historical Landmark in 1976. It is a private residence and is not open to the public.

Frogmore, South Carolina
Penn Center

Penn Center has been a community of history and achievement since 1862. Penn Center was known as Penn School for its first 85 years, as the first school for free slaves in America. When Union Troops invaded St. Helena Island in 1861, they confiscated the property of a slave owner including over 10,000 slaves listed as "Contrabrand of War." In 1862 Laura Towne and Ellen Murray, two Quaker abolitionists from Philadelphia established the Penn School to educate the newly freed slaves.

In late 1862 Charlotte Forten, from Philadelphia became the school's first African-American teacher, like her wealthy grandfather James Forten and her Uncle Robert Purvis.

Charlotte Forten was acquainted with the plight of slaves though her family's connection with the Underground Railroad in Pennsylvania. Her friend, antislavery poet John Greenleaf Whittier sent her his "St. Helena Hymn" written for the scholars of St. Helena Island. Forten taught her students to sing Whittier's verses for the Emancipation Proclamation exercise of January 1, 1863. Harriet Tubman, the great Underground Railroad conductor was also connected with the St. Helena and Beaufort area serving as a union army spy scout and nurse.

Designated in 1974 as a National Historic Landmark by the United States Department of Interior, the center displays photographs and artifacts depicting lifestyles of the Sea Islands from the 1800's. Today the school is the Penn Community Service Center.

Location: Situated on St. Helena Island between the inland waterway and the Atlantic Ocean about 30 miles from I-95.

For further information about Penn Center contact:
    Greater Beaufort Chamber of Commerce at (803) 838-5400 or Penn Center (803) 838-2432

South Carolina/Georgia
South Carolina and Georgia Sea Islands

The Sea Islands off the coast of South Carolina and Georgia have been one of the most thoroughly researched areas in the South. No complete story about the Underground Railroad would be complete without mentioning the Sea Islands. The Islands served as a connection between African-Americans, the Caribbean and Africa as the islands were separated from the mainland by a system of tidal creeks and salty inlets, wide bays, live oak trees and marshes. The island names are pure music: Bull Pawley, Dewees, Murphy Cedar, and the Isle of Palms; then James and Johns, Kiawah, Wadmalaw, Edisto, famous Parris Island, the Hilton Head, and Daufuskie, and on down to Tybee, Wassaw, Ossabaw, St. Catherine, Sapelo, St. Simons, Jekyll and Cumberland. The African-American community lived long (over one hundred years) in isolation on the islands as slaves and many of their customs and beliefs closely resemble those of the IBO, Yoruba, Kongo, Mandingo, and other West African tribes from whom they are probably descended. This region of the Low Country was noted for its long-stable sea island cotton. Profits for the slave owners were enormous.

Before and during the Civil War many city slaves from Charleston, South Carolina and Savannah, Georgia seeking freedom simply escaped by small boats and barges and united with their Gullah speaking neighbors living on the Islands. On Jekyll Island, in 1858 the slave ship *Wanderer* debarked one of the last cargoes of slaves ever to land in the United States. A historic marker records the site today. As the Confederacy collapsed, freed slaves mobbed into the Sea Island region in large numbers. Signs of the Sea Islands' Gullah culture are vivid today, in fact, the Gullah dialect and culture is seen and heard during the Annual Gullah Festival held in Beaufort, and the Sea Island Festival held at St. Simons Island. Many African-Americans held onto their lands, bequeathing their property to heirs.

Many old African words and expressions are still used among the Gullah speakers of the Sea Islands today.

For further information about the Sea Islands contact:

> Division of Parks and Tourism
> 1205 Pendleton Street
> Columbia, SC 29201
> (803) 734-0122

For tours contact:

> Extended Kinship Appeal/Afrikan
> Kultural Arts Network
> Attn: Marquetta Goodwine
> P.O. Box 40-0199
> Brooklyn, NY 11240-0199
> (212) 439-1026

Georgia

Savannah, Georgia
First African Baptist Church

The First African Baptist Church was established in 1773 at Brompton Plantation by a small group of African-American men and women longing for religious expression. The church became an organized body in 1775, the oldest organized African-American church in America. Completed in 1859, the church building is now located at Franklin Square. The Underground Railroad took concrete from here when the congregation began to harbor escaped slaves who came through Savannah's many subterranean passageways to the church. There they were hidden in a four-foot-wide tunnel underneath the floor, which had diamond-shaped air holes carved in it to provide them with air. Also carved into the church's pews are the initials of both free blacks and slaves who worshiped in First African Baptist Church. Many of the symbols that accompany the initials are African in their origin.

Location: 23 Montgomery Street
             (912) 232-5526

Macon, Georgia
Harriet Tubman Historical and Cultural Museum

One of the boldest and most ingenious events in the history of the Underground Railroad occurred here in 1848

William and Ellen Craft, escaped slaves from Macon, Georgia, who made one of the boldest escapes to freedom. Courtesy William Still Underground Railroad Records.

when William and Ellen Craft made their daring escape; William dressed his young wife, Ellen who possessed a light complexion, in the top hat and well-cut suit of a planter. They continued with a bandage for a "toothache" and a sling for a "border arm" to conceal her beardlessness and her inability to write. Masquerading as master and slave, the two traveled northward with Ellen sleeping in first-class accommodations in southern cities along the way, until they reached Philadelphia and relative safety.

The Underground Railroad is still connected with the city of Macon, by a museum named for the great conductor Harriet Tubman. The Harriet Tubman Historical and Cultural Museum features exhibits of African-American history and crafts. A large wall mural depicting the voyage people of African descent have taken from early American culture to contemporary life is the major feature of the museum.

Georgia

Location: The Harriet Tubman Historical and Cultural
Museum 340 Walnut Street (on the Northern
edge of city.)
Macon, GA 31201
(912) 743-8544

Native Americans were among the earliest friends of fugitive slaves.

Osceola, the Seminole chief, married a woman whose mother was Indian and whose father was a fugitive slave.

Florida

Jacksonville (Fort George Island), Florida
Kingsley Plantation

"For what purpose does the master hold the servant?" asked a Southerner in the *Farmer's Journal* in 1853. He answered himself frankly, "It is not that by his labor, he, the master, may accumulate wealth?" The romantic charm of plantation life was lost on the slaves who made it possible. Although the African slave trade was abolished by federal law in 1808, Zephaniah Kingsley circumvented the law by transporting slaves on his own vessels. Kingsley believed, as most planters did, that the person of the slave was not property, but the right to his labor was property and might be transferred like any other property. Slaves were doomed to turn vast tracts of cheap land into productive plantations of indigo, rice, cotton, sugar and tobacco destined for foreign markets. After training in field and shop, they were sold at 50% above market value.

Known as the largest slave trading plantation in Florida, Fort George Island Plantation housed anonymous Africans in tabby-walled, palmetto-roofed cabins after their importation by owner and slave-trader Zephaniah Kingsley. From 1813 to 1839 Kingsley's slaves grew long-stemmed Sea Island cotton, sugarcane, corn and citrus on his plantation. The "task" system of slavery was used, whereby white overseers and their slave "drivers" assigned, on a daily basis, specific work to individual slaves. Upon completion of this work, the slaves were permitted to use the remainder of the day as they chose. This system had proven profitable to the owners of the low country rice plantations and was adopted on the neighboring Sea Island cotton plantations.

Kingsly married an African woman named Anna Madgigine Jai, whom he had purchased as a slave in Havanna, Cuba. Her African name, Jai or Ndiays, is an old and important name among the Wolof people of Senegal. After Kingsley freed her in 1811, she became a landowner and successful businesswoman in her own right. Today visitors to Kingsley can see Kingsley's residence, barn and ruins of slaves' houses.

Kingsley prohibited the playing of drums; he feared that his slaves would send coded messages to forment revolts. On one of his voyages to West Africa, he married Anna Madegigine Jai, the daughter of a Senegalese tribal ruler. Kingsley's plantation offers one of the best illustrations of slave quarters in the National Park Service system. The main house and slave quarters are still standing on the site.

Location: Kingsley Plantation is about 25 miles northwest
             of Jacksonville. Access by ferryboat from
             Florida AIA, or by way of I-95 eastbound to
             Florida 105 to Fort George Island.

For further information contact:
             National Park Service
             Fort Caroline National Memorial
             Timucuan Ecological and Historical Preserve
             12713 Fort Caroline Road
             Jacksonville, FL 32225-1229
             (904) 251-3537
             or
             (904) 251-2473

An escaped slave with the Seminole Indians in Florida; courtesy of artist Jerry Pinkney.

Sumatra, Florida
Fort Gadsden State Park

Hundreds of slaves took matters into their own hands with their escape from southern Georgia into the Florida Everglades, where they made their home for many years with the Seminole Indians. Like the Creek of Georgia and eastern Alabama, Seminole Chief Osceola was a Native American who welcomed fugitives. When the British abandoned Fort Gadsden in 1816, it was taken over by Indians and African-Americans and renamed Fort Negro. General Andrew Jackson was ordered to "destroy the fort and return the stolen African-Americans and property to their rightful owners." Thus began the first of the Seminole Wars. The fort was eventually blown up by a cannon, exploding the fort's powder magazine to kill almost 300 men, women and children. The survivors were sent into slavery.

When the Seminoles were removed to Indian Territory in the early 1830s, 450 to 500 African-American members of the tribe, representing about 15% of the tribe's total number, went with them. After finding that Indian Territory was not exempt from the activities of slave raiders, some African-American Seminoles moved in 1849 to Mexico, where today their descendants are known as Seminole Freedmen or Black Seminoles. Today only a historical marker, some earthworks and a network of trenches remain to tell the story of Fort Negro.

Location: Six miles southwest of Sumatra or 20 miles north of Apalachicola on State Road 65, in Florida's pan handle.

Tennessee

Gallatin, Tennessee
Fairvue Plantation

During the great plantation era from the early eighteenth century until the Civil War, many planters became immensely wealthy, erecting large plantation houses, many with classic architecture and luxurious furnishings.

Isaac Franklin built Fairvue in 1832 largely from money he made on the slave trade. His two-thousand-acre plantation was the largest slave trading operation in the South. Franklin also owned thousands of acres in Texas and Louisiana. Slaves worked this vast plantation called Fairvue, and they also kept the "big house." Set back from the mansion at some distance were sixteen brick slave houses, each with a large chimney, forming a long street in the manner of a small village. Between the slave quarters and Fairvue lived the ominous presence of an overseer.

On various occasions a number of slaves escaped to freedom in northern states. Throughout the years the plantation has been subdivided to less than one-third of its original size. This site is a National Historic Landmark, but is closed to the public.

Location: Fairvue is about 3 miles west of Gallatin on U.S. 31 East.

THE OLD SOUTHWEST

Missouri

Hannibal, Missouri
Mark Twain House

Hannibal, the home of Samuel Clemens, or Mark Twain as he is better known, was the heart of the region called "Little Dixie," a haven for slave hunters from Kentucky, Tennessee, and elsewhere. In 1841, three abolitionists, George Thompson, John Burr and Alanson Work, had attempted to help five escaped slaves but were betrayed by one of the fugitives and caught. Since Missouri had no law under which they could have been charged, false witnesses were drummed up and a kangaroo court sentenced the men to 12 years in the state penitentiary. They were released before five years had elapsed. Mark Twain's father was on the jury that sentenced the men; Twain himself wrote about the trial in his story, "A Scrap of Curious History."

In 1847, George Thompson, one of the abolitionists, described the trial in his book, *Prison Life and Reflection: or A Narrative of the Arrest, Trial, and Conviction, Imprisonment, Treatment, Observation, Reflection and Deliverance of Work, Burr and Thompson, who suffered an Unjust and Cruel Imprisonment in Missouri Penitentiary for Attempting to Aid some Slaves to Liberty*. Thompson's last plea in his book was for others to use their pens and their tongues "in opposing Slavery—the 'Mother of Abominations' in our land."
Location: 208 Hill Street

Hannibal, MO 63401
(314) 221-9010
For further information on Missouri, contact:
Missouri Division of Tourism
P.O. Box 1055
Jefferson City, MO 65102
1-800-877-1234

St. Louis, Missouri
Knights of Liberty

In 1846 Moses Dickson and eleven other free African-Americans organized the Knights of Liberty in St. Louis for the purpose of overthrowing slavery. Ten years were spent working slowly and secretly making their preparations and extending the society. At the end of this time, because of changes in slavery conditions North and South, the plan of operation was altered and Underground Railroad work was done. It is said that the Knights of Liberty assisted hundreds of slaves to escape yearly. After Emancipation, Dickson established The Knights and Daughters of Tabor Society in 1871 in memory of the original organizations.

St. Louis, Missouri
The Old Courthouse and the Dred Scott Case

Missouri was a slave state prior to the Civil War and was divided in its sympathies during the conflict. Slaves were sold on the courthouse steps in St. Louis. In 1857, the Old Courthouse became the subject of national attention when a slave named Dred Scott appeared in the courtroom to bring suit for his freedom. His litigation had continued for eleven years and the case ultimately went to the Supreme Court, where Chief Justice Roger Taney ruled that slaves could not become free by escaping or being taken into free territory. Dred Scott was emancipated by his owner and

Dred Scott

died a year later in 1858. He is buried in the Calvary Cemetery, St. Louis, MO.

While Scott eventually received his freedom from his master, other slaves liberated themselves on the Underground Railroad. As early as 1854 branches of the fugitive slave network led from St. Louis to Chicago, and lines of the Underground passed through the following Missouri towns and cities: Bethany, Joplin, Potosi, Kansas City and Theopolis. Fugitives were assisted by both African-American and white conductors.

Of course, John Brown's name is connected with the Underground Railroad in Missouri. Late in 1858, he raided the state and rescued eleven slaves from their owners, delivering them to safety in Canada. Their journey was the longest in Underground Railroad history.

Location:　The Old Courthouse stands at 11 North Fourth St. at Broadway and Market Streets; part of the Jefferson National Expansion Memorial

and is administered by the National Park
Service.
For further information contact:
Bob Moore, Historian
Jefferson National Expansion Memorial
11 N. 4th St.
St. Louis, MO 63102
(314) 425-4465

Kansas

Osawatomie, Kansas
John Brown Memorial Park

Captain Brown, the Old Man, Osawatomie Brown, Brown of Kansas— called by whatever name, he was known to all among abolitionists warriors and martyrs. Others, including the U.S. government, regarded him as a murderous insurgent. John Brown arrived in Kansas in 1855, in response to appeals for arms from his sons, five of whom preceded him to the territory and settled at Osawatomie. It was not to make a home for himself in Kansas nor to aid his sons in their wilderness struggle that John Brown came to Kansas. Rather, it was his conviction that there was an opportunity to make Kansas, rather than Canada a terminal on the Underground Railroad. Here he fought in several border skirmishes near Osawatomie. A cabin where he lived still stands, and a life-sized bronze statue of the famous abolitionist was erected in 1935 in Osawatomie on the 135th anniversary of John Brown's birth.

Location: Osawatomie is about 50 miles southwest of Kansas City by way of U.S. 169. John Brown Memorial Park is west of the center of town. (913) 755-4384

Baldwin, Kansas
Robert Hall Pearson (Black Jack) Park

Believing that slavery must be eliminated by force, John Brown organized guerrillas to preserve Kansas from slavery, and at Baldwin and Potawotomie in 1856 fought several battles with federal troops. Brown's men killed five men in revenge for an attack by pro-slavery forces at Lawrence.

Location: Three miles east of Baldwin City on KS 56, then south a quarter of a mile is Robert Hall Pearson (Black Jack) Park. Open 24 hours.

For further information about Kansas contact:

Kansas Department of Commerce
400 Southwest 8th Street, 5th Floor
Topeka, Kansas 6603-3957
(913) 296-2009

Kansas City, Kansas
Old Quindaro Underground Railroad Site

Oral tradition states that John Brown, whose statue stands near the south end of old Quindaro town site, assisted fugitive slaves from Missouri by way of secret tunnels. The statue was the first monument in the United States to be raised for the famous abolitionist.

In 1856, the Quindaro Town Company was founded by an alliance of abolitionists, Wyandot Indians and the New England Emigrant Aid Company. Quindaro became a safe haven on the Underground Railroad, conveying fugitive slaves out of Missouri into freedom in Kansas Territory. During the Civil War, the once bustling 100-acre town, with churches, hotels, saloons, Underground Railroad stations and a stagecoach line linked with Lawrence, became empty. In 1862 the Kansas legislature repealed the town's charter.

Today, a dedicated group of citizens continues to fight to save the Quindaro town site as a memorial to the great abolitionist movement that lead to the formation of the state of Kansas. Currently a landfill is the proposed fate that looms over the area.

Location: On the Missouri River in the northern part of the present-day Kansas City.

For further information contact:

        Fred Whitehead, Secretary
        Quindara Town Preservation Society
        Kansas City, KS 66119

        Marivin S. Robinson
        Quindaro Ruins Underground Railroad Exercise
        P.O. Box 2603
        Kansas City, KS 66110
        (913) 371-0576

Rivers and waterways were used by escaping slaves.

A Note on Rivers and Waterways

Rivers and waterways were intimately connected with the Underground Railroad, providing lines of escape and sources of direction for many an escaped slave. One should remember this in traveling along automobile routes, because geographical features like rivers and mountains were often more helpful to fugitive slaves than were the roadways. Among the great arteries was the Mississippi, a pathway to the Gulf of Mexico and the southern terminus of the Underground Railroad in Mexico, which was also reached by the Pecos River and the Rio Grand in Texas.

Northwards, the Mississippi could be used to reach the midwestern states, along with the Missouri. The Great Lakes, where friendly ship captains ferried slaves, should also be kept in mind as one follows the Underground Railroad. The Detroit River in Michigan was a favorite place for escaped slaves to cross into Canada. The Ohio has always been linked historically and romantically with the Underground escape of thousands of slaves, witness the real-life experience of the woman that the fictional Eliza in *Uncle Tom's Cabin* was based on. The Chesapeake Bay and the Susquehanna were other great routes for slaves from the Eastern Shore area, while the Big and little Choptank Rivers in Maryland and Delaware, as well as the Nanticoke, were also of importance. In southeastern Pennsylvania, the Dela-

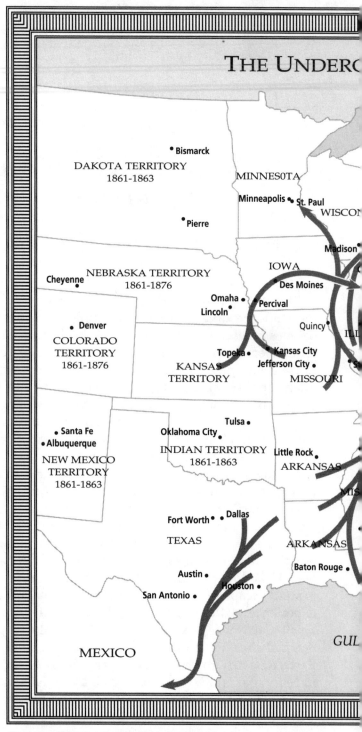

THE UNDERG

DAKOTA TERRITORY
1861-1863

• Bismarck

MINNESOTA

Minneapolis • St. Paul

WISCON

• Pierre

Madison

NEBRASKA TERRITORY
1861-1876

Cheyenne •

IOWA

• Des Moines

Omaha •
Lincoln •

• Percival

Quincy

ILLI

• Denver

COLORADO TERRITORY
1861-1876

Topeka •
KANSAS TERRITORY

• Kansas City
Jefferson City •

St

MISSOURI

• Santa Fe
• Albuquerque

NEW MEXICO TERRITORY
1861-1863

Oklahoma City •

Tulsa •

INDIAN TERRITORY
1861-1863

Little Rock •

ARKANSAS

MIS

Fort Worth • • Dallas

TEXAS

ARKANSAS

Austin •

San Antonio •

Houston •

Baton Rouge •

MEXICO

GUL

Courtesy Charles L. Blockson and Mark Mattson.

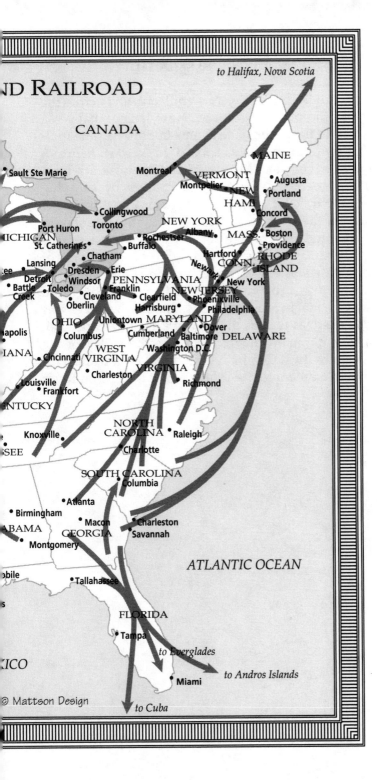

...ND RAILROAD

CANADA

to Halifax, Nova Scotia

- Sault Ste Marie
- Montreal
- Collingwood
- Port Huron
- Toronto
- St. Catherines
- Buffalo
- Chatham
- Lansing
- Dresden
- Erie
- Detroit
- Windsor
- Battle Creek
- Toledo
- Cleveland
- Oberlin
- Harrisburg
- Uniontown
- Columbus
- Cincinnati
- Louisville
- Frankfort
- Knoxville
- Charleston
- Richmond
- Raleigh
- Charlotte
- Columbia
- Atlanta
- Birmingham
- Macon
- Charleston
- Montgomery
- Savannah
- Tallahassee
- Tampa
- Miami

MICHIGAN

VERMONT
Montpelier

MAINE

NEW HAMP.
Concord

Augusta
Portland

NEW YORK
Albany

MASS. Boston
Providence

Rochester
Hartford
CONN.

RHODE ISLAND

Newark
New York

PENNSYLVANIA
Franklin
Clearfield
Phoenixville
NEW JERSEY
Philadelphia

OHIO
MARYLAND
Cumberland
Dover
Baltimore
DELAWARE
Washington D.C.

WEST VIRGINIA

VIRGINIA

KENTUCKY

TENNESSEE

NORTH CAROLINA

SOUTH CAROLINA

ALABAMA

GEORGIA

ATLANTIC OCEAN

FLORIDA

to Everglades
to Andros Islands
to Cuba

...ICO

© Mattson Design

ware and Schuylkill Rivers were significant, and across the Delaware in the port of Camden, New Jersey, many sea captains would flash signals to agents in Philadelphia indicating that they had fugitives aboard. In western Pennsylvania, the Allegheny and Monongahela Rivers, which form the Ohio, were waterways frequently used by escaping slaves. As the traveler crosses the Tappan Zee Bridge, the importance of the Hudson River in New York State should be kept in mind; the bridge itself was named after the abolitionist Tappan Family. Up through the Finger Lakes of New York State was a favorite route, and some slaves followed the northeast corridor of the St. Lawrence River into Montreal, Canada. In Massachusetts, the Charles River was commonly used, as well as the seaways around Cape Cod. Once in Canada, many slaves settled in the valley of the Thames, especially at Chatham, Dresden, London and Wilberforce, while others found refuge along the Huron River area.

CANADA

Former home of Josiah Henson (Uncle Tom) in Dresden, Ontario, Canada. Courtesy Uncle Tom's Cabin Museum.

Canada

Dresden, Canada
Uncle Tom's Cabin and Museum

Over the years thousands have been thrilled by the mesmerizing story of Josiah Henson, so trustworthy a slave that his owner made him an overseer, but who later became an advocate for people of African descent. Henson was at first so devoted to his owners that while transporting slaves in Kentucky, he resisted other's efforts to free them all. However, his master's plan to sell Henson's children was more than Henson could bear, and he made a daring escape from slavery with his entire family on the Underground Railroad to Canada. He later returned many times to the United States, leading slaves to the "Promised Land," where he had established a haven near the present town of Dresden. His plan was to give fugitive slaves an opportunity to learn self-supporting skills, and he visited England to raise money for his "Uncle Tom's British Institute," which became the first vocational school in Canada.

In the current museum building there is a collection of rare books and other items pertinent to the anti-slavery era. Displayed also is a signed portrait of Queen Victoria that was presented to Henson in 1877, on one of his trips to Great Britain. Harriet Beecher Stowe's character Uncle Tom in *Uncle Tom's Cabin* is reported to have been based upon Henson's Life.

Henson's fictional counterpart became a byword for servility in the usage of a later generation. Henson, who became a minister, died in 1883 at the age of 94. The Reverend Josiah Henson is buried with his family in the cemetery near the museum. On his gravestone are chiseled the words, "Uncle Tom."

Location: Dresden is located in Kent County, on No. 21 Highway, 70 miles from the American border at Detroit and 45 miles from the border at Port Huron, Michigan.

For more information contact:
Uncle Tom's Cabin Historic Site
P.O. Box 700
Curunna, ONT N0N 1G0
Canada
(519) 683-2978

Amherstburg, Canada
North American Black Historical Museum and Cultural Center

Amherstburg, adjacent to Fort Malden, was the most important of the refugee settlements, and in the 1820s fugitive slaves helped make it the center of a modest but flourshing Canadian tobacco culture. Amherstburg itself is situated in Canada's southernmost province, snuggled between Lake St. Clair and Lake Erie. Just south of Detroit, Michigan, was a route over which hundreds of fugitive slaves traveled to the "Promised Land." Even before the Underground Railroad was organized, Amherstburg served as a port of entry for escaped slaves during the War of 1812, when it was a British shipyard and naval base. Because the Detroit fugitive slave network was closely watched by slave hunters, some runaways were smuggled aboard river boats and carried to Canada. Other more daring fugitives risked everything and swam towards the Canadian shore.

Mary Ann Shadd (Cary), daughter of an African-American agent in Wilmington, Delaware, was a teacher and lecturer. She moved to Canada where she edited the Provincial Freeman. *After her marriage she became known as Mary Shadd Cary.*

Due to the increasing number of escaped slaves arriving in Amherstburg and vicinity, the Nazery African Methodist Episcopal Church was established in 1850. Many of the descendants of escaped slaves still live in Amherstburg. On display in the North American Black Historical Museum and Cultural Center is a wooden trunk, once used to ship a young slave girl from the United States across the Detroit River to freedom in Canada. The focus of the exhibitions in this museum is on the Underground Railroad and its influence on Canadian history.

Location: Amherstburg is 18 miles south of Windsor using Ontario Route 18. The museum is at:
271 King Street
P.O. Box 12
Amhersburg, Ontario
N4V 2C7

North Buxton, Canada
Raleigh Township Centennial Museum

According to the first report of the Anti-Slavery Society of Canada, there were 30,000 former slaves in the country in the 1850s. Most of them from the United States and most of them arrived via the Underground Railroad. Fugitives fled to Canada in 1850 as a result of the Fugitive Slave Law, which legalized their recapture and return to slavery regardless of where they were captured in the U.S. A large number of fugitive families settled in the Elgin settlement that had been founded by the Reverend William King, of Louisiana, who freed his slaves in 1849 and brought them to Canada. By 1862 more than 2,000 men, women and children lived in the community, which was then called North Buxton. Abraham D. Shadd, a free African-American Underground Railroad agent in Wilmington, Delaware, and West Chester, Pennsylvania, emigrated from Pennsylvania with his 13 children in 1851 and settled in North Buxton. Mary Ann, his attractive, fiery, Quaker-educated daughter, used her talent as a writer, editor, speaker, teacher and lawyer to promote the anti-slavery and women's suffrage causes. Shadd is credited with being the first woman in North America to establish and edit a weekly newspaper, *The Provincial Freedman*, whose offices were in North Buxton.

Mary Ann Shadd also published an important pamphlet, *A Plea for Emigration, or Notes on the Canada West in its Moral, Social and Political Aspect*, in 1852. A majority of families living in North Buxton today are descended from former slaves who elected to remain in Canada. A one-room school house and adjacent cemetery hold memories of these ancestors, while a museum founded in 1967 also preserves the Elgin settlement's rich Underground Railroad history.

Location: Village of North Buxton, Ontario, Canada, 4 miles to Bloomfield Road, south on Bloomfield, west on Eighth Concession, south on Country Road No. 6.
(519) 354-8693

St. Catherine, Canada
The British Methodist Episcopal Church: Salem Chapel

Canada was called the "Promised Land" by fugitive slaves because it held great promise for a better way of life, and the British Methodist Episcopal Church in St. Catherine has often been called the last stop on the Underground Railroad. The most famous Underground Railroad conductor, Harriet Tubman, who lived in St. Catherine from 1851 to 1858, was a member of this church when it was called Salem Chapel. Originally built in 1840 and located on Queenston Street, it was rebuilt in 1855 and has since been renamed the British Methodist Episcopal Church. Today there is a blue and gold historical marker located in front of the church building honoring the memory of Harriet Tubman. It reads as follows:

Harriet Ross Tubman

A legendary conductor on the Underground Railroad, Harriet Tubman became known as the "Moses of Her People." Tubman was born into slavery on a Maryland plantation and suffered brutal treatment from numerous owners before escaping in 1849. Over the next decade she returned to the American South many times and led hundreds of freedom seekers north. When the Fugitive Slave Act of 1850 allowed slave owners to recapture runaways in northern free states, Tubman extended her operation to the Canadian border. For eight years, she lived in St. Catherine and at one point rented a house in this neighborhood. With the outbreak of the Civil War, she returned to the United States to serve the Union.

The marker is written in English and French, and was erected by the Ontario Heritage Foundation, Ministry of Culture and Communication.

Location: Salem Chapel
92 Geneva Street
St. Catherine, ONT Canada
(905) 682-0993

Edgar, Canada
The African Episcopal Church

The area around Edgar in what is now known as Oro Township was noted for its gold and also for its slave trade. At one time this township or a portion of it was intended to be set apart as a colony for liberated slaves. To make the slaves feel at ease, the township was called Oro after the river Rio del Oro on the west coast of Africa; ironically, "oro" is the Spanish word for gold. A number of escaped slaves from the American South settled at Edgar; by 1828 about 28 fugitive slave families had made their homes in the area. Following the North Star, many of these self-emancipated slaves had found their way through the deep woodland to Oro, feeling for the moss that grew on the north side of the trees when the North Star could not be seen. James Dixon Thompson, who died in 1947, was the last escaped slave to live in Oro Township. The first regular minister of this community was the Reverend Ari Raymond, who supervised the building of the African Episcopal Church that served the community in 1849. There are several burial sites throughout the area.

Location: African Episcopal Church, Wilberforce Street, at Lot 11, Con. 4 Edgar, Oro Township

For further information contact:

    Colored Methodist Episcopal Church of Canada
    R.R. 2
    Oro Station, Ontario
    L0L 2E0

Sandwich, Canada
Sandwich First Baptist Church

Sandwich was another refugee settlement that arose out of the migration of escaped slaves. One of the first things slaves did when they reached freedom was build a church: the escaped slaves who settled in Sandwich made hundreds of bricks with clay from the Detroit River and in 1844 built

Sandwich First Baptist Church, which still stands not far from the river near Amherstburg. The Detroit River was clearly a powerful factor in the life of the community; during this mid-ninteenth century period members of the congregation were baptized in it. Most of those who came over the border brought with them nothing but the clothes on their backs, and border communities were faced with the serious problem of providing food, shelter and whatever further assistance they could. Churches were an obvious focal point for such charitable commitment, and Sandwich First Baptist Church was known as such a stop on the Underground Railroad. This area became home to many of the most daring and courageous escaped slaves. Buried in the St. Catherine cemetery is the Reverend Anthony Burns, hero of the Boston Riots of 1854. He was the subject of one of the most violent and costly fugitive slave rescues in the history of the Underground Railroad.

Not far away in Essex County, Henry Bibbs, also a former fugitive slave, became editor of anti-slavery newspaper, *The Voice of the Fugitive*, and later wrote a popular narrative describing his escape to Canada. Both Burns and Bibbs visited Sandwich First Baptist Church.

Location: 3652 Peter Street, Windsor
Ontario, CANADA
(519) 252-4917

Maidstone, Canada
John Freeman Walls Historic Site and Underground Railroad Museum

The Walls family site is still owned and operated by the descendants of John Freeman Walls, an escaped slave from Rockingham County, North Carolina. Walls fell in love with and married his late owner's Scotch-Irish wife, and with her and their children fled to Canada. He purchased land in 1846 and built a log cabin, now restored, that is the centerpiece for the historic site. Although it is located in Canada, the log cabin once served as a station of the Underground Railroad because some slave owners and slave hunters were known to travel to Canada to recapture their human property. Slaves were hidden within the stone walls of the hideaway cellar.

John Freeman Walls was a multi-talented individual: a skilled carpenter, he was also the first man to introduce tobacco to this part of Canada, and he also planted apple orchards.

Today, in a clearing, a sign that indicates the exact number of miles escaped slaves walked from various states serves as a reminder to visitors of how desperately slaves wanted freedom. Visitors are led along a wooded path, where for verisimilitude sounds of vicious dogs pulling on leashes held by slave hunters can be heard. John Freeman Walls' flight to freedom is recounted by Dr. Bryant Walls in his book, *The Road That Led Somewhere*.

Location: John Freeman Walls Historic Site and
            Underground Railroad Museum are located
            eight miles east of the Windsor-Detroit border
            in Maidstone Township, a mile north on Puce
            Road after exiting off Route 401.

Contact: Allen E. Walls
            1307 Pelissier Street
            Windsor, Ontario, Canada
            N8X 1M4
            (519) 258-6253

Chatham, Canada
The First Baptist Church

Founded by fugitive slaves in 1841, the First Baptist Church was where John Brown drew up a new government that he dreamed would follow his attack on the Harpers Ferry arsenal, some time before he actually marched to his apotheosis along the route used by escaped slaves. After meeting with Harriet Tubman in Ingersoll, near St. Catherine, Canada, Brown organized a convention with prominent American and Canadian black abolitionists. In the First Baptist Church, Brown drafted his *Provisional Constitution for the People of the United States* in 1858. Only seven copies of this rare and tremendously important document have survived. Mary Ann Shadd, who was present at this historic meeting, assisted with its writing. Dr. Martin R. Delaney, the Harvard-educated militant Underground Railroad agent, was also present at the convention. Brown believed that he and his followers could organize a slave insurrection and destroy the American institution of slavery. When Brown was hanged for his attack on Harpers Ferry, Harriet Tubman took his execution very seriously and later proclaimed, "John Brown was one of the greatest emancipators of his people."

A simple wooden table around which Brown and his fellow conspirators met is still on display here. Throughout the church, John Brown's tumultuous spirit seems to reside. A plaque in the church commemorates the convention. This church will be open for tours in April, 1994.

Location: 135 King Street East, Chatham
             Ontario, Canada
             (519) 352-9553
Tour Information:
             Toni Addy
             Chatham Tourist Bureau
             c/o City Call
             Sixth Street
             Chatham, Ontario
             CANADA
             (519) 354-6125

Chatham, Canada
Chatham-Kent Museum

Most of the fugitive slaves who inhabited Chatham departed after the Civil War, while those who stayed blended into its society. Scarred by branding irons, bullwhips and shackles, Chatham's ancestors eluded brutal slave hunters and bloodhounds to get there and to other Canadian settlements. Hundreds of others died in the attempt to reach "Canaan," as Canada was referred to by some of them. Chatham became known as the Canadian capital for fugitive slaves.

For some escaped slaves, however, Canada was not the "haven" that they had sung about. This is how one fugitive expressed his feelings upon his arrival: "There is not a town in Canada, in which the feelings against Negroes is stronger than in Chatham. Most of the white settlers in Chatham were low, degraded persons, in early and former life. They are the Negro-haters. The more gentlemanly, as true almost everywhere, treat blacks according to their character and position." This statement is recorded in Benjamin Drew's *A North-Side View of Slavery: The Refugee, Or the Narratives of Fugitive Slaves in Canada, Related by Themselves*, published in 1856. Drew gathered information at random as he journeyed through Canadian cities. During his travels he managed to transcribe the oral narratives of some 117 fugitives.

The Chatham-Kent Museum displays exhibitions centering around refugee communities of former escaped slaves.
Location: 59 William Street North, Chatham, Ontario, about
            60 miles from Detroit, Michigan
            (519) 354-8338

Niagara-on-the-Lake, Canada
Parliament Oak School

The first person of African descent to enter Canada was a young slave boy named Olivier Le Jeune who came in 1628. However, it was not until the early 1700s that the French transported other slaves into what was then called New France. When the British won control of Canada in 1759, Canadians were still holding Africans in bondage.

In 1792, Chloe Cooley, an African-Canadian slave girl

Lieutenant-Governor John
Graves Simcoe of
Upper Canada.

Dr. Alexander Ross of Toronto,
Canada.

who was the property of William Vrooman of Queenston,
resisted violently when she learned that her owner had sold
her to an American across the Niagara River. She was still
screaming and resisting when she was delivered to her new
owner. As a result of the Chloe Cooley slave incident, Lieutenant Governor John Graves Simcoe led the Executive
Council of Ontario to pass the Imperial Act of 1793, which
outlawed the importation of slaves into Upper Canada.

Lieutenant Governor John Graves Simcoe, to whom much
of the credit for the foundation of Upper Canada belongs,
left as one of his most important legacies the Imperial Act
of 1793. It provided for the gradual abolition of slavery in
Upper Canada, and no more slaves were introduced to
Niagara-on-the-Lake. It was followed by the Abolition Act
of 1833, which terminated slavery in Canada 30 years before
Lincoln's Emancipation Proclamation was to do the same in

the United States. As a result of the Act of 1793, a substantial number of fugitive slaves from the United States sought safety behind Canada's humanitarian policies. At first the numbers arriving were small, but they increased with each decade, reaching their greatest volumes in the 1840s and particularly the 1850s after the passing of the Fugitive Slave Law. A plaque on the grounds of the Parliament Oak School, the site where Simcoe signed the Imperial Act into existence, bears a relief depicting the historic scene.

Location:　Parliament Oak School
　　　　　　325 King Street
　　　　　　Niagara-on-the-Lake, Ontario
　　　　　　(416) 468-3912

Dartmouth, Canada
Black Cultural Centre for Nova Scotia

Nova Scotia has a long and interesting history of harboring people of African descent. During the Revolutionary War, Lord Dunmore, the British Royal Governor of Virginia, promised freedom to all slaves who would leave their owners and join the King's forces. When the British were defeated, several hundred blacks fled on vessels bound for Nova Scotia. These men and women who remained loyal to the British were called "Black Loyalists." Many found Nova Scotia's winters harsh and farming difficult, and did not stay; however, those who remained were the progenitors of today's black Nova Scotian community. Following this first immigration by people of African descent, 600 Jamaican Maroons arrived in 1796. The third influx occurred when fugitive slaves arrived between 1812 and 1820.

The Underground Railroad into Nova Scotia has until recently been Canada's best-kept secret. Although the largest number of these destitute escaped slaves was settled at Preston and Hammond Plains, other terminals of emigration were established in Guysborough, Lincolnville, Tracadie, Milford Haven and Boylston. In these locations today

there are people who are able to trace their roots to escapees on the Underground Railroad. Memorabilia and documents relating to Nova Scotia's early history and the Underground Railroad may be seen at the Black Cultural Centre.
Location: No. 7 Highway at Cherrybrook Road
For further information contact:
        Robert French
        Program and Marketing
        or
        Mr. Henry Bishop
        Curator
        Black Cultural Centre
        P.O. Box 2128
        East Dartmouth, Nova Scotia
        B2Y 3Y2
        1-800-465-0767
        (902) 434-6223
For further Canadian touring information contact:
        Devara Goodman
        Footloose Tours, Inc.
        2126 W. Newport Pike Ste. 203
        Wilmington, DE 19804
        (302) 994-9451
        1-800-433-4212

STEAL AWAY TO JESUS

Steal a-way, steal a-way, steal a-way to Je-sus!

Steal a-way, steal a-way home, I ain't got long to stay here!

My Lord calls me, He calls me by the thun-der;
Green trees are bend-ing, Poor sin-ner stands a-trem-bling;
Tomb stones are burst-ing, Poor sin-ner stands a-trem-bling;
My Lord calls me, He calls me by the light-ning,

(die away)

The trum-pet sounds with-in-a my soul, I ain't got long to stay here.

Songs of the Underground Railroad

For those travelers who would like to experience the sense of community and the full spirit of the Underground Railroad, there are a number of coded spirituals that could give them the feeling of the adventure as they are traveling between sites.

These coded spirituals conveyed every hidden signal imaginable, signals for escaping, hiding, and expressing danger. Slaves used the Bible as a source for the religious interpretation of lyrics, when singing innocent seeming spirituals. One song, for example, "Steal Away," was an obvious invitation to the slave to steal way to freedom.

> *Steal away, steal away*
> *Steal away to Jesus*
> *Steal away, steal away*
> *I ain't got long to stay here*

Harriet Tubman, the noted Underground Railroad conductor, composed her original spiritual:

> *Lie de friends of endless days*
> *Dark and thorny is the path,*
> *Where the Pilgrim make his way*
> *But beyond this vale of sorrow*

"Swing Low, Sweet Chariot," the song, beloved by Har-

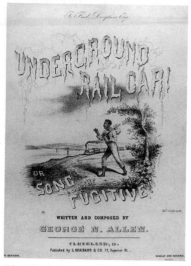

The Fugitive's Song, dedicated to Frederick Douglass was sung at many anti-slavery meetings.

The Underground Rail Car was a popular song sung by abolitionists and other friends of freedom.

riet Tubman was sung by her friends the evening that she died March 10, 1913.

Frederick Douglass once said, "A keen observer might have detected [Canada] in our repeated singing of: O' Canaan, sweet Canaan, I am bound for the land of Canaan."

"Follow the Drinking Gourd," for example was a metaphoric allusion to the Big Dipper and North Star. Knowledge of the North Star was shared by most slaves. This traditional spiritual served as a map for escaping slaves.

Slaves took advantage of every possible opportunity to escape from bondage, and when their owners deployed packs of bloodhound dogs to track them down, fellow slaves alerted them to the oncoming peril so that they could elude their would-be captors by singing:

Wade in the water
Wade in the water children
Wade in the water
God's gonna trouble the water

The time of the meeting and plans for escape were coded in the verses of many spirituals:

Let us break bread together on our knees
When I fall on my knees
With my face to the rising sun
O Lord have mercy, if you please.

On the eve of the planned escape, when fear engulfed them, these words gave courage as well as dignity to the possibility of death.

Sinner please don't let this harvest pass
and die and lose your soul at last.

Those who remained in slavery would have been consoled by such spirituals as "You'd Better Get Ready"; "Go Where I Send Thee, Deep River"; "The Gospel Train is Coming"; "I have a Robe"; "Go Down Moses"; "There is a Highway to Heaven, Oh, Sinners, You'd Better Get Ready"; "Good News, de Chariot's Coming"; and "I Hear from Heaven To-Day"; "This Train; and "Many Thousands Gone."

The song "John Brown's Body" is recommended when visiting Harpers Ferry, West Virginia and his grave at North Elba, Near Lake Placid, New York.

Upon reaching their final destination, they sang the spirituals "Great Day" and the soul stirring words of "Amazing Grace."

If books about African-American spirituals and slave songs are not found in bookstores; they should be available for copying in local libraries.

Chatham Hill Games produces an adventure game and music cassette set entitled "The Underground Railroad

Game and Songs." For more information about the set contact:

Chatham Hill Games
P.O. Box 253
Chatham, NY 12037

Suggested Reading for Slave Songs and Spirituals

Allens, William, Ware, Charles, and Garrison, Lucy McKim, eds. *Slave Songs of the United States.* New York, 1867; modern paperback ed. with arrangements by Irving Schlein, New York, 1965.

Barton, William F. *Old Plantation Hymns,* Boston, 1899.

Douglass, Fredrick. *The Narrative of the Life of Frederick Douglass.* Boston, 1845, New York, 1969.

Fisher, Miles. *Negro Slave Songs in the United States.* Ithaca, New York, 1953.

Frances, Mary and Ludlow, Helen. *Hampton and Its Students with Fifty Cabin and Plantation Songs,* arranged by Thomas P. Fenner (New York, 1874).

Higginson, Thomas Wentworth. "Negro Spirituals." *Atlantic Monthly Magazine* (1867), *Army Life in a Black Regiment,* Boston, 1870; reprinted New York 1962.

Johnson, James Weldon and Johnson, J. Rosamond. *The Book of American Negro Spirituals and the Second Book of Negro Spirituals.* New York, 1925, 1926, issued in one volume, New York, 1969.

Lomax, John A. and Lomax, Alan, eds. *Folk Songs; U.S.A.* New York.

Marsh, J.B. *The Story of the Jubilee Singers, with Their Songs.* (Boxton, 1880).

Odum, Howard W., and Johnson, Guy B. *The Negro and His Songs.* Chapel Hill, 1925.

Parrish, Lydia. *Slave Songs of the Georgia Sea Islands.* New York, 1942, 1965.

Southern, Eileen. *The Music of Black America*. New York, 1971.

Work, John Wesley and Work, Fredrick J. *Folk Songs of the American Negro*. Nashville, 1907.

Work, John Wesley. *American Negro Songs and Spirituals*. New York, 1940.

GIT ON BOARD, LITTLE CHILLEN

Arranged by Lawrence Brown

To Laura J. Heathfield

board, lit-tle chil-len, Dere's room for ma-ny a mo', De fare is cheap, an' all can go, De

rich an' poor are dere,— No sec-ond class a-board dis train, No

diff-runce in de fare. Git on board, lit-tle chil-len, Git on board, lit-tle chil-len, Git on

board, lit-tle chil-len, Dere's room for ma-ny a mo'.____

The Ballad

of the Underground Railroad

Charles Blockson and James McGowan

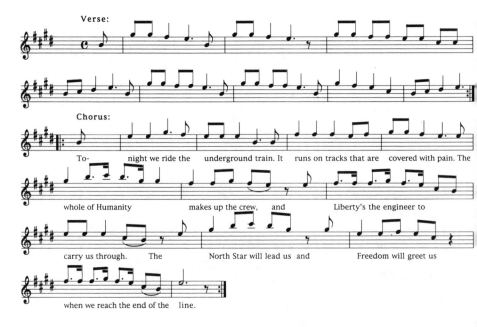

Repeat chorus after every 3 verses.
Music arranged by B. David Krivit.

THE BALLAD OF THE UNDERGROUND RAILROAD

by Charles L. Blockson

The Underground Train,
Strange as it seems,
Carried many passengers
And never was seen.

It wasn't made of wood,
It wasn't made of steel;
A man-made train that
Ran without wheels.

The train was known
By many a name.
Bu the greatest of all
Was "The Freedom Train."

The Quakers, the Indians,
Gentiles and Jews,
Were some of the people
Who made up the crews.

Free Blacks and Christians
And Atheists, too,
Were the rest of the people
Who made up the crews.

Conductors and agents
Led the way at night,
Guiding the train
By the North Star Light.

The passengers were
The fugitive slaves
Running from slavery
And its evil ways.

Running from the whip
And the overseer,
From the slave block
And the Auctioneer.

They didn't want their masters
To catch them again,
So the men dressed as women
And the women as men.

They hid in churches,
Cellars and barns,
Waiting to hear the
Train's alarm.

Sleeping by day,
And traveling by night,
Was the best way they knew
To keep out of sight.

They waded in the waters
To hide their scent,
And fool those bloodhounds
The slavemasters sent.

They spoke in riddles
And sang in codes,
To understand the message,
You had to be told.

Those who knew the secret
Never did tell
The sacred message
Of the "Freedom Train's" bell.

Riding this train
Broke the laws of the land,
But the laws of God
Are higher than man's.

THE UNDERGROUND RAILROAD

O, WASN'T DAT A WIDE RIVER?

Arranged by J. Rosamond Johnson

Following Harriet Tubman's Trail: A Suggested Tour

In the years since my Underground Railroad article appeared in the *National Geographic Magazine* in 1984, many people have come to me requesting self-guided tours. To my mind, the most exciting and historically informative tour is to follow Harriet Tubman's most frequently used route from the Delmarva Peninsula to St. Catherines, Canada.

Starting at Bucktown in Dorchester County, Maryland, where Tubman was born into slavery on the Edward Brodas plantation, the traveler can go up the Choptank River to Cambridge, still in Dorchester County, an area that still preserves its untouched scenic tranquility. It must be much like the plantation fields and woods that Tubman knew.

Still following the Choptank, the next step would be from Cambridge to Camden, Delaware, and from there up through Dover, Smyrna, Blackbird and Odessa. While passing through Odessa, Delaware, Tubman often stopped at the little red brick Friends' Meetinghouse that still stands today on Main Street.

Moving through Delaware City and Newcastle, she went on to Wilmington, Delaware, to the station at the home of her Quaker friend, the noted Thomas Garret. Although his house has not survived, there is a historical marker dedicated to him at Peter Spencer Plaza on French Street between Eighth and Ninth Streets.

From Wilmington, Tubman came through Chester County, Pennsylvania, stopping at the Hosanna A.U.M.P. Church, bordering the property of Lincoln University, and on into the Kennett Square area where she had many allies. Many of the homes that were most heavily involved in the Underground Railroad are now in private hands, but at Longwood Gardens Meetinghouse there is a museum that tells the story of Harriet Tubman's journey, with further Underground Railroad information. In front of the Longwood Gardens Meetinghouse is a graveyard where many of the Chester County conductors are buried. For further information on Longwood Gardens, see the text entry for the Brandywine Valley Tourist Information Center.

Moving from Chester County to Philadelphia, Tubman stayed with friends in the free black community such as William Still, Robert Purvis and Frances Ellen Watkins Harper. A historical marker is located at the former site of Still's house at 244 South Twelfth Street, while Mother Bethel A.M.E. Church at South and Lombard Streets was a reliable haven for Tubman and other agents, and gives tours by appointment.

From Philadelphia, the next leg of the journey was to New York City which may now be taken via Lawnside, in Camden County, New Jersey (where the Still family resides and the Peter Mott home still stands), and on up the New Jersey Turnpike. In New York, the visitor can stop at the A.M.E. Zion Church at 140 West 136th Street in Harlem, which had a rich tradition of involvement in the Underground Railroad, although this is not the site that Harriet Tubman knew. While in Harlem, the traveler should explore the Schomburg Research Center at 103 West 135th Street, which has the world's largest collection of information pertaining to people of African-American descent, as well as Sylvia's Soul Food Restaurant at Lenox Avenue and 126th Street, which serves the traditional food that Tubman and her passengers would have been familiar with. There are many soul food kitchens in the New York City vicinity—try as many as possible.

The trail continues along the Hudson River to Albany, then up to Troy, New York, where a marker at First and State Streets commemorates Tubman's involvement in the violent rescue of Charles Nalle from an adjacent building. From Troy, Tubman moved on through Schnectady to Peterboro, Canandaigua, Oneida and Syracuse. All these towns are located in the scenic Finger Lakes region. The tiny town of Peterboro in particular is full of associations with the Underground Railroad and the abolition movement, especially the museum, which is open by appointment. Further on, in Syracuse, there is a statue dedicated to Jerry McHenry, an escaped slave, at Clinton and West Water Streets.

After Syracuse, the road leads toward Auburn and Harriet Tubman's home, which she purchased in later years for her parents. It is now operated as a museum with information and memorabilia about her activities, although it was never a station on the Railroad. Be sure to ask the curator about the little church in which she worshipped and her gravesite.

Leaving Auburn, the trail continues to Rochester, the last major stop in the United States. Although the home of Tubman's close friend, Frederick Douglass, no longer stands, there is a monument on Central Avenue and St. Paul Street that commemorates his endeavors. While in Rochester, Tubman was also very likely to visit the home of her friend Susan B. Anthony, which is located at 177 Madison Street. From Rochester, she went on to Buffalo, where the weary traveler, then as now, can look across Lake Erie to Canada, the Promised Land.

Next is the city of Niagara Falls. In her day, Tubman led her passengers across the old suspension bridge that is now called the Whirlpool Bridge into St. Catherines, Canada. This was her last stop, where she gave thanks at the Salem Chapel Church that still can be seen at 92 Geneva Street, at the corner of North Street.

Underground Railroad Tour Organizations

For further information about African-American tours contact:

Brandywine Valley Tourist Information Center
Includes displays, exhibits and information pertaining to the Underground Railroad in Chester County, Pennsylvania.
Located at the entrance to Longwood Gardens
Route 1
Kennet Square, Pennsylvania 19348
(215) 388-2900

Marquetta Goodwine
Extended Kinship Appeal Inc./
Afrikan Kultural Arts Network
P.O. Box 40-0199
Brooklyn, New York 11240-0199
(212) 439-1026

Friends of Frederick Douglass
Dr. Juanita Pitts
353 West Avenue
Rochester, New York 14611
(716) 328-7866

Capitol Entertainment Services, Inc.
Attn. Vinnie Best
3629 18th Street NE
Washington, DC 20018
(202) 636-9203

Le'Obs Tours
Attn: Lucille Le'Obia
4625 Touro Street
New Orleans, Louisiana 70122
(504) 288-3478

Soul Journey Enterprises, Inc.
Attn: Ron Powell/Bill Cunningham
235 Ben Franklin Station
Washington, DC 20044
(202) 337-5132

Cline Transportation Service, Ltd.
Attn. Linda Cline
Post Office Box 552
Malden, Massachusetts 02148
(617) 322-3998

Douyon
Afro-American Tours
339 South 2nd Street
Philadelphia, PA 19106
(215) 925-4136

Kevin Contrell & Denise Easterling, Directors
Motherland Connection
P.O. Box 564
2815 Highland Avenue
Niagara Falls, New York, 14305
(716) 282-3501
(716) 278-1773

Norman E. Jones - Cultivator
The Art of Living, Inc.
Christopher Columbus Station
P.O. Box 151515
Columbus, Ohio 43215-8515
Has information on Underground Railroad
sites in Columbus, Ohio (614) 258-9035

The Harriet Tubman Coalition, Inc.
P.O. Box 1164
Cambridge, Maryland 21613-5169
(410) 228-0401

Laise International Inc.
501 Fifth Avenue
New York, New York 10017
(212) 922-1522

Tuxedo Tours
Diane Gordon
2050 Cataract
Fonthill, Ontario, Canada LOS 1E6
(416) 682-0431

The Road That Led to Freedom
African-American Heritage Tour is operated
by Group Travel Designers Inc.

Donna Spiner
Group Travel Designers, Inc.
1812 W. Pershing Rd.
Chicago, Illinois 60609
(312) 927-7676.

For site information in Windsor contact the Convention
and Visitors Bureau of Windsor, Essex County, Canada
333 Riverside Dr. West
Suite 103
Windsor, Ontario, Canada
N9A 5K4
1-800-265-3633

Detroit Upbeat Tours
18430 Fairway Dr.
Detroit, Michigan 48221
Contact: Tim Dagg
(313) 341-6810

A.M. DATA Systems
Contact: Shirley Wilcox
(609) 845-3750

Footloose Tours Inc.
Contact: Sharon Walklett
2126 W. Newport Pike
Ste. 203
Wilmington, Delaware 19804
(302) 994-9451 or
(800) 433-4212

Black Cultural Center for Nova Scotia
P.O. Box 2128 East
Dartmouth, Novia Scotia, Canada
B2W 3Y2
(902) 434-6223

Underground Railroad
P.O. Box 1136
Madison, Tennessee 37116-1136
Attention: UMARU Jutte
(615) 868-1997

Kevin Cottrell
Denise Easterline
New State Park
Prospect Park
P.O. Box 1132
Niagara Falls, New York 14303-0132
(716) 278-1773

For Free (or low-cost) Information

Many states provide free or low cost information regarding African-American related cultural museums, local sites to see, and activities. Not all may be connected to the history of the Underground Railroad, but do provide one of a kind information.

The Insider's Guide to African-American Atlanta
>This is a two-paneled color fold-out with today's hot spots and historic and cultural sites. It costs $3.95 plus .95 cents to cover postage.
>Treadwell Travel Enterprizes
>441 W. 24th Street
>New York, NY 10011

African-American Heritage Brochure (free)
>Baltimore Area Convention and
>Visitors Association
>300 W. Pratt Street
>Baltimore, MD 21201
>1-800-282-6632 or (410) 837-4636

Preserving the Legacy (free)
>Georgia Department of Industry,
>Trade, and Tourism
>Box 1776
>Atlanta, GA 30301
>1-800-847-4842

Illinois Generations (free)
>From the Illinois Department of Tourism
>1-800-727-0630

Philadelphia's Guide to African-American Historical and Cultural Sites (free)
    Philadelphia Convention and Visitors Center
    16th and JFK Boulevard
    Philadelphia, PA 19102
    1-800-537-7676 or (215) 636-1666

To Walk the Whole Journey: African-American Resources in South Carolina (free)
    South Carolina Department of Parks,
    Recreation, and Tourism
    Box 71
    Columbia, SC 29202
    (803) 734-0235

The Roots of Tennessee (free)
    Tennessee Department of Tourist Development
    Box 23170
    Nashville, TN 37202
    1-800-636-8100

AFRICAN-AMERICAN ANTI-SLAVERY NEWSPAPERS

In connection with the anti-slavery movement a number of papers were published by African-Americans. A list of papers published by African-Americans before the Civil War follows:

Name	City	Date of lst Issue
Freedom's Journal	New York, N.Y.	March 30, 1827
Rights of All	New York, N.Y.	March 28, 1828
The Weekly Advocate	New York, N.Y.	Jan. — 1837
Colored American		March 4, 1837
(*Weekly Advocate* changes to) *National Reformer*	Philadelphia, PA	Sept. — 1838
African Methodist Episcopal Church Magazine	Albany, N.Y.	Sept. — 1841
The Elevator	Philadelphia, PA	1842
The National Watchman	Troy, N.Y.	1842
The Clarion	Troy, N.Y.	1842
The Peoples Press	New York, N.Y.	1843
The Northern Star	Philadelphia, PA	
The Mystery	Pittsburg, PA	1843
(*Northern Star* changes to) *The Genius of Freedom*	—	1845
The Rams Horn	New York, N.Y.	Jan. l, 1847

The North Star	Rochester, N.Y.	Nov. 1, 1847
The Imperial Citizen	Boston, Mass.	1848
The Christian Herald	Philadelphia, PA	1848
The Colored Man's Journal	New York, NY	1851
The Alienated American	Cleveland, Ohio	1852
The Paladium of Liberty	Columbus, Ohio	
The Disfranchised American	Cincinnati, Ohio	
The Colored Citizen		
(The *Disfranchised American* changes to)		
The Christian Recorder	Philadelphia, PA	1852
(*Christian Herald* changes to)		
The Mirror of the Times	San Francisco, Cal.	1855
The Herald of Freedom	Ohio	1855
The Angelo African	New York, N.Y.	July 23, 1859

GLOSSARY

Abduction Network—A group of citizens protecting fugitives.

Abolitionist— A person who demanded the immediate emancipation of the slaves.

Active Committee, The—another name for the Vigilance Committee.

Agent—A person who plotted the course of escape for fugitive slaves.

American Colonization Society—This society was founded in 1816 with idea of establishing free African-Americans in a land of their own in Africa. A colony was established in Liberia. In fact, many African-Americans did return to the motherland, while others opposed the plan.

Amistad— A Spanish word meaning "friendship," the term was made famous in America during the *Amistad* Mutiny Slave Case in 1839. The Amistad Research Center, located at Tulane University in New Orleans, Louisiana, uses a relief of the boat for its logo, as does the Amistad Press. The Research Center houses one of the largest collections of African-American archives, dating from the 1700s to the present.

Antebellum—Events taking place before the Civil War.

Baggage—A code word used for escaping slaves.

Black Grapevine—A method of communication in the black community.

Bondage—The institution of slavery.

Brakeman—A person in charge of making contacts for fugitive slaves.

Christiana Resistance—Events that occurred in September 1851, in Christiana, Lancaster County, Pennsylvania, when a Maryland slaveowner confronted and demanded the return of his escaped slave. The slaveowner was killed by a member of the local African-American slave-defense organization.

Conductor—The person who directly transported escaping slaves.

Creole Code—A mixing of French, Spanish and African coded language used by escaping slaves on the Underground Railroad. The term is generally associated with Louisiana.

Drinking Gourd, The—A code term for the North Star.

Emancipation Car, The—A name for the Underground Railroad.

Emancipation Proclamation—On January 1, 1863, President Abraham Lincoln declared that all those slaves residing in territory that was in rebellion against the Federal government were free, "as a fit and necessary war measure for suppressing said rebellion."

Flying Bondsmen—A number of escaping slaves.

Forwarding—Taking fugitive slaves from station to station.

Freedom Line, The—Another name for the Underground Railroad.

Freedom Road—The fugitives' route of travel.

Freedom Train—A term used to describe the Underground Railroad.

French Leave—A secret departure without paying one's debts.

Friends of Liberty—A group of people who worked for emancipation.

Fugitive Slave—A runaway slave.

Fugitive Slave Law of 1850—The law provided that any federal marshal who did not arrest on demand an alleged fugitive slave might be fined one thousand dollars. Anyone obstructing the recovery of a fugitive slave or assisting a fugitive slave to escape was liable to a fine of one thousand dollars and a prison sentence of six months. The law gave slaveowners the power to organize a posse at any point in the United States to aid them in recovering their slaves.

Go Free—Code word used by runaway slaves.

God's Poor—A term used by Thomas Garrett for escaping slaves.

Gospel Train, The—A name for the Underground Railroad.

Grand Central Station—A major station.

Guineas—People of African descent sold into slavery from the coast of Guinea. During the period of slavery some free black communities were called Guineatown, Guinea Hill and Guinea Run. Some of these communities still exist.

Gullah—A person who mixes English words and syntax with those from the Caribbean and especially West Africa to create a speech that is all but incomprehensible to outsiders. This tongue, sometimes called "Geechee" is still spoken in the Sea Islands of South Carolina and Georgia.

Harpers Ferry—Formerly in Virginia and a part of West Virginia since the Civil War, Harpers Ferry is located in the easternmost section of the state on bluffs at the confluence of the Potomac and Shenandoah Rivers. Harpers Ferry was the scene of John Brown's famous raid in 1859.

Haven—A place of shelter for escaping slaves.

Heaven—A code word for Canada.

Homestead Act—Passed by the United States Congress in 1862, the act allowed the U.S. government to sell land to settlers in the West for the acquisition of revenue. As the West became politically stronger, however, pressure was increased on Congress to guarantee free land to settlers. The Homestead Act was sponsored by Gulusha A. Grow of Pennsylvania.

Illegal Caravans—Groups of fugitive slaves.

Imperial Act of 1793—In 1792, Chloe Cooley, an African-Canadian slave girl who was the property of William Vrooman of Queenston, resisted violently when she learned that her owner had sold her to an American across the Niagara River. She was still screaming and resisting when she was delivered to her new owner. As a result of the Chloe Cooley slave incident, Lieutenant Governor John Graves Simcoe led the Executive Council of Ontario to pass the Imperial Act of 1793, which outlawed the importation of slaves into Upper Canada. It was followed by the Abolition Act of 1833, which terminated slavery in Canada.

John Brown's Trail—A route of travel for fugitives.

Juba—An African name given to female slaves, it was also the name of a dance done by slaves and free African-Americans in which hands, knees and thighs are clapped in a rhythmic pattern.

Jumping Off Place—A place of shelter for fugitives.

Jumping the Broom—Enslaved Africans were denied the right to marry by their owners, so an engaged couple would literally jump a broom as a spiritual gesture announcing their commitment to each other.

Juneteenth—An African-American independence day celebration of the Emancipation Proclamation. Although President Lincoln signed the document on January 1, 1863, sections of the Southwest did not receive the news until June 19th, 1863. Juneteenth is a state holiday in Texas and is celebrated primarily in the Southwest.

Lightning Train, The—A name for the Underground Railroad.

Lines—Routes of Travel used by fugitive slaves.

Load of Potatoes—A code to indicate a wagon of fugitives hidden under the produce.

Make Free—Escaping to freedom.

Maroon—A runaway slave; when the fugitive lived with other escaped slaves, the settlement was called a "maroon" community.

GLOSSARY

Mason-Dixon Line—Boundary between Pennsylvania and Maryland popularly designated as the boundary dividing the slave states from the free. Named for surveyors Charles Mason and Jeremiah Dixon.

Middle Passage, The—The route of travel between slavery and freedom to the North.

Mulatto—Spanish term derived from the word for mule, meaning a half-breed, a person with white and black or mixed parentage.

Mysterious Tracks—A name for the Underground Railroad.

Nigger Stealer—A term used by slavewoners for Underground Railroad workers.

Operator—A person who aided fugitive slaves as a conductor or agent on the Underground Railroad.

Overflow Stations—Places of hiding for a number of slaves.

Passengers—Escaping slaves.

Patrollers—Southerners who guarded roads against escaping slaves.

Pilot—A person serving as a guide for runaways.

Preachers, Cows and Courthouse—Code words for conductors, fugitives and a station.

Prison House, The—Term for slavery, especially in the South.

Promised Land, The—Code word for Canada.

Puttin' De Mouth On a Person—Many slaves placed a curse or worked voodoo on their owners for the cruelty they experienced during slavery.

Puttin' On Ole Massa—Making fun of or practicing deception on the slaveholder, as did many slaves in dealing with their owners.

Railroad, The—Code for the Underground Railroad.

Railroad Telegraphy—Term for Underground Railroad.

Rufugees—Escaping slaves.

Safe House—Hiding place for escaped slaves.

Sanctuary—A place of hiding.

Scattered Way Stations—A number of hiding places.

Shepherds—People who enticed slaves to escape.

Society of Friends—A religious body whose members are commonly called Quakers. The organization of this society includes meetings of worship and monthly, quarterly and yearly meetings.

Soul Food—Food handed down from the days of slavery to the present generation of African Americans. Soul food cooking consists of collard greens, wild rice, fried cabbage, chitterlings, ham, chicken, pigs feet, cornbread, grits, black-eyed peas, sweet potato pie and ash cake.

Slave Haven—A settlement of fugitive slaves.

Star Pointed North, A—Code word for the North Star.

Station—A place of sanctuary where slaves could be sheltered.

Stationmaster—A person in charge of a hiding place.

Stockholder—A person contributing food, clothing or money to the Underground Railroad.

Stop and Start—A place of shelter for fugitive slaves.

Ticket Office—A station on the Underground Railroad.

Trackless Train, The—Another name for the Underground Railroad.

Travelers—Runaway slaves.

"The wind blows from the South today"—A warning to Underground Railroad workers that fugitive slaves were present in the area.

Underground Railroad or Railway—A method of trasporting fugitive slaves.

Underground Railroad Managers—People who worked on the Underground Railroad.

Way Stations—Hiding place for fugitive slaves.

Bibliography

Aptheker, Herbert. *A Documentary History of the Negro People.* Secaucus, NJ: Citadel Press, 1973.

Bearse, Austin. *Reminiscences of a Fugitive: Slave Law Days.* Boston: Warren Richardson, 1880.

Bennett, Jr., Lerone. *Wade In The Water.* Chicago, Ill. Johnson Publishing Co., 1979.

Blackett, R.J.M. *Building an Antislavery Wall.* Baton Rouge, LA: Louisiana State University Press, 1983.

Blassingame, John W., ed. *Slave Testimony.* Baton Rouge, LA: Louisianna State University Press, 1983.

Blockson, Charles L. "Escape from Slavery: The Underground Railroad, "*National Geographic,* July 1984, pp. 3-39.

Blockson, Charles L. *The Underground Railroad First Person Narratives of Escapes to Freedom in the North.* New York, Prentice Hall Press, 1987.

Boyer, Richard O. *The Legend of John Brown.* New York: Alfred A Knopf, 1973.

Brandford, Sarah H. *Harriet, the Moses of Her People.* New York: J.J. Little, 1901.

Buckmaster, Henrieta. *Let My People Go.* New York: Harper & Brothers, 1941.

Chace, Elizabeth Buffum, and Lovell, Luch Buffum. *Two Quaker Sisters: Diaries of Elizabeth Chace and Lucy B. Lovell.* New York: Liveright, 1937.

Child, Lydia Maria. *Isaac T. Hopper.* Boston: J.P. Jewett & Co., 1853.

Conrad, Earl. *Harriet Tubman*. Washington, DC: Associated Publishers, 1942.

Davidson, John Nelson. *Negro Slavery and the Underground Railroad in Wisconsin*. Milwaukee: Park Club, 1981.

Douglass, Fredrick. *Life and Times*. Hartford, CT: Hartford Park Publishing Company, 1882.

Drew, Benjamin. *A North-Side View of Slavery: The Refuge: Or, The Narratives of Fugitive Slaves in Canada*. Boston: J.P. Jewett & Co., 1856.

Drew, Benjamin. *Reminiscences*. Cincinnati: Robert Clarke & Co., 1876. Commonwealth. July 17, 1863. Collection of interviews with Levi Coffin.

Dumond, Dwight Lowell. *Anti-Slavery: The Crusade for Freedom in America*. Ann Arbor: University of Michigan Press, 1961.

Fairchild, James Harris. *The Underground Railroad*. Cleveland: Western Historical Society, 1895.

Foner, Philip. *The Making of Black America*. Westport, CT: Greenwod Press, 1983.

Franklin, John Hope. *From Slavery to Freedom*. New York: Alfred A. Knopf, 1967.

Gara, Larry. *The Liberty Line: The Legend of the Undegound Railroad*. Lexington: University of Kentucky Press, 1961.

Genovese, Eugene. *Roll Jordan, Roll, The World the Slaves Made*. New York: Pantheon Books, 1974.

Harding, Vincent. *There Is a River: The Black Struggle for Freedom in America*. New York: Vintage Books, 1981.

Haviland, Laura S. *A Woman's Life Work*. Chicago: C.V. Waite, 1881.

Higginbotham, Leon A., Jr. *In the Matter of Color*. New York: Oxford University Press, 1978.

Hill, Daniel G. *The Freedom Seekers: Blacks in Early Canada*. Agincourt, Canada: Book Society of Canada, 1981.

Johnson, Homer U. *From Dixie to Canada: Romances and Realities of the Underground Railroad*. Orwell, OH: H.U. Johnson, 1896.

Katz, Jonathan. *Resistance at Christina: The Fugitive Slave Rebellion,*

Bibliography

Christiana, Pennsylvania, September 11, 1851. New York: Thomas Y. Crowell Co., 1974.

Littlefield, Daniel. *Africans and Seminoles.* Westport, CT: Greenwood Press, 1977.

Litwack, Leon. *North of Slavery: The Negroes in the Free States.* Chicago: University of Chicago Press, 1961.

Loguen, J.W. *The Rev. J.W. Loguen, as a Slave and as a Freeman.* Syracuse, NY: J.G.K. Truair & Co., 1859.

Lumpkin, Katherine DuPre. "The General Plan Was Freedom: A Negro Secret Order on the Underground Railroad." *Phylon* (Spring 1967). Atlanta, GA: Atlanta University. pp. 63-76.

May, Samuel. *The Fugitive Slave Law and Its Victims.* New York: American Anti-Slavery Society, 1861.

McGowan, James A. *The Life and Letters of Thomas Garrett, Station Master on the Underground Railroad.* Moylan, PA: Whimsie Press, 1977.

Merril, Arch. *The Underground, Freedom's Road.* New York: American Book Statford Press, 1963.

Nicholas, Charles H. *Many Thousand Gone: The Ex-Slaves' Account of Their Bondage and Freedom.* Leiden: Brill, 1963.

Northup, Solomon. *Twelve Years a Slave, Narrative of Northup.* Wilson, N.Y.

Pettit, Eber M. *Sketches in the History of the Underground Railroad.* Fredonia, NY: W. McKinstry & Son, 1879.

Pickard, Kate. *The Kidnapped and the Ransomed, Being the Personal Recollections of Peter Still and His Wife "Vini."* Fredonia, NY: W. McKinstry & Son, 1856.

Price, Clement Alexander, ed. *Freedom Not Far Distant: A Documentary History of African Americans in New Jersey.* New Jersey Historical Society, 1980.

Quarles, Benjamin. *Black Abolitionists.* New York: Oxford University Press, 1969.

Robbins, Arlie C. *Legacy to Buxton, Ontario.* New York: Oxford University Press, 1969.

Ross, Alexander M. *Recollections and Experiences of an Abolitionist.* Toronto: Rowell and Hutchinson, 1875.

Siebert, Wilbur H. *Mysteries of Ohio's Underground Railroad.* Columbus, OH: Long's College Bookstore Co., 1951.

_____. *The Undeground Railroad: From Slavery to Freedom.* New York; MacMillan Company, 1898.

_____. "The Underground Railroad in Massachusetts," Proceedings of the American Antiquarian Society, Vol. 45 (April 17, 1935).

_____. *Vermont's Anti-Slavery and Underground Railroad Record.*

Smedley, Robert C. *History of the Undeground Railroad in Chester and the Neighboring Counties of Pennsylvania.* Lancaster, PA: Office of the Journal, 1883.

Stampp, Kenneth M. *The Peculiar Institution.* New York: Random House of Canada Limited, 1956

Sterling, Dorothy. *We Are Your Sisters: Black Women in the Nineteenth Century.* New York: W.W. Norton, 1984.

Still, William. Underground Railroad Records. Philadelphia: W. Still, 1872.

Stowe, Harriet Beecher. *Key to Uncle Tom's Cabin.* Cleveland: Jewett, Proctor & Worthington, 1853.

Wade, Richard C. *Slavery in the Cities.* New York: Oxford University Press, 1964.

Walls, William J. *The African Methodist Episcopal Zion Church: Reality of the Black Church.* Charlotte, NC: A.M.E. Zion Publishing House, 1974.

Winks, Robin W. *The Blacks in Canada: A History.* New Haven: Yale Universtiy Press, 1971.

Wood, Peter. *Black Majority.* New York: Alfred A. Knopf, 1974.

Woolman, John. *Some Consideration in the Keeping of Negroes, 1754.* Philadelphia: James Chattin, 1754.

Index of Sites

Index of Towns

HIPPOCRENE U.S.A. TRAVEL BOOKS

IRISH AMERICA by *Russ Malone*
Over 40 million Americans claim Irish roots—That's one in five of us! In the spirit of traditional Irish good humor, Russ Malone creates an outstanding guide that will aid any Irish American traveler in need of a glimpse of their heritage or a new favorite pub anywhere across the United States.
250 pages ISBN 0-7818-0173-7 $14.95

BLACK AMERICA by *Marcella Thum*
"A useful acquisition for all travel collections."—*Library Journal*
"An admirable guide."—*Choice Magazine*
Organized by state, this fully indexed guide describes more that 700 historic homes, art and history museums, parks, monuments, landmarks of the civil rights movement, battlefields, colleges and churches across the U.S., all open to the public.
325 pages ISBN 0-87052-045-8 $11.95

BLACK WASHINGTON by *Sandra Fitzpatrick and Maria Goodwin*
"The authors provide a much-needed corrective and show how black Washingtonians affected not only this city but the nation and indeed, the world."—*The Washington Post Book World*
Explore over 200 sites in our nation's capital, central to the African-American experience. Gain insight into the heritage that had a profound impact on African-American culture and American society.
288 pages ISBN 0-87052-832-7 $14.95

HISTORIC BLACK SOUTH by *Joann Biondi and James Haskins*
"The book provides some wonderful reading and inspires tourists to go and explore a part of the south that has not been emphasized in travel."
—*Library Journal*
This unique guide describes over 1,000 sites which pay tribute to the significant and often overlooked contribution of the southern African-American community. Includes a description of attractions open to the public, listing hours, fees, directions, and phone numbers.
300 pages ISBN 0-7818-0140-0 $14.95

HISTORIC HISPANIC AMERICA by *Oscar and Joy Jones*
"This is an unusual guide that any serious traveler to the southwest would find informative."—*Library Journal*
This guide focuses on uncovering the living heritage in the southwestern U.S., where both Spanish and Indian presence is still felt.
300 pages ISBN 0-7818-0141-9 $14.95

POLISH HERITAGE TRAVEL GUIDE TO U.S.A. & CANADA by *Jacek Galazka and Albert Juszczak*
"A very useful contribution to an understanding of the Polish heritage in North America."—Zbigniew Brzezinski
For travelers seeking to visit important Polish points of interest in North America.
272 pages ISBN 0-7818-0035-8 $14.95

THE U.S.A. GUIDE TO BLACK NEW YORK by *James Haskins and Joann Biondi*
Find the best of the best of African and African American culture and history in the city with the greatest concentration of black culture in America. Jazz joints and clubs; soul food, Caribbean and other cuisines; historic monuments; museums, libraries and contemporary art spaces are all listed here with addresses and phone numbers for all to easily enjoy.
200 pages, map ISBN 0-7818-0172-9 $14.95

THE COTTON CLUB by *James Haskins*
The famous chronicle of THE COTTON CLUB by James Haskins relating the story of New York City's once-roaring mecca of black entertainment is back.
When jazz was a new, raw music, THE COTTON CLUB launched the best of that hip edge: Duke Ellington, Lena Horne, Ella Fitzgerald, Cab Calloway, Louis Armstrong, and others adored by thousands of fans. Read about THE COTTON CLUB in the exciting book that inspired the Coppola movie starring Richard Gere and Gregory Hines. With first hand accounts from the great players, and true tales of the gangster-run Jazz Age, the book THE COTTON CLUB is a lesson in fad, fashion and the life and death of Renaissance Harlem. Contains: •new preface •over 125 black and white photos
213 pages ISBN 0-7818-0248-2 $14.95

NEW!
NAMIBIA: THE INDEPENDENT TRAVELER'S GUIDE by *Lucinda and Scott Bradshaw*
This in-depth, up-to-date travel guide shows the cultural or adventurous traveler around the expanse of a newly independent southwest African country. Now it's easy to enjoy the wildlife and unspoiled wilderness found in its four geographic sections—the Namib Desert, the Great Escarpment, the northern plains and the lower lands. Learn about the nooks and crannies of Namibia's intriguing towns, both large and small,and their people. Geared for travelers of any means, it covers eating, lodging, and sites with a cultural history that enhances any part of the country. Contains: •6 detailed maps •20 black and white photos and illustrations
278 pages ISBN 0-7818-0254-7 $16.95

(All prices subject to change.)
TO PURCHASE HIPPOCRENE BOOKS contact your local bookstore, or write to: HIPPOCRENE BOOKS, 171 Madison Avenue, New York, NY 10016. Please enclose check or money order, adding $4.00 shipping (UPS) for the first book and $.50 for each additional book.

HIPPOCRENE AFRICAN LANGUAGE LIBRARY

For travelers to Africa, for African-Americans exploring their roots, and for everyone interested in learning more about Africa and her languages, we offer the new African Language Library.

ENGLISH-SOMALI/SOMALI-ENGLISH DICTIONARY
Somali, the national language of Somalia, is spoken by 6 million in this easternmost African country, as well as 1 1/2 million in Ethiopia, and 300,000 in Kenya. Features 11,000 up-to-date entries with clear pronunciation.
276 pages 5 1/2 x 9 $29.50 cloth 0-7818-0269-5

SWAHILI PHRASEBOOK
T. Gilmore and S. Kwasa
Presented simply, with a minimum of grammar, this is a straightforward guide to basic communication in many African countries from Botswana in the south to centrally situated Zaire to Kenya and Ethiopia in the east.
184 pages 4 x 5 3/8 $8.95 paper 0-87052-970-6

TWI-ENGLISH/ENGLISH-TWI CONCISE DICTIONARY
Paul Kotey
Twi is the major language of Ghana and it is spoken by 6 million people. Brand new and easy-to-use, this is **the only Twi-English/English-Twi dictionary available in the U.S.**
425 pages 3 5/8 x 5 3/8 $11.95 paper 0-7818-0264-4

A NEW CONCISE XHOSA-ENGLISH DICTIONARY
J. McLaren
One of the Bantu languages, Xhosa is spoken by about 4 million people, primarily in the Transkei territory of South Africa, which borders Lesotho and faces the Indian Ocean. A standard among students of Xhosa since 1914, this edition of *A New Concise Xhosa-English Dictionary* contains approximately 6,000 modern entries.
194 pages 4 3/4 x 7 1/8 $14.95 paper 0-7818-0251-2

YORUBA-ENGLISH/ ENGLISH-YORUBA CONCISE DICTIONARY
Olabiyi Yai
One of the major languages of Nigeria, Yoruba is spoken by 15 million people, principally in the southwestern region of the country. This is **the only Yoruba-English/ English-Yoruba dictionary to be offered in the U.S.**
375 pages 3 5/8 x 5 3/8 $11.95 paper 0-7818-0263-6

ZULU-ENGLISH/ENGLISH-ZULU DICTIONARY
G.R. Dent and C.L.S. Nyembezi
Zulu is one of the major Bantu languages of South Africa, originating in the easternmost part of the country. Over 4 million people speak Zulu.
519 pages 7 1/4 x 4 3/4 $29.50 paper 0-7818-0255-5

U.S.A. TRAVEL

MIDWESTERN TRAVEL

AMERICA'S HEARTLAND: A Travel Guide to the Backroads of Illinois, Indiana, Iowa, Kansas and Missouri, *2nd Edition*, by Tom Weil
$14.95 • 528 pages • maps • 0-7818-0044-7

EXPLORING MID-AMERICA: A Guide to Museum Villages, by Gerald and Patricia Gutek
$14.95 • 172 pages • b/w photos • 0-87052-643-X

CHICAGOLAND & BEYOND, by Gerald and Patricia Gutek
$14.95 • 288 pages • maps, b/w photos • 0-87052-036-9

SOUTHERN TRAVEL

AMERICA'S SOUTH: The Atlantic States, by Tom Weil
Includes Florida, Georgia, North and South Carolina, and Virginia
$14.95 • 400 pages • maps • 0-7818-0139-7

AMERICA'S SOUTH: The Gulf and Mississippi States, by Tom Weil
The companion which completes award winning author Tom Weil's tour of the entire South includes Mississippi, Louisiana, Kentucky, Arkansas, Tennessee and Alabama.
$14.95 • 400 pages • maps • 0-7818-0171-0

THE KEY TO FLORIDA: A City Breaks Guide, by Reg Butler
$7.95 • 112 pages • maps •0-87052-178-0

WESTERN TRAVEL

THE ROCKY MOUNTAIN STATES, by Henry Weisser
$14.95 • 366 pages • b/wphotos • 0-7818-0043-9

THE SOUTHWEST: A Family Adventure, by Tish Minear and Janet Limon
$16.95 • 440 pages • b/w photos, illust. • 0-87052-640-5

(Prices subject to change.)
TO PURCHASE HIPPOCRENE BOOKS, contact your local bookstore, or write to: HIPPOCRENE BOOKS, 171 Madison Avenue, New York, NY 10016. Please enclose check or money order, adding $4.00 shipping (UPS) for the first book and .50 for each additional book.